A
Warning

A
Warning

A
Warning

A
Warning

A
Warning

A Warning in Daniel 12

Marian G. Berry

Let us read and study the 12th chapter of Daniel. It is a warning we shall all need to understand before the time of the end.
Letter 161, July 30, 1903 Ellen G. White

TEACH Services, Inc.
PUBLISHING
www.TEACHServices.com • (800) 367-1844

World rights reserved. This book or any portion thereof may not be copied or reproduced in any form or manner whatever, except as provided by law, without the written permission of the publisher, except by a reviewer who may quote brief passages in a review.

The author assumes full responsibility for the accuracy of all facts and quotations as cited in this book. The opinions expressed in this book are the author's personal views and interpretations, and do not necessarily reflect those of the publisher.

This book is provided with the understanding that the publisher is not engaged in giving spiritual, legal, medical, or other professional advice. If authoritative advice is needed, the reader should seek the counsel of a competent professional.

Copyright © 2006 Marian G. Berry

Copyright © 2015 TEACH Services, Inc.

ISBN-13: 978-1-4796-0559-0 (Paperback)

Library of Congress Control Number.: 2015906903

Published by

www.TEACHServices.com • (800) 367-1844

TABLE OF CONTENTS

Ellen G. White Reference List vi
A Word from the Author vii
The Author's Foreword viii
Acknowledgements x

Chapter I. What are the "Principles of Interpretation"? 1
    Part 1. What is "The End"? Past or Future? 2
    Part 2. What is "The Literal Approach" to Daniel 12? 4
    Part 3. What is an "Interpretation"? 5
    Part 4. What is an "Application"? 6
    Part 5. What is an "Historicist"? A "Futurist"? 8
    Part 6. What is the Progressive "Forward Movement" of the Book of Daniel?....9
    Part 7. What are the "Objections to Former Applications" of Daniel 12?..........12
    Part 8. What "Prophetic Time Shall be no Longer"? 14
    Part 9. What is the "Problem"? 15
    Part 10. What is the "Dilemma"? 16
    Part 11. What are the "Hermeneutic Principles"? 17
    Part 12. What is the "Context and Historical Setting" of Revelation 10:5,6? 18
    Part 13. What is "Prophetic Time" in Revelation 10? 19
    Part 14. What are the "Prophetic Periods"? 20
    Part 15. What was the "Circumstantial Setting"? 22
    Part 16. What was the "Focus of Daniel 8:14"? 23
    Part 17. What "Will Never be a Test Again"? 24
    Part 18. What are the "Times and Timelines" of the Future? 25
    Part 19. What is the "Year-day Computation Principle"? 27
    Part 20. What "Would Jesus Say"? 28
    Summary of Chapter I 29

Chapter II. What is the "Warning" in Daniel 12? 31
    Part 1. What is "The Question"? 32
    Part 2. What is "The Answer"? 33
    Part 3. What is the "Abomination"? 35
    Part 4. What is the "Desolation"? 38
    Part 5. What is the "Abomination of Desolation"? 40
    Part 6. What is a "Dual Application"? 41
    Part 7. What is the "First Application" of Matthew 24:15 43
    Part 8. What is the "Second or Endtime Application" of Matthew 24:15? 46
    Part 9. What is the "Warning"? 48
    Part 10. What is the "Final Test"? 50

Part 11.	What is the Formation of "The Image of the Beast"?	51
Part 12.	What is the Sabbath-Sunday Controversy that is the "Great Test" to the Last Generation?	52
Part 13.	What is "The Judgment of the Living"?	53
Part 14.	What is "The Shaking"?	54
Part 15.	What is the "Seal of God"?	56
Part 16.	What is the "Loud Cry" Warning?	58
Part 17.	What is the "Third Angel's Warning Message"?	59
Summary of Chapter II		60

Chapter III. What is the "1335 Days" Timeline? 62
Part 1.	What are the "Precedent Voices" of Timelines?	64
Part 2.	What "Event Begins" the 1335 Days of Daniel 12:12?	67
Part 3.	What is the "Voice" or "Speaking" of a Nation?	68
Part 4.	What is "The Wait" of Daniel 12:12?	69
Part 5.	What is "The Blessing" of the 1335 Days?	70
Part 6.	What is the "Voice of God"?	71
Summary of Chapter III		74

Chapter IV. What is the "1260 Days" Timelines of Daniel 12:7? 76
Part 1.	Who is "The Man" Clothed in Linen?	78
Part 2.	Who are the "Holy People" of Daniel 12:7?	80
Part 3.	What is "To Scatter the Power" of the Holy People?	82
Part 4.	Who is "He" that shall have accomplished to Scatter the Power of the Holy People in Daniel 12:7?	83
Part 5.	What is the "Historicist View" of Daniel 12:7?	85
Part 6.	What is "Time, Times, and an Half" of Daniel 12:7?	86
Part 7.	What is "Revelation 13" Past? or Future?	88
Part 8.	What is "Papal Supremacy No. 2"?	90
Part 9.	What are the "Voices" which Begin and End the 1260 Days?	92
Part 10.	What "Event" Begins the 1260 Day Timeline?	93
Part 11.	What "Event" Ends the 1260 Day Timeline?	95
Part 12.	What is the "Universal Death Decree"?	97
Part 13.	What is the "One Hour" of Revelation 17:12,13?	98
Part 14.	What is the "Year-day Computation Principle" of Prophetic Interpretation?	100
Part 15.	What is the "Relationship" between the 1335 Day Timeline and the 1260 Days?	101
Part 16.	What is "The Time of Jacob's Trouble"?	103
Part 17.	What are "All These Things" that "Shall be Finished" in Daniel 12:7?	106
Summary of Chapter IV		108

Chapter V. What is "The Daily" of the 1290 Days of Daniel 12:11? 110
| Part 1. | What is the Daily "Sacrifice"? | 113 |
| Part 2. | What is the "Daily" "Tamiyd"? | 115 |

Part 3.	What is the "Context" of the "Daily"?	116
Part 4.	What is the "Daily"-"Tamiyd"-Continuum?	118
Part 5.	What is the "Scepter"-"Tamiyd"-"Daily"?	120
Part 6.	How is the "Daily"-"Tamiyd"-"Scepter of Power" "Taken Away"?	122
Part 7.	What were the "Advent Pioneers"?	126
Part 8.	What did the Prophet say about the "Daily"?	128
Part 9.	What is the "Importance" of the "Daily"?	130
Summary of Chapter V		133

Chapter VI.	What is the "1290 Day Timeline" of Daniel 12:11?	135
Part 1.	Why is the "Daily" Scepter of Power taken away?	136
Part 2.	What "Event" Begins the 1290 Day Timeline?	137
Part 3.	What "Event" Ends the 1290 Day Timeline of Daniel 12:11?	139
Part 4.	What is "The Fall of Babylon"?	140
Part 5.	What is the "One Hour" of Revelation 18?	142
Part 6.	What is the "Thirty Days Difference"?	143
Part 7.	What is "About the Space of Half an Hour"?	144
Part 8.	What is the "Drama" of the 6th and 7th Plagues?	148
Part 9.	What are the "Thunderings and Lightnings"?	149
Summary of Chapter VI		152

Conclusion	153
Chart of Daniel 12 Timelines	154
The Interlocking Nature of the Three Timelines of Daniel 12	155
The Structure of the Book of Daniel	157

Appendix A.	What are the Seven Angel's Messages of Revelation 14 and 18?	159
Appendix B.	Daily	169
	White Estate Letter	174
	The Daily and the Ministry of Christ	175
	E.G.W. Office Document on "Daily"	182
	How Does Satan Attempt to Seize the "Daily" (Scepter of Power, Seat and Authority)?	185
Appendix C.	Additional Notes on Daniel 12	194
	The Man on the Water in Daniel 8:16	197

v

ELLEN G. WHITE REFFERENCE LIST

4-8 BC	SDA Bible Commentary, Vol. 4,5,7,8
COL	Christ's Object Lessons
DA	Desire of Ages
EW	Early Writings
Ev	Evangelism
GC	Great Controversy
Ltr	Letter
MAR	Maranatha—The Lord is Coming
MB	Mount of Blessings
PP	Patriarchs and Prophets
1,2 RH	Review and Herald, Vols. 1,2
1-3 SM	Selected Messages, Vols. 1,2,3
1-5 T	Testimonies, Vols. 1,2,5
1-3 SG	Spiritual Gifts, Vols. 1,2,3

A WORD FROM THE AUTHOR

"Repairing the Fan"

This study of Daniel 12 may be likened to the repair of an electric fan, which had numerous blades bent out of shape and covered with globs of muck. Some of the blades have been removed and hidden for years, while others have been put in backwards by inept repairmen.

This study of Daniel 12 requires an enormous amount of work! Each blade of the fan, each definition and concept, must be removed, scraped, cleaned, polished, bent back into its original shape, aligned with the others and mounted correctly into socket.

This fan in its present condition, when turned on, clatters, shatters, and throws off chunks of debris! Whoever touches it is smeared from head to foot with black dirt. Most people prefer to keep their distance! But since this fan has an excellent Power Source and the Manufacturer stands behind His product, someone needs to put on work-clothes, an apron, get out the tool box and go to work. This has been the aim of the author in construction of this book.

The weather will soon be turning hot. This fine old fan will be needed. When well cleaned and repaired, and each blade mounted in its correct socket, it runs perfectly. It will then produce a current of air that can be identified easily with the Holy Spirit which moves as a wind upon the hearts of men.

Each chapter of this book is one more blade repaired and put into place. The author hopes that the reader will be patient with this long process, enjoying the idea that each part of it has been thoroughly and expertly placed back into its originally intended function. By the end of this book (fan), the reader should be able to turn it on and enjoy refreshing breezes, regardless of the temperature out there.

THE AUTHOR'S FOREWORD

> In **every age** there is **a new development of truth**, a message of God to the people of **that generation**. The old truths are all essential; **new truth is not independent of the old, but an unfolding of it**. It is only as the old truths are understood that we can comprehend the new. When Christ desired to open to His disciples the truth of His resurrection, He began "at Moses and all the prophets" and "expounded unto them in all the Scriptures the things concerning Himself." Luke 24:27. But it is the light which shines in the fresh unfolding of truth that glorifies the old. **He who rejects or neglects the new, does not really possess the old.** For him it loses its vital power and becomes but a lifeless form. COL 127,128.

Just prior to 1844, one prophetic timeline of Scripture—Daniel 8:14, took precedence over all others. Not that it was more important than other elements of the gospel, but **its time had come**.* The object of this book is to reveal that in like manner, the prophetic timelines of Daniel 12:7-13 now take priority because their time has come to speak to the last generation.

The Daniel 8:14 prophetic timeline warned that 1844 generation of the **beginning** of the Investigative Judgment. This study shows that the Daniel 12:7-13 timelines warn the last generation of events connected with the **ending** of the Investigative Judgment; whereas the Daniel 8:14 timeline announced the beginning of the Investigative Judgment of the **dead** in 1844, the Daniel 12:7-13 timelines announce the Investigative Judgment of the **living**.

The Daniel 8:14 timeline did not give a date for the coming of Jesus and the Daniel 12:7-13 timelines do not give date, day nor hour of His coming. But all of these timelines of Chapter 8 and 12 are warnings concerning the Investigative Judgment and events connected with the close of probation. Regarding events connected with the 1844 timeline, the prophet wrote: "It was needful that men should be awakened to their danger; that they should be aroused to prepare for the solemn events connected with the close of probation." GC 310. The Daniel 12:7-13 timelines are intended to rouse the last generation to prepare for the solemn events connected with the close of probation for The Church and the world. The three timelines of Daniel 12 do not give the date for the close of probation nor Christ's coming but are a delineation of events connected with them.

> We want the past message and the fresh message. 2 RH 378.

The Daniel 8:14 prophetic timeline was a proclamation of the first and second angels' messages

---

* Daniel 8:14 "Unto two thousand three hundred days" timeline. The 2300 day timeline began in 457 B.C. and ended on October 22, 1844. The timeline is computed in detail in Daniel 9:24-27. Its time of proclamation was 1833-1844. The proclamation was called "The Great Advent Movement."

of Revelation 14:6-8, "The hour of his judgment is come" and "Babylon is fallen." The Daniel 12:7-13 timelines are also a proclamation of the first and second messages but give special emphasis to the third angel's warning of Revelation 14:9-12[*]

The third angel's message is not "hung on time," not dependent on time. However, the Loud Cry of the third angel combined with the fourth angel of Revelation 18 are relevant to events which occur in a specific endtime setting. It is these events which are elucidated and clarified by a study of the Daniel 12:7-13 timelines.

> Surely the Lord God will do nothing, but he revealeth his secrets unto his servants the prophets. Amos 3:7.

If the prophecy of Daniel 8:14 specified the very day—October 22, 1844, on which the Investigative Judgment of the dead was to begin, is it not reasonable that God would reveal to the last generation those events connected with the judgment of the living and the closing of the Investigative Judgment? Does He not reveal His "secrets" to the prophets and are they not recorded and preserved there for our benefit? It is the last generation, those who come to final crisis who most need the guiding light of prophetic assurance. Will God not give them clear vision for their own day by prophetic passages of the Scripture?

> We have also a more sure word of prophecy; whereunto ye do well that ye take heed, as unto a light that shineth in a dark place.... 2 Peter 1:19.

> Increased light will shine upon all the grand truths of prophecy and they will be seen in freshness and brilliance because the bright beams of the Sun of Righteousness will illuminate the whole. (Ms 18, 1888) Ev 198.

---

[*] The Third Angel's Warning Message is the subject of the Daniel 12:7-13 timelines. *And the third angel followed them, saying with a loud voice, If any man worship the beast and his image, and receive his mark in his forehead, or in his hand, The same shall drink of the wine of the wrath of God, which is poured out without mixture into the cup of his indignation; and he shall be tormented with fire and brimstone in the presence of the ... Lamb: Rev 14:9,10.*

ACKNOWLEDGMENTS

The author expresses praise to God who answers many prayers for wisdom and understanding of prophetic Scriptures. The author does not claim "Inspiration Revelation" as given to the prophets. However, in exactly the same way that the minister seeks aid of the Holy Spirit as he prepares to stand in the pulpit, or the Christian who prays before opening the Bible, the author has sought "Inspiration Illumination" of the Holy Spirit for insight to truth. All glory, praise, and honor must be directed to Him.

We are all indebted to Godly students of the Word who have gone before us. Historians, prophets, and pioneers over the centuries have resolved many complexities of Bible doctrine and prophecy. These have made their contributions and on such solid foundations, this study of Daniel 12 builds the final segments in the edifice of truth.

The writings of Ellen G. White, especially her descriptions of future events, as she saw them in vision, have brought the concepts presented in Daniel 12 into sharp focus. Her comments confirm, explain and enrich the total picture—the scenes of the endtime drama, as they have been outlined in the Bible itself.

Appreciation is expressed to my husband, Kenneth, who has given his continuing support in all aspects of production. Jim Riggs has invested time and energy putting the MS on the computer and getting it ready for publication. Pat Robertson, also has labored much in proof-reading through the many steps in perfecting copy. Gratitude is expressed to the committee, who spent eight days in critical analysis of content, and to many friends who have pointed out various matters of concern along the way. Those who have attended Endtime Prophetic Seminars have contributed from their stores of knowledge in regard to their own research and days of interaction with each other. All of these exercises have had their part in clarifying the issues at hand.

To those who have contributed substantially to the cost of publication, and to those in the future who continue to actively promote this project, we simply ask the Lord to reward you according to His loving kindness.

CHAPTER I

WHAT ARE THE  "PRINCIPLES OF INTERPRETATION"?

Before the three timelines of Daniel 12:7-13 can be understood, certain words must be defined and specific questions must be stated and answered. These questions are as follows:

1. What is "THE END"? Past or Future?
2. What is the "LITERAL APPROACH" to Daniel 12?
3. What is an "INTERPRETATION"?
4. What is an "APPLICATION"?
5. What is an "HISTORICIST"? A "FUTURIST"?
6. What is the "PROGRESSIVE, FORWARD MOVEMENT" of the book of Daniel?
7. What are the "OBJECTIONS TO FORMER APPLICATIONS" of Daniel 12?
8. What "PROPHETIC TIME SHALL BE NO LONGER"?
9. What is the "PROBLEM"?
10. What is the "DILEMMA"?
11. What are the "HERMENEUTIC PRINCIPLES"?
12. What is the "CONTEXT AND HISTORICAL SETTING" of Revelation 10:5,6?
13. What is "PROPHETIC TIME" in Revelation 10?
14. What are the "PROPHETIC PERIODS"?
15. What was the "CIRCUMSTANTIAL SETTING"?
16. What was the "FOCUS OF DANIEL 8:14"?
17. What "WILL NEVER BE A TEST AGAIN"?
18. What are the "TIMES AND TIMELINES" in the future?
19. What is the "YEAR-DAY COMPUTATION PRINCIPLE"?
20. What "WOULD JESUS SAY"?

Part 1. WHAT IS "THE END" ? PAST OR FUTURE?

> Let us read and study the twelfth chapter of Daniel. It is a warning that we shall all need to understand before the time of the end. EGW Letter 161, 1903. [To A. G. Daniells and W. W. Prescott].

The above statement written in 1903, makes no reference to the past! It directs attention to that "warning that we **shall** [FUTURE TENSE] all need to understand before the time of the end." This statement places Daniel 12 in an endtime setting. To be specific, an endtime setting is that **which pertains to the last generation** which will be living on the earth when Jesus comes.

Seven times in Daniel 12, the questions and answers refer to the very end of time, as follows:

1. Verse 4 "...even to the time of the **end**."
2. Verse 6 "...How long shall it be to the **end** of these wonders?"
3. Verse 7 "...all these things shall be **finished**."
4. Verse 8 "...what shall be the **end** of these things?"
5. Verse 9 "...till the time of the **end**."
6. Verse 11 (implied) "...from the time...shall...days." (to the end)
7. Verse 13 "...stand in thy lot at the **end** of the days."

Therefore, from the contextual emphasis of Daniel 12 and from the inspired comment, it is a "warning we shall [FUTURE TENSE] all need," it is self-evident that this is a prophecy with an endtime application to future closing events at the very end of time.

Daniel 12 is **not** a repetition of previous chapters! Daniel 12 with its three timelines should be consigned to the future in its proper endtime setting. This application is the final chapter of the historicists' view of fulfilling prophecy.

Historicists view prophecy, not only as "history written in advance," but also as a continuum, covering past, present and **future** events. For example, the image of Daniel 2 is viewed by historicists to cover past empires. It also pinpoints our own day as living in the time of the "toes of the image," and includes the **future** in the coming stone kingdom. By such an historicist-continuum, historicists link the past to the present and ALSO SEE INTO THE FUTURE. This does not make them "futurists!"

Historicists in the early Advent Movement did not anticipate nearly two centuries until the coming of Christ! Their eyes searched their recent past for an "interpretation" of Daniel 12. These great men were "prisoners of history" and could not comprehend the endtime events of Daniel 12—that was left to the last generation!

> Perhaps one of the most conspicuous lessons of all prophetic testimony through the years is the contemporary recognition, or interpretation of each major epoch or event in the prophetic outline at the very time of fulfillment. L.E. Froom: *The Prophetic Faith of Our Fathers*, (Washington, D.C.: Review and Herald Publishing Association, 1950), Vol. I, p. 890.

> ...whenever a major epoch or event of prophecy is reached, always there are reverent students whose minds are led by the Spirit of God to special study and recognition of the fulfillment. This is ever contemporaneous with the event. Ibid., Vol III, p.9.

The last generation should not expect men who lived nearly two centuries before the end to have completed all prophetic exposition! This was certainly not the view of the pioneers as revealed in the following quotation:

> And the most marked guidance of prophecy, they believed would yet be experienced just before the world's final crisis.... It is the luminous torch in the hands of the faithful...that will enlighten man in his final march toward the kingdom of God. Ibid., Vol. IV, p. 1171.

Today, prophetic expositors look at Daniel 12 by an indepth study of the Word, by observation of current events, which make up history, and by the guidance of the Spirit of Prophecy. They find their gaze irresistibly drawn to a future fulfillment of Daniel 12 which "is a warning that we shall [FUTURE TENSE] all need" before the end of time.

> In every age there is a new development of truth, a message of God to the people of that generation. The old truths are all essential; new truth is not independent of the old, but an unfolding of it. It is only as the old truths are understood that we can comprehend the new. COL 127.

It is the last generation in the endtime who will have the broad panorama of all past history behind them, and the "unrolling of the scroll" will be complete! If the last generation had no new development of truth and were to rest only on that which was understood two centuries ago, they could not recognize the final deliverance and understand the final crisis! Prophecy is given to provide hope and joy to those living at the time of its fulfillment.

Part 2. WHAT IS "THE LITERAL APPROACH" TO DANIEL 12 ?

> Every declaration of Scripture is to be taken in the most obvious and literal sense, except where context and the well-known laws of language show that the terms are figurative, and not literal, and whatever is figurative must be explained by other portions of the Bible which are literal. G. M. Hyde, Ed.: *A Symposium on Biblical Hermeneutics.* (Washington, D.C.: Review and Herald Publishing Association, 1979), Statement by Don Neufeld. (See also GC 599).

The above quotation defines one of the most important hermeneutic rules to be used in a study of the Bible. This is called THE LITERAL APPROACH and it applies to **all** parts of the books of the Bible. It is the **only** approach approved by Seventh-day Adventists. By this literal approach all foundations were laid for Adventism, the doctrines now held by the church, as well as its valid expositions on prophecy. This means that Daniel 12 must **also** be subjected to this literal approach and guarded by this hermeneutic principle.

In Daniel 12 there is no prophetic symbolism—no image, no beasts, no horns, no crowns, no mountains, no stone, no winds, no eyes, no mouth, none of the prophetic symbolism otherwise used in Daniel or Revelation. It is true that Daniel was in vision when he heard the conversation recorded in Daniel 12, but still there is no symbolism in the text. Therefore **DANIEL 12 SHOULD BE READ IN ITS MOST LITERAL SENSE.**

When prophetic time periods are couched in the context of symbolic figures, these time periods should be treated as symbolic time and decoded by the Year-day Computation Principle. The timelines of Daniel 12 are **not** couched in symbolic context and should therefore be considered literal time. Prophetic expositors do not have the right to attempt to decode literal statements of Scripture but must take them in the most "obvious and literal sense." Therefore the "days" spoken of in Daniel 12 should be regarded as **literal** days.

The "days" timelines of Daniel 12 are as follows:

> ...the man clothed in linen...sware...that it shall be for a time[*], times, and an half...to scatter the power of the holy people,.... Dan. 12:7.

> And from the time that the daily, shall be taken away, and the abomination that maketh desolate set up, there shall be a thousand two hundred and ninety **days**. Dan. 12:11.

> Blessed is he that waiteth and cometh to the thousand three hundred and five and thirty **days**. Dan. 12:12.

---

[*] Note: "time, times, and an half" is prophetic terminology, **not** symbolic or "prophetic" time. See the full explanation in Chapter IV, Part 6:
    a. What is "Prophetic Terminology"?
    b. What is "Prophetic Time"?

Part 3. WHAT IS AN "INTERPRETATION"?

Some prophecy is written in figurative-symbolic language, such as that of Daniel 2, 7, 8, and parts of Revelation. These symbols are that of an image, beasts, horns, eyes, mountains, stones, etc. Other prophecies are written in literal language, such as that of Matthew 24:7, "...there shall be famines, pestilences, and earthquakes, in divers places." It is prophecy because it points to the future but it uses no symbolism. It simply points to specific events to occur.

Only those prophecies which are couched in symbols or figurative language must have those symbols **decoded** or **interpreted**. This decoding process or "interpretation" is the **first step** toward understanding. After the symbol or figure of speech is "interpreted"—decoded, then an application can be made. Prophecies which are written in literal language do not need to be decoded or interpreted. They need only to be **applied** to the correct circumstance.

The process of decoding or "interpreting" symbolism is circumscribed to a procedure in which the Bible **must** be its own interpreter or expositor! We are given the following warning which is the first hermeneutic rule of exposition:

> Knowing this **first,** that no prophecy [prophetic symbol] of the Scripture is of any private interpretation. 2 Peter 1:20.

In this process of decoding or interpretation of symbolism, no man is permitted to insert his own private opinions or conjecture as to the meaning of a symbol or figure or type. These meanings must be derived by cross reference Bible study in which other portions of the Scripture unlock or decode the meaning. This process is described in Isaiah 28:9-13 (KJV).

> Whom shall he teach knowledge? and whom shall he make to understand doctrine? ...For precept must be upon precept, precept upon precept; line upon line, line upon line; here a little, and there a little; ...the word of the Lord was unto them precept upon precept, precept upon percept; line upon line, line upon line; here a little, and there a little;.... Isa. 28:9-13.[*]

---

[*] Note: Regardless of the various Bible translations of Isaiah 28, in which there has been an attempt to discard the cross-reference or topical study of the Scripture, there remains the context which reinforces this basic hermeneutic in which the Bible remains its own expositor or "interpreter" of prophetic symbolism.

Part 4. WHAT IS AN "APPLICATION"?

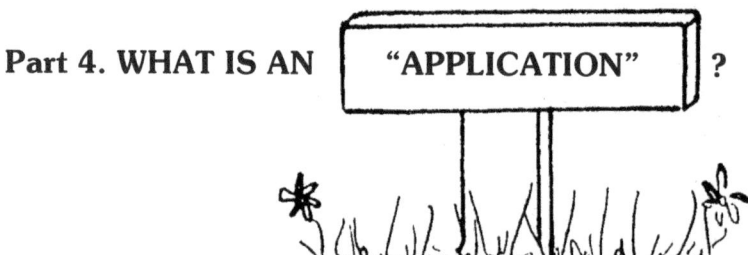

If a prophecy is written in symbolism, the first step toward understanding is the decoding or interpretation of the symbol. Only after that is carefully "nailed down" by Scriptural cross-reference, can the next step be taken—that of **application**. An example follows:

THE SYMBOL: "I saw in my vision...four great **beasts**..." Daniel 7:2,3.

THE DECODING: **Step No. 1 Interpretation**
The Bible interprets the symbols as follows: "These great beasts... are four kings." Daniel 7:17.

APPLICATION: **Step No. 2 Application**
The four kings, representing kingdoms, are: Babylon, Medo-Persia, Greece, and Rome.

Only after such "interpretation" of the symbol is complete, can the prophetic expositor make an **APPLICATION** to the correct persons or circumstances. When prophecy is written without symbolism, then Step No. 1 is eliminated. It then needs no "interpretation." It requires only Step No. 2—that of application.

Daniel 12 uses **NO SYMBOLISM.** It needs only an application to the correct circumstances. Therefore this book, A WARNING is not an "interpretation" of Daniel 12. Daniel 12 uses no symbolism, but it contains perplexing terminology which needs to be defined. Therefore the objectives of this book are to:

1. Classify the language form of Daniel 12 as "literal."
2. Define its terms with reference to the original Hebrew language.
3. Reduce the KJV's baffling terminology to simple everyday language.
4. Provide linkage between Daniel and Revelation.
5. Apply its plain, literal statements to circumstances as described in other passages with endtime prophetic significance.
6. Proclaim the warning, "that we shall all need to understand."
7. Bring confidence to God's people as the end approaches.

Skillful prophetic expositors see no tension or conflict between literal and symbolic forms of prophetic utterance. The Historicist "School" of Prophetic Interpretation and application has used both forms to identify historical-political-spiritual events of the past, present and future. Skillful exposition requires that the Bible student:

1. Recognize the difference between literal and symbolic language.
2. Understand the harmonious relationship between the two prophetic forms.

3. Permit the Scriptures to decode or "interpret" the symbols.
4. Use consistently the historicist methods with both forms.
5. Make consistent applications, using either form, extending the historical view as new concepts emerge as time advances the "unrolling of the scroll."

Part 5. WHAT IS AN "HISTORICIST"? A "FUTURIST"?

If one should declare that Daniel 12 is literal and applies it to the future, will he not be classified as a **"futurist"**?

First, consider Daniel 7:

Many years ago, Roman Catholic prophetic expositors **ignored the symbolism** of Daniel 7 with its symbolic "little horn." This little horn would persecute the saints for a "...time and times and the dividing of time,...and think to change times and laws...." This prophecy was a threat to them and they worked to make it ineffective. They **displaced the symbolism and substituted literal time.** They would not acknowledge the Year-day Computation Principle—the interpretation of prophetic-symbolic time, and declared this period of Daniel 7 to be a literal three and a half years to be fulfilled at the very end of time. This stance drew the accusing finger away from Rome.

Therefore, a "futurist" is one who substitutes literal applications in place of a true historicist interpretation of those prophecies which are written in symbolism and have time couched within the symbolic context. A "futurist" was one who was determined to divert the gaze from Papal Rome.

On the other hand, those of the Historicist "School" of Prophetic Interpretation[*], from the days of the Protestant Reformation, recognized symbolic-prophetic passages to be couched in figurative language. They used the cross reference method of study to interpret the symbols and the Year-day Computation Principle to interpret the times couched in symbolic text. They pointed the finger directly at Papal Rome as the fulfillment and persecutor of God's people, past and future! (See Revelation 13:1-10).

Now consider Daniel 12:

The historicist uses both symbolic and literal prophecy to provide an historical continuum of **past, present and future.** If one declares Daniel 12 to be written in literal language, to apply to the future he will take his place with the great historicists of the centuries.

Froom's statement is made concerning "Catholic Futurists" positions. He does not deny the historicist the right to view history as a continuum of past, present and future; nor does he deny the literal approach to prophecy written in literal language.

---

[*] ...the basic conflict between Catholic Futurist and the Protestant Historical schools is forcefully and inescapably portrayed. The utter irreconcilable conflict of opposites still stands—with Catholicism consistently the same, and Protestantism seriously shorn of its testimony, confused, capitulating and helpless when surrendering its historicist ground." L.E. Froom: *The Prophetic Faith of our Fathers*. Vol. III, p. 733.

Part 6. WHAT IS THE PROGRESSIVE "FORWARD MOVEMENT" OF THE BOOK OF DANIEL?

The book of Daniel presents seven lines of prophetic time.

1. Dan. 2   The metallic image and the stone kingdom established
2. Dan. 7   The four beasts and the little horn Papal power—1260 year-days
3. Dan. 8,9   The two beasts, horns and 2300 year-days to the judgment
4. Dan. 11   The kings involved in Judeo-Christian history to the **end**
5. Dan. 12:7   The "...time, times and an half...."
6. Dan. 12:11   The 1290 days
7. Dan. 12:12   The 1335 day wait

The Daniel 2 image sequence lays the historical foundation of scope and succession. The following timelines reiterate and lock in on Daniel 2. This enables the Bible scholar to get a secure footing in past history. Each additional timeline surges **forward giving additional details.** Daniel 7 moves forward to the little horn **Papal supremacy** which ended in **1798.** Daniel 8 and 9 timelines move still further forward to **1844.** Daniel 11 moves even to our own day and into the future. This forward, progressive movement of the book of Daniel, by the last chapter focuses on the climactic events of earth's history and endtime events.

In Summary:
1. The Daniel 2 sequence presents a succession of empires or kingdoms until Christ's kingdom is securely established.
2. The Daniel 7 sequence of "beasts" locks into the Daniel 2 timeline by reiterating the same succession of kingdoms but **adds** one significant feature—the rise of the "little horn" Papacy and defines its reign as a Papal Supremacy over Europe for "...a time, times and a half..." or 1260 years ending in 1798.
3. The Daniel 8-9 timelines of "beasts" and "horns" again reiterate that succession of empires and the Papal reign but **adds** one more significant factor moving forward to 1844, to the 2300 year-days, which specify the beginning of the Investigative Judgment.
4. The Daniel 11 timeline of kings reiterates Daniel 2, 7, 8, 9 with the same succession of kingdoms, but **moves forward** again to "the time of the end" (vs. 40-45) even to our own day and into the future.
5. The three timelines of Daniel 12 are simply extensions of Daniel 11, giving additional detail.

The progressive, forward movement of the entire book of Daniel carries the reader to final events in the last chapter. Chapter 12 deals exclusively with the **END** time.

DISCLAIMER

1. The three timelines of Daniel 12 are **NOT** rooted in, nor an extension of, the "seventy weeks" prophecy of Daniel 9:24-27. The "time, times and an half" of Daniel 12 is **NOT** the same time period as that of Daniel 7:25 nor the three and a half years from 31 A.D. to 34 of Daniel 9:24-27.

   The three timelines of Daniel 12 **ARE NOT** to be used in connection with the last three and a half years of the seventy weeks prophecy of Daniel 9 to support any form of "gap theory," whether originating within or without Adventism. The "gap theory" was instigated by Roman Papal futurists to thwart the identification of the "little horn" of Daniel 7 and 8 as Papal Rome. Modern Apostate Protestantism adopted it as a basis for those conclusions which ultimately lead to the rapture theory.

   Ellen G. White states plainly that the seventy weeks **ENDED** IN 34 A.D. They do **NOT** extend to the endtime. See PK 699, DA 233, and GC 410 where she says that "The one week [seven years] **ENDED** in 34 A.D."

2. The Daniel 12 timelines must stand alone as the last segment of fulfilled prophecy at the very end of time. The forward movement of the book of Daniel (see chart on page 11) places the Daniel 12 timelines at the very END of the book, describing the very end of time. When correctly understood they are the LAST SEGMENT of prophecy fulfilled by closing events of history. (Prophecy is simply history written before it happens). It is the LAST SEGMENT of application within the historicist school of prophetic interpretation. It is the last round of the "unrolling of the scroll."

3. It is imperative that the Bible student extricate the Daniel 12 timelines from any concept of dual application of Daniel 7:25 and especially from any "gap theory" proposed in regard to Daniel 9. To not do so is to cloud these timelines with error.

There is a similarity or parallel between the first three and a half years of the Christian church (31 to 34 A.D.) and the last three and a half years of Daniel 12, just as the early rain of the Holy Spirit was poured out at Pentecost to begin the Christian church, so also the latter rain will be poured out at the end of the Christian era.

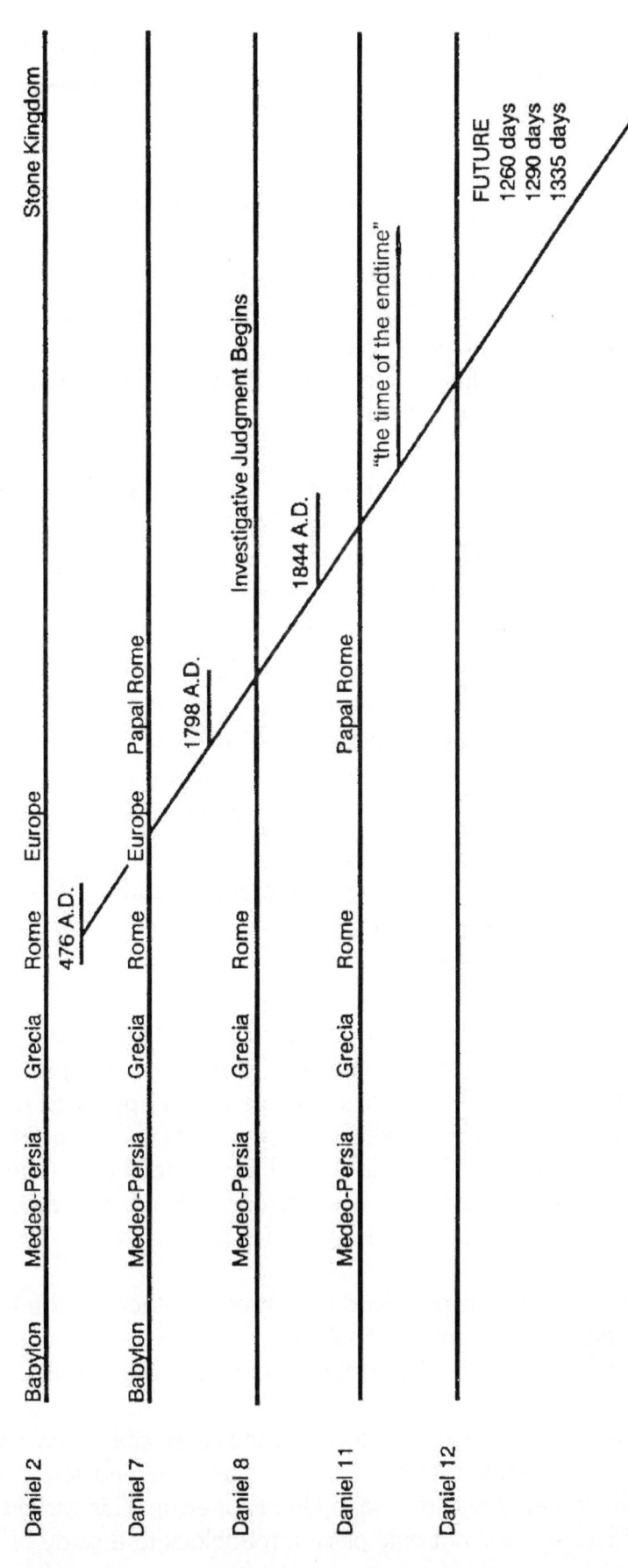

Part 7. WHAT ARE THE "OBJECTIONS TO FORMER APPLICATIONS" OF DANIEL 12?

The pioneers of Adventism studied the three timelines of Daniel 12. They attempted to fit them into their recent past, ending the timelines in 1798 and 1844. They viewed Daniel 12 as a reiteration of the 1260 and 2300 year-days of the prophecies of Daniel 7, 8, 9. Therefore they **assumed** the prophetic timelines of Daniel 12 to be symbolic time. From our vantage point in time, this presents problems as follows:

1. Daniel 12 is written without symbolism, in literal language. The timelines, in literal context, should be understood as literal days. Neither they, nor we, are permitted to decode literal language! In the providence of God, their secondary application was used to strengthen their prophetic stance for their time in history. We cannot stand on that same ground today. The unrolling of the scroll gives the last generation a wider perspective.

2. The literal language of Daniel 12 states plainly that it is dealing with the **END** when **ALL THINGS SHALL BE FINISHED.** This was not true in 1798 or 1844. It is still future!

3. Prophecy opens at the time of fulfillment. Over a century ago the pioneers were "prisoners of history" and could not be expected to open up prophecy which was then more than a hundred years before its time of fulfillment. The Lord did not burden them with "warnings" which were not pertinent to their day.

4. "In every age there is a new development of truth, ...COL 127. The truth for each age comes from the Bible. It is improper for this generation to expect the past generations to have done their Bible study for them.

Some approach the study of the prophecies of Daniel and Revelation, especially those prophetic elements which deal with time or timelines, with fear and apprehension. These feelings are due to certain statements made by Ellen G. White which appear to say that all prophecy pertaining to time or timelines ended in 1844. Those who have such consternation need to make a careful study of such statements. Truth is denied by a violation of hermeneutic principles. Wicked Babylon has prevented men from a study of the Bible and devised many kinds of error. The simple hermeneutic principles which are violated are:

1. One text shall not be permitted to destroy all others on the topic.
2. Statements must be read in context.
3. Historical settings and circumstances must be considered.

There are among us also, those who violate these principles, not only in a study of the Bible, but also in the use of Ellen G. White's writings. This is a Babylonish device to deflect men from a study of the Bible and it results in many kinds of error. This wicked mechanism, when applied to the Spirit of Prophecy will not only place a roadblock to a study of prophecy needed for endtime crisis, but gives great difficulty to any study of the Daniel 12 timelines. Those who have concern, should give concentrated study to the next section.

Part 8. WHAT "PROPHETIC TIME SHALL BE NO LONGER"?

Babylon claims that her doctrines come directly from the Bible! Her manifold errors rest upon an **unbalanced** use of Scripture. Her methods of theology are:

1. Use one text while ignoring all others on the subject.
2. Ignore the context—verses before and after the text in question.
3. Ignore the historical and circumstantial settings.

The same pernicious techniques can be applied to the writings of Ellen G. White!

1. One statement is used exclusively ignoring all others pertinent to the subject.
2. Statements are taken out of their historical and circumstantial settings.
3. Specific applications are presumed to be generalities with unlimited applications.

Today some are using both the Scripture, which says "...there should be time no longer...." (Revelation 10:6) and Ellen G. White's statements on the 2300 year-day prophecy in this same manner, by which to frighten men and women away from the study of endtime prophecies in the Word of God. They would wall off all those prophecies which deal with time, or endtime, or timelines in the books of Daniel and Revelation relating to the coming crisis and closing events of earth's history. Such movements are not of God, but are Satan's attempt to blind men's sight to those very prophetic truths which they shall most need to prepare them for events which lie right before us.

If such tactics are not recognized for their perversity, and if they are continued, their proponents will lead themselves and their followers right back in the darkness and confusion of Babylon! The following is a careful look at the statements of Ellen G. White, not only to observe correct hermeneutic rules in study of the Scripture but also to use the same integrity and techniques when examining her writings.

Part 9. WHAT IS THE "PROBLEM" ?

The angel of Revelation 10:6 declared, "...that there should be time no longer...." Ellen G. White explained that text, saying:

> This time, which the angel declares with a solemn oath, is not the end of this world's history, neither of probationary time, but of prophetic time, which should precede the advent of our Lord. That is, the people will not have another message upon definite time. After this period of time, reaching from 1842 to 1844, there can be no definite tracing of the prophetic time. The longest reckoning reaches to the autumn of 1844. (Ms. 59, 1900) 7 BC 971.

Again she wrote:

> This message announces the end of the prophetic periods. 2 SM 108.

In addition to these inspired statements, there are those who add uninspired assumptions, concluding that the Year-day Computation Principle, which converts prophetic time to literal time, became invalid in 1844. Some feel that it is dangerous to study any prophecy which mentions time or pertains to endtime applications.

The problem is that God's people become fearful of the Word of God, especially those portions which they most need to guide them through the time of trouble, to give them hope of final deliverance and an understanding of the endtime crisis so soon to fall upon the world.

Part 10. WHAT IS THE  "DILEMMA"?

The true worshiper must obey the words of Jesus: "Search the Scriptures...." John 5:39. "**All** Scripture is given by inspiration of God, and **is profitable**...." 2 Timothy 3:16. There is **NO** safety or logic in excluding certain portions of Scripture from study. True worshipers must **search** for the **Present Truth**, and **proclaim** it. God's people of the last generation must find guiding light from the prophetic Word, which applies to their own day as outlined in the books of Daniel and Revelation. They must focus on endtime prophecies which will prepare them for final crisis and deliverance. It is not safe to conclude that the endtime prophecies, which mention elements of time, must be read in a vague and meaningless manner without specific application. What hermeneutic rules can guide the people of God in their study of endtime prophecy of Daniel and Revelation and other parts of the Bible?

Part 11. WHAT ARE THE "HERMENEUTIC PRINCIPLES" ?

Those hermeneutic principles which bring harmony between the admonition to study all the Scripture and the statements of Ellen G. White are simple. Special emphasis should be placed on the following:

1. One Bible text shall not be permitted to destroy all others on the same subject!
2. One quotation by Ellen G. White shall not be permitted to destroy all others on the same subject.
3. Bible verses must be kept in context.
4. Quotations by Ellen G. White must be kept in context of the discussion.
5. Statements by Ellen G. White must be kept in circumstantial setting as explained in the following Part 12.

When such hermeneutic principles are followed, the statements of Scripture and Ellen G. White will be found in harmony. A good hermeneutic will solve the problem of careless assumptions making up excuses to ignore the Scriptures which deal with closing events!

Part 12. WHAT IS THE "CONTEXT AND HISTORICAL SETTING" OF REVELATION 10:5,6?

What is the context and historical setting of Revelation 10:5,6?

> And the angel which I saw stand upon the sea and upon the earth lifted up his hand to heaven, and sware by him that liveth for ever and ever,...that there should be time no longer." Rev. 10:5,6.

For over a century Seventh-day Adventists have recognized the context of Revelation 10:9, which describes the little book as honey in my mouth ...bitter in the belly, (author's paraphrase), as referring to the **sweetness** of the message given by the Great Advent Movement and to the **bitterness** of the Great Disappointment of October 22, 1844. This provides the historical setting. The theological context specifies that the message of the Great Advent Movement was based on **one** text—Daniel 8:14, and its explanation of the **prophetic time[LINE]** of the 2300 year-days which ended in 1844.

When Ellen G. White is commenting on Revelation 10:5,6 it must be remembered that she refers to prophetic **time** as the prophetic **timeLINE** of the 2300 year-days.

Part 13. WHAT IS  IN REVELATION 10?

It is imperative that the prophetic expositor and those who read the writings of Ellen G. White understand that her use of the phrase "prophetic time," **in connection with Revelation 10**, is like that of the angel himself in reference to the "prophetic **time[line]**" of Daniel 8:14 regarding **the 2300 year-days**. Neither the angel nor Ellen G. White was canceling out all other prophecies which deal with time as found in Revelation 16-22 and Daniel 12. The angel was not canceling out all prophetic utterances after 1844, and neither was Ellen G. White.

Therefore, when we read her statement it should be understood as follows:

> This time, which the angel declares with a solemn oath, is not the end of this world's history, neither of probationary time, but of [the] prophetic **time[line** of Daniel 8:14]**, which should precede the advent of our Lord. 7 BC 971.

When thus understood, this statement does not destroy any other prophecy! It has nothing to do with those timelines or events which follow 1844.

The PROPHETIC TIME LINE
[of the 2300 year-days]
ENDED IN 1844

Part 14. WHAT ARE THE "PROPHETIC PERIODS"?

> This message announces the end of the prophetic periods. (Ms. 32, 1896) 2 SM 108.

> After this period of time reaching from 1842 to 1844, there can be no definite tracing of the prophetic time. (Ms. 59, 1900) 7 BC 971.

Remember the historical setting and context! What **prophetic periods** were included in the 2300 year-day prophetic timeline of Daniel 8:14 and 9:24-27?

1. The seventy weeks Dan. 9:24.
2. The seven weeks Dan. 9:25.
3. The threescore and two weeks Dan. 9:25.
4. The seventieth week which includes events at the beginning of the week Dan 9:26.
5. The midst of the week Dan. 9:27.
6. The end of the week Dan. 9:27.
7. The 2300 year-days, ending in 1844 Dan. 8:14.

These prophetic periods contained within the 2300 year-day timelime cannot be restructured or retraced in a different manner than that which was done by the early Advent Movement. These **statements had nothing to do with prophecy or timelines regarding events pertaining to the last generation**. It is imperative that Ellen White's comments be kept in context or they will contradict each other! To misappropriate such comments effectively cuts off all study of Daniel and Revelation which apply to times after 1844.

When the quotations of the prophet are taken out of historical setting and out of context they do appear to contradict each other. Look at such so-called **contradictory** statements as follows:

This message [of Revelation 10:5,6] announces the end **of the prophetic periods**. 2 SM 108.	In the Scriptures are truths that relate especially **TO OUR OWN TIME** to the period just prior to the appearing of the Son of man,...The **prophetic periods**...extending to the very eve of the great consummation, **throw a flood of light upon events then to transpire.** (RH Sept. 25, 1883) 1 RH 367.

Whereas the quotation on the left refers to the prophetic periods **prior to** 1844 (as contained in the Daniel 8:14, 2300 year-day timeline), the prophetic periods in the right quotation refer to those **after 1844 extending to the eve of the great consummation**.

The PROPHETIC TIME [LINE of the 2300 year-days—and its PROPHETIC PERIODS contained therein] ENDED IN 1844

Part 15. WHAT WAS THE "CIRCUMSTANTIAL SETTING"?

After the 1844 Disappointment, there were those who did not accept the explanation that Jesus had not come to this earth as expected, but rather had entered into the Most Holy Place to begin the Investigative Judgment. Such persons returned to the timeline of Daniel and especially the 2300 year-day prophecy seeking new dates and ways in which to arrange it and the prophetic periods contained therein to predict various times for the Lord to come. These persons who were continually setting new dates and having more disappointments were told by Ellen G. White that there could be no more **definite tracing** of those 2300 year-day prophetic periods to establish a date for the coming of Jesus. Regarding such efforts she gave counsel:

> ...the people will not have another message upon definite time [**expecting the Lord to come on a definite date**]. After this period of time, reaching from 1842 to 1844, there can be no definite tracing of **the** prophetic time. (Ms. 59, 1900) 7 BC 971.

This problem is spelled out in the following quotations:

> Different times were set **for the Lord to come**, and were urged upon the brethren. But the Lord showed me that they would pass by, for the time of trouble must take place before the coming of Christ. 1 T 72.

> Time after time will be set by different ones, and will pass by; and the influence of this time setting will tend to destroy the faith of God's people...for the time of trouble must come before the coming of Christ,.... 1 T 72,73.

The circumstantial setting for Ellen G. White's statements that there can be **no definite tracing of the time** and that the prophetic periods (of the 2300 year-day prophecy) had come to its end pertained to **date-setting for the Coming of Christ**. Again let it be said that we cannot know the day nor hour of His coming! However, we may study the timelines of Daniel and Revelation in order to delineate closing events and we are obligated to know when it is "near even at the door."*

---

* Note: "The First-day Adventists have set time after time, and notwithstanding the repeated failures, they have gathered courage to set new times. God has not led them in this. Many of the have rejected the true prophetic time, and ignored the fulfillment of prophecy.... The Great Test was in 1843 and 1844; and all who have set time since then have been deceiving themselves and deceiving others." 1 T 73

She was referring, not to prophecy in general, but specifically to the 2300 Year-day timeline of Daniel 8:14. It was this prophecy and timeline which was abused by unbelievers.

Part 16. WHAT WAS THE "FOCUS OF DANIEL 8:14"?

The focus of the Daniel 8:14 timeline prophecy was not designed to provide a date for the Second Coming of Jesus. To assume that it did was a mistake which caused the Great Disappointment of 1844. Neither is the Second Coming of Jesus and its exact date the focus of any other prophecy, including that of Daniel 12. Then what was the focus of the 2300 year-day timeline? **IT GAVE THE DATE FOR THE BEGINNING OF THE INVESTIGATIVE JUDGMENT!** It pointed to the changing ministry of Christ and His movement from the Holy Place to the Most Holy Place of the heavenly sanctuary. It drew attention to the Ten Commandment Law and the sacredness of the fourth commandment, the true seventh-day Sabbath. It called for the perfecting of a people to meet judgment. It signaled the beginning of the judgment of the dead, after which would follow the judgment of the living. It never was intended to focus on the Second Coming of Jesus.

Evangelists point to the Second Coming of Jesus as a doctrine. It is the Blessed Hope toward which all Scripture, including prophecy, points. But prophecy and prophetic timelines never have and never will set a date for the coming of Jesus. The day and hour will not be known until it is announced by the Voice of God under the 7th plague. (See GC 640). **We have no need to know the date**, day and hour, of His coming. What we need to know is the information **REGARDING EVENTS WHICH PERTAIN TO THE CLOSING UP OF THE INVESTIGATIVE JUDGMENT**. Daniel 12 focuses on the end-time scenario to help us endure the time of trouble just before us.

Prophecy is that light spoken of in 2 Peter 1:19 which helps us get our bearings and sense of direction as to where we are in the unrolling of the scroll. It identifies God's true people as well as the enemy. It warns us when to get out of the large cities and tells us how to wait patiently for God to work out the great controversy. It assures us that deliverance is on the way. Prophecy does not give dates for the falling of the latter rain, nor the close of probation, nor the coming of Jesus. The Daniel 12 timelines focus on the legislative and judicial actions which lead into final crisis and provide a delineation of events in their order. It gives us that warning which we shall all need before the time of the end. In summary, we do need help to get through the time of trouble, but we **DO NOT** know and **DO NOT** need the date of His coming.

Part 17. WHAT "WILL NEVER BE A TEST AGAIN"?

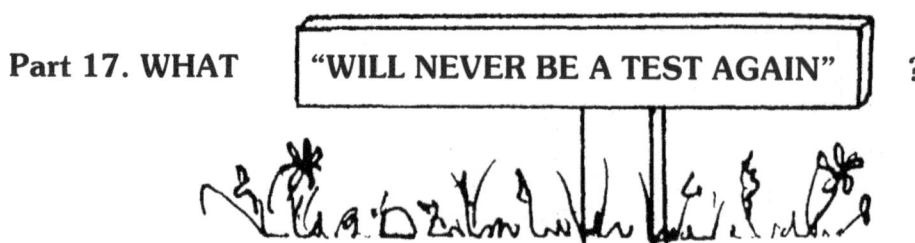

It was not the timeline of Daniel 8:14 which was the test; it was the mistake by those who assumed that it pointed to the date of the coming of Jesus which made it a test. God held His hand over that mistake and permitted it to become a test. That test became an instrument in His hand so that only the true in heart might be gathered to become that last great remnant to give the true gospel to all the world.

Now we know what that mistake was. That prophecy and timeline will never again be a test to God's people. We will not make that same mistake again. Never again will we use Daniel 8:14 timeline, nor any other timeline to set a date for His coming. These facts should not stand in the way of our study of the timelines which delineate endtime events that precede His coming.

The First-day Adventists did not accept the full meaning of the Daniel 8:14 timeline, concerning the judgment, the Ten Commandment Law and the true seventh-day Sabbath. Consequently, they continued to set dates by that timeline using arguments that Ellen G. White declared to be **unscriptural and unsound.**

> The First-day Adventists have set time after time, and notwithstanding the repeated failures, they have gathered courage to set new times. God has not led them in this. Many of them have rejected the true prophetic time, and ignored the fulfillment of prophecy.... The great test was in 1843 and 1844; and all who have set time since then have been deceiving themselves and deceiving others. 1 T 73.

The studies of the timelines of Daniel 12 do not present a **test** on time for the coming of Jesus, but they delineate future events leading us to the eve of the great consummation!

Part 18. WHAT ARE THE 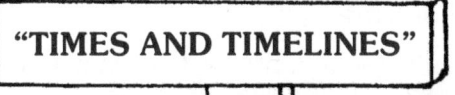 **OF THE FUTURE?**

There are several times and timelines in Daniel and Revelation which pertain to the future. Ellen G. White also commented on some of them, placing them in a future setting. For example, she wrote:

> Trumpet after trumpet is **TO BE** sounded, vial after vial poured out one after another upon the inhabitants of the earth. Scenes of stupendous interest are right upon us (Letter 109, 1890). 7 BC 982.

The above statement places the trumpets in the future. In these trumpets **time** is mentioned as follows:

> ...**the day**...a third part of it, and **the night** likewise. Rev. 8:12.
>
> ...**five months**. Rev. 9:5,10.
>
> ...an **hour**, and a **day**, and a **month**, and a **year**,.... Rev. 9:15.*

The plagues mentioned in Revelation 11:6 and 16 are yet future. In that chapter **time** is mentioned again:

> ...**a thousand two hundred and threescore days**,.... Rev. 11:3.
>
> ...**three days and an half**.... Rev. 11:11.
>
> ...**the same hour**.... Rev. 11.13.

Revelation 13 refers to the beast whose wounded head is finally healed so that "all the world wondered after the beast." This has not yet been fulfilled as all nations are not yet wondering after the Papacy to the extent that he has the power to "make war with the saints" in the final "scattering" or persecution of God's people. That prophecy continues to say:

> ...power was given unto him to continue **forty and two months**. Rev. 13:5.

Revelation 17 also mentions **time**:

> ...ten kings...receive power as kings one **hour**.... Rev. 17:12.

Revelation 18 mentions **time**:

> Therefore shall her plagues come in **one day**.... Rev. 18:8.
>
> ...for in **one hour** is thy judgment come. Rev. 18:10.
>
> For in **one hour** so great riches is come to naught. Rev. 18:17.
>
> ...for in **one hour** is she made desolate. Rev. 18:19.

---

*   Or a period of time

Revelation 20 also has a unit of **time**:

> ...for the witness of Jesus... with Christ **a thousand years**. Rev. 20:4.

> ...the rest of the dead lived not again until **the thousand years** were finished. Rev. 20:5.

There is also a reference to **time** which is yet future in Revelation 8:

> ...silence in heaven **about the space of half an hour**. Rev. 8:1.

Shall we just ignore all these sections of Revelation? Shall we conclude that God never intended His people to understand the meaning of any such prophecies after 1844? Is this all forbidden territory? If so, why are these time prophecies there? Did Ellen G. White take this attitude toward all such prophecy?

Shall we all just close our eyes to the last chapter of Daniel of which E. G. White said plainly:

> Let us read and study the twelfth chapter of Daniel. It contains a warning that we shall all need before the time of the end. Letter 161, July 30, 1903.

Shall we just write off the three timeliness of Daniel 12 which delineate closing events?

Part 19. WHAT IS THE "YEAR-DAY COMPUTATION PRINCIPLE"?

Is the **Year-day Computation Principle** obsolete? Did Ellen G. White ever declare this instrument of conversion of symbolic-prophetic time to literal time was done away with in 1844? Of course not! Shall we forbid ourselves to use the Year-day Computation Principle now to convert time (couched in prophetic symbolism) to literal time, by which the symbolism of Revelation can be joined to the literal statements of Daniel 12? Must we cast a web of our own making around ourselves so that we cannot link Revelation with Daniel?

Shall we just ignore all those sections of Revelation pertaining to time, especially those that have to do with **definite** measurements of time such as an hour, a month, a year as being indefinite time, "just a short space" or "a while"?

> For I testify unto every man that heareth the words of the prophecy of this book, If any man shall add unto these things, God shall add unto him the plagues that are written in this book: And if any man shall take away from the words of the book of this prophecy, God shall take away his part out of the book of life, and out of the holy city, and from the things which are written in this book. Rev. 22:18,19.

There are many references by Ellen G. White which urge God's people to study the books of Daniel and Revelation together. She places these prophecies in an endtime setting. It is therefore imperative that the Bible student open his mind and heart to study anew the treasures in the Word which await their correct timing for perfect understanding.

Therefore, we may conclude that the **Year-day Computation Principle** is simply a unit of conversion—a mathematical tool. It is like a yardstick which is kept in the corner until needed. It is used for measurement and conversion of prophetic time. This is essential for use in combining the symbolism of Revelation with the literal parts of Daniel.

When the Jesuit futurist expositors determined to divert attention from the persecuting "little horn" in Daniel 7:25, as it existed for 1260 years in a Papal supremacy, their first move was to discard and deny the "Year-day Computation Principle."

If the endtime prophetic expositor follows in the Jesuit futurist footsteps, he also will declare that the "Year-day Computation Principle" ended in 1844. By denying it, he has destroyed the linkage between Daniel and Revelation. Endtime prophecy in Daniel 12 concerns literal time whereas the endtime prophecies of Revelation are couched in symbolism. The "Year-day Computation Principle" provides the only linkage in time between the two!

If Satan can get rid of the "Year-day Computation Principle" he knows that he can prevent an understanding of the 30 day difference between the Daniel 12 timelines (1260 days and 1290 days) so that they cannot be linked with the prophetic time of Revelation 17 and 18. The times referred to in Revelation 17 and 18 cannot have meaning until they are decoded by the "Year-day Computation Principle" and linked to Daniel 12.

Denying the "Year-day Computation Principle" will be as effective in blocking prophetic understanding in the endtime as it was in the middle ages!

Part 20. WHAT "WOULD JESUS SAY"?

What did Jesus say?

> But of that day and hour knoweth no man, no, not the angels of heaven, but my father only. Matt. 24:36. **BUT**

> So likewise ye, when ye shall see all these things, know that it is near, even at the door. Matt. 24:33.

> We have also a more sure word of prophecy; whereunto ye do well that ye take heed, as unto a light that shineth in a dark place until the day dawn, and the day star arise in your hearts: 2 Peter 1:9.

> Search the Scriptures;.... John 5:39.

We find as we search Daniel 12 and related prophecies that it does not give the day nor hour of the coming of Jesus. The timelines of Daniel 12 do not give any clue to that information. There is no date-setting for His coming!

The timelines of Daniel 12 give information so His saints can know "that it is near, even at the door...." The Father will announce the day and hour Himself!

The timelines of Daniel 12 are to:

1. Give warning that the endtime scenario has begun.
2. Provide focus on the warning signs to God's people to flee the large cities.
3. Give warning regarding the messages of Revelation 13.
4. Delineate major events and their sequence in the endtime scenario.
5. Clarify political conditions which will surround the people of God in the final crisis.
6. Give hope of protection in time of trouble.
7. Assure the saints of final deliverance from the wicked.
8. Provide insight into the significance of the legislative enactments of earth and heaven.
9. Spur interest in the study of closing events.
10. Link many prophetic passages together in a clear picture of endtime events.

SUMMARY OF CHAPTER I

WHAT ARE THE PRINCIPLES OF INTERPRETATION?

1. Daniel 12 is "A WARNING" which we shall (future tense) all need to understand before the time of the end of the earth's history.
2. Daniel 12 concentrates on the "end," "when all these things shall be finished" and it pertains to the future.
3. The forward, progressive movement of the entire book of Daniel propels the last chapter (12) to endtime events and future fulfillment.
4. Prophecy is "history written in advance." It is the "unrolling of the scroll,"—a continuum of historical past, present and future. Prophetic expositors who apply Daniel 12 to future events are "historicists" not Jesuit "Futurists"!
5. Whereas the Daniel 8:14 timeline gave warning of the **beginning** of the Investigative Judgment, the Daniel 12 timelines are a warning of the nearness of the **closing** of the Investigative Judgment.
6. Daniel 12 must be treated in the same consistent manner as all other Scripture—with "THE LITERAL APPROACH."
7. Daniel 12 is written in literal language—not symbolism.
8. The literal language of Daniel 12 cannot be "decoded"—interpreted. It can be given only an historical application—applied to future events.
9. This book, *A WARNING* is not an "interpretation" of Daniel 12. It is an exposition or clarification of terms and an application of prophecy to future events.
10. The Daniel 12 timelines do not give a date, day nor hour for the Second Coming of Jesus. They do reveal that He is "near, even at the door."
11. The principles of integrity which are the basis for hermeneutic rules apply, not only to a study of Scripture, but also to the use of the writings of Ellen G. White:
    a. One statement shall not destroy the effect of all others on the topic.
    b. Statements must be understood in context.
    c. Statements must be placed in correct circumstantial settings.
12. Spirit of prophecy statements, taken out of context and setting, are given perverse meanings which stifle prophetic studies.
13. The "Prophetic time[LINE] which ended in 1844" was the 2300 year-days of Daniel 8:14.
14. The "Prophetic periods which ended in 1844" were those periods within the 2300 years as interpreted in Daniel 9:24-27.

15. The "definite tracing" of prophetic time which ended in 1844, pertained to the computation and dating of the 2300 year-day prophecy.
16. Time will never be a test again as it was in 1844 because the "great test" or "final test" will concern the true Sabbath and the Law of God.
17. Many prophecies of Revelation, yet to be fulfilled, refer to time periods of definite specifications: a day, an hour, a half hour, a month, a year, one third of a day and a night.
18. God's people are forbidden to ignore or "take away" from Revelation any part and that includes the references to time.
19. The "Year-day Computation Principle" is a mathematical tool. It did not end in 1844.
20. The "Year-day Computation Principle" is a necessary tool to link Daniel and Revelation. It links the symbolic time of Revelation to the literal time of Daniel 12.
21. The time has come for the last generation to understand the three timelines of Daniel 12.
22. Daniel 12, when given a future application, is "a new development of truth" for this age, and as such is a "**primary**" application for the last generation.

CHAPTER II

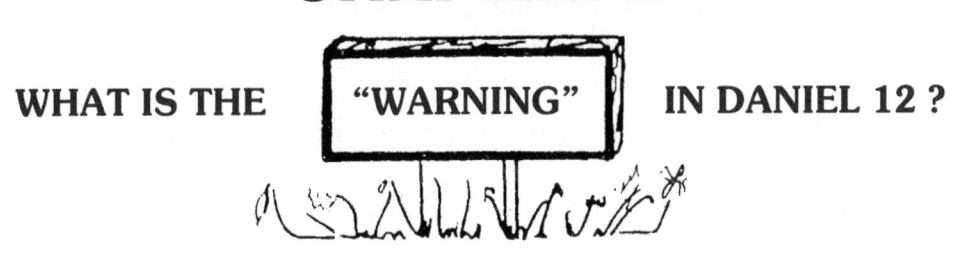

WHAT IS THE "WARNING" IN DANIEL 12 ?

Daniel 12 is not written in prophetic symbolism. It does not need to be decoded; but it does contain prophetic "terminology"—words and phrases, which need to be (a) traced in the original Hebrew language, (b) "translated" into modern language, (c) cross-referenced for historical association (d) correlated with other prophetic passages (especially those of Matthew 24 and Revelation 13 which have references to the same endtime events.)

Therefore, Chapter II is an attempt to: (a) define the content of Daniel 12, (b) determine the basic concepts addressed therein, (c) define the terminology, (d) correlate it with related prophecies in Revelation and (e) define the concepts involved in this study.

The following questions must be answered to discover the nature of the **WARNING** in Daniel 12:

1. What is "The Question" of Daniel 12?
2. What is "The Answer" given by Jesus?
3. What is "The Abomination"?
4. What is "The Desolation"?
5. What is "The Abomination of Desolation" referred to in Daniel 12?
6. What is a "Dual Application"?
7. What is "The Warning"?
8. What is "The Final Test"?
9. What is "The Judgment of the Living"?
10. What is "The Shaking"?
11. What is "The Seal of God"?
12. What is "The Loud Cry" Warning?
13. What is "The Third Angel's Warning Message"?

When these questions are answered and the terminology defined, the reader will know what the **WARNING** is in the endtime prophetic timelines of Daniel 12.

Part 1. WHAT IS "THE QUESTION"?

First the question. Then the answer. What is the Question? The disciples asked it. The saints who already inhabit heaven asked it. (See Daniel 8:13). We are asking it. Daniel asked it in Daniel 12. What is the question?

> Tell us...what shall be the sign of thy coming, and of the end of the world? Matt. 24:1-3.

> Then I Daniel looked, and, behold, there stood other two [saints],.... And one said.... **How long shall it be to the end**?.... Dan. 12:5,6.

> ...O my Lord, **what shall be the end of these things**? Dan. 12:8.

How long shall it be to the end?

Daniel asked it. Five hundred years later the disciples were asking the same question! It is a most vital question considered by students of Scripture in all the ages, but it becomes urgent and consuming to those who are the last generation!

This **question** and its **answers** are the key to understanding the three timelines of Daniel 12. What is the answer?

Part 2. WHAT IS "THE ANSWER"?

It is Jesus who answered the question! It was He who answered the disciples in Matthew 24 and again it is Jesus ("the man clothed in linen, which was upon the waters of the river")[*], who answered Daniel's question by giving him the three timelines found in Daniel 12. The prophecies of Matthew 24 and Daniel 12 are **related**!

THE QUESTION

Matthew 24:3	**Daniel 12:6**
...the disciples came unto him privately, saying tell us, when shall these things be? and what shall be the sign of thy coming and of the end of the world?	And one said to the man clothed in linen.... How long shall it be to the end of these wonders?

The questions are related and the answers are related.

THE ANSWER

Matthew 24:15,16	**Daniel 12:11**
When ye therefore shall see the **abomination of desolation**, spoken of by Daniel the prophet, stand in the holy place, (whoso readeth, let him understand:) Then let them which be in Judea flee into the mountains:	And from the time that the daily shall be taken away, and the **abomination that maketh desolate** set up, there shall be a thousand two hundred and ninety days.

Jesus, in the most specific manner, connected the events spoken of in Matthew 24 with the book of Daniel. His answer to the disciples' question plainly reveals this relationship when He told them (and us) to keep our eyes focused on "the abomination of desolation, **spoken of by Daniel the prophet**" Matthew 24:15.

The "abomination of desolation" (or transgression of desolation) was spoken of by Daniel in the following references: Daniel 8:12, 13, 23; 9:27; 11:31 and 12:11. Each of these references is prophecy because the fulfillment would occur after Daniel's day. However, several of these references refer to different historical events and therefore each must be given its correct application.

---

[*] To identify "the man clothed in linen" in Daniel 12:7 as Jesus see 4BC 858, 879. It is Jesus, in His priestly ministry "clothed in linen," who walked upon the water!

There must be a definition and identification of the "abomination of desolation" before:

   a. the relationship between Matthew 24 and Daniel 12:11 can be established,
   b. the prophetic timelines of Daniel 12 can be understood, and
   c. the historical events connected with their prophetic utterance.

What or who was the abomination of desolation in the days of the disciples when they saw fulfillment? Who was it in the dark ages? Who will it be in the future?

Part 3. WHAT IS THE "ABOMINATION"?

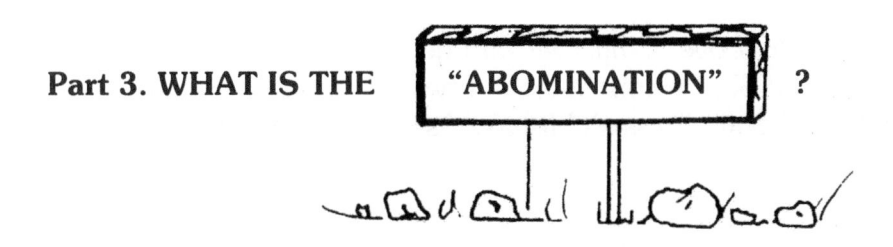

It is astonishing as to how many students of the Scriptures will ignore the **One** who gave the prophecy, the **ONE** who repeated it to His disciples, and the **One** who so plainly identified it in another parallel passage of Scripture! It is incredible that so many ignore the words of Jesus, and labor to construct some other complicated explanation to focus on some peripheral idea rather than on the specific identification as given by Jesus Himself!

This "abomination of desolation" was shown to Daniel in prophetic vision and given to him, as in all other prophetic Scripture, from "**Jesus Christ**, which God gave unto him, to show unto his servants things which must shortly come to pass; and he sent and signified it by his angel unto his servant John"[or Daniel] Revelation 1:1. About 500 years later, it was Jesus who again called attention to it in Matthew 24:15. And it is this same Jesus who identifies exactly who this abomination is in the parallel Scripture of Luke 21:20,21.

Matthew 24:15,16	Luke 21:20,21
When ye therefore shall see the **abomination of desolation,** spoken of by Daniel the prophet, stand in the holy place, (whoso readeth, let him understand:) Then let them... flee into the mountains:	And when ye shall see Jerusalem compassed with **armies**, then know that the **desolation** thereof is nigh. Then let them which are in Judea flee to the mountains;....

Matthew 24 refers to the "abomination of desolation" but in Luke 21:20,21 the term is shortened simply to "desolation." The meaning is the same which is evidenced by similar context and admonition to "flee into the mountains." In Matthew, Jesus referred to the enemy as the "abomination," but in Luke that "abomination" is simply spoken of as "armies" (the armies of **Rome**). It is the Scripture itself, in the very words of Jesus, by Bible cross-reference which identifies the "abomination" to be **ROME**!

For more than a century, God's Sabbath-keepers have identified the "abomination of desolation" in Matthew and Daniel as Rome, first Pagan, then Papal, in its past and future historic role. The most recent comprehensive statement of definition is as follows:

> When "the abomination of desolation, spoken of by Daniel the prophet" is set up (Matt. 24:15), Jesus' people are to pray that their flight from their persecutors will not be on the Sabbath day. Jesus was referring to Dan. 8:13 and 9:27. The little-horn power of Daniel 8 represents both Pagan and Papal Rome. It first set up the "abomination of desolation" (Matt. 24:15), or "the desolating sacrilege" (RSV) when the Roman armies threatened Jerusalem (A.D. 66-70). The context of Jesus' statement indicates that a second fulfillment came in the Middle Ages. (See Matt. 24:15-29.) Because Matthew chapter 24 is using historical events as a type of end-time events, we know that just prior to the Second Advent "the abomination of desolation" once more will become a threat to the religious liberty of the people of God. *Adult Sabbath School Lessons.* Lesson 6, November 5,

1988, page 48. *God Reveals His Love. What Seventh-day Adventists Believe.* October, November, December 1988. Lesson Authors: Erwin R. Gane, J. Robert Spangler, Leo R. Van Dolson. Pacific Press Publishing Association, Nampa. ID 83687.

Let us lay aside all conjecture and lines of reasoning and begin with the words of Christ! Permit the Bible to be its own expositor! Not until the Bible student gets this fundamental understanding is he ready to understand Daniel 12! Enter it into the mental notebook. THE **ABOMINATION OF DESOLATION WAS, IS, AND WILL BE ROME**.

It is imperative that those who seek to understand Daniel 12 align themselves with the historicist school of interpretation. How have the historicists identified the "abomination of desolation" down through the centuries?

> **The abomination of desolation**. See on Daniel 9:27, 11:31, 12:11.... The parallel passage in Luke reads, "When ye shall see Jerusalem compassed with armies, then know that the desolation thereof is nigh" (ch. 21:20). The event foretold is obviously the destruction of Jerusalem by the **Romans** in A.D. 70,.... (Emphasis supplied by author). (Comment on Matthew 24:15). 5 BC 499

> ...Daniel saw **Rome** first in its Pagan, imperial phase, warring against the Jewish people and the early Christians, and then in its Papal phase, continuing down to our own day **and into the future**, warring against the true church. On this double application see on vs. 13, 23. (Comment on Daniel 8:5-11). 4 BC 841.

> ...This has reference in part at least to the horrors and atrocities that were perpetrated upon the Jewish nation by the Romans in A.D. 70. (Comment on Daniel 9:27). 4 BC 855.

Historicists have consistently understood the "abomination of desolation" to refer to **Rome**. This has been the consistent view of the Protestant Reformation and Adventism. When would-be prophetic expositors leave this platform, darkness and confusion are the inevitable result. Without this understanding there can be no insight into the meaning of the three timelines of Daniel 12.

In summary of the Bible Commentary quotations it should be noted that Daniel, the prophet, saw the "abomination of desolation" to be:

1. **ROME** in its Pagan phase in the destruction of Jerusalem in 70 A.D.
2. **ROME** in its Papal phase in the persecutions of Christians. (538-1798)
3. **ROME** in its Papal phase in future persecutions.

The "abomination of desolation" in its future persecutions is described in Daniel 12:7 and 11 timeline prophecies. It is the warning of these future persecutions of which Ellen G. White wrote:

> Let us read and study the 12th chapter of Daniel. It is a warning we shall all need to understand before the time of the end. Ellen G. White Ltr. 161, July 30, 1903.

It is this warning in Daniel 12 which links it with the same warning found in Revelation chapters 13 and 14. When "all the world wondered after the beast... all...nations...." This is also the warning found in Revelation 13:15.*

---

* Note: This warning is comprehensive. It has dimensions of political and spiritual significance. The distress of God's people involves persecution **and** a warning of the closing of probationary time.

Part 4. WHAT IS THE "DESOLATION"?

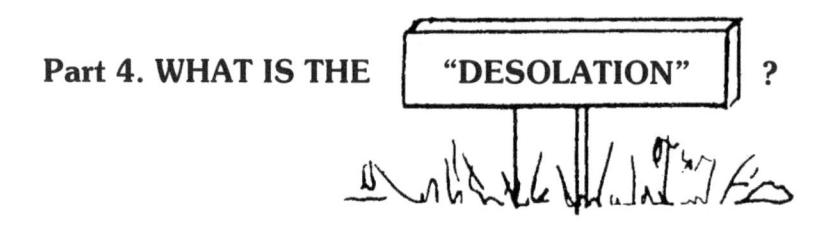

Definition:

> **Desolation**: "laying waste; ruin, destruction, havoc, ravage." Webster's Dictionary

The prophet Daniel saw three specific **desolations** in prophecy:

Dan. 9:26,27	The destruction of the temple and Jerusalem 70 A.D.
Dan. 7:20,21,25; 8:9-13,24; 11:31	The desolation or persecution of the Christian church in Europe which was called **The Papal Supremacy (No.1)** 538-1798 A.D.
Dan. 12:11; 12:7; 11:41-44 Rev. 13:7	The **desolation** or persecution as described in Revelation 13 will be known as **The Papal Supremacy (No. 2) coming in the Future**.

****

Papal Supremacy (No. 2) will be different from that which existed from 538 to 1798 in Europe. **Papal Supremacy (No. 2)** as described in Revelation 13 will be, not merely over Europe, but over **ALL** the world!

> ...his deadly wound was healed: and **ALL** the world wondered after the beast. Rev. 13:3.

> And it was given him to make war with the saints, and to overcome them [desolate them]: Rev. 13:7.

> ...and power was given him over **ALL** kindreds and tongues and nations. Rev. 13:7.

> And **ALL** that dwell upon the earth shall worship him, whose names are not written in the book of life.... Rev. 13:8.

> ...as many as would not worship the image of the beast should be killed [desolated] Rev. 13:15.

The abomination of desolation spoken of by Daniel the prophet, quoted in Matthew 24:15, is the same abomination of desolation mentioned in Daniel 12:7 and 11, and this **Daniel 12 prophecy is a parallel of Revelation 13**!

In every prophetic timeline of Daniel, **ROME** is brought to view:

			ROME IS THE
Daniel 2	The Image	The Legs of Iron	Iron
Daniel 7	The Beasts	The Fourth Beast	Little Horn
Daniel 8	The Horns	The Little Horn	Transgression of Desolation
Daniel 11	The Kings	(Verse 15-45)	Abomination that Maketh Desolate
Daniel 12		(No Symbols—only a name)	Abomination that Maketh Desolate

The legs of the image, and **iron** and clay, representing Rome, continue until "all the chaff is blown away." The fourth beast of Daniel 7 continues even with its "little horn" until Daniel saw it destroyed, and "given to the burning flame." Daniel 7:11. In every timeline **Rome** continues until the end of time! It is one of the main characters of Daniel and Revelation. It is, in every age since its beginning, the great persecutor and desolator of God's people. In the days of Jesus, it was the Roman Empire (Pagan Rome) which "made desolate" or persecuted God's people. It was Rome which ruled over the Jews, gave authority to crucify Jesus, and persecuted the early Christians.

It was Papal Rome which persecuted (desolated) the Christian Church according to the prophecies of Daniel 7:25, Revelation 12:6, 14, and Revelation 13:2, 3 for one thousand two hundred and sixty years during what was known as the Papal Supremacy over Europe. It was Papal Rome which received a deadly wound in 1798, but which has been healing ever since. It is Rome, in the future, that will be a healed power. In Revelation 13, it will establish **Papal Supremacy (No. 2)**. It will reign not merely over Europe but "all the world shall wonder after the beast." Revelation 13:3-7.

In the days when Jesus answered His disciples, he referred to the armies of Rome as the **abomination of desolation**. He spoke of Rome as the **abomination** and the destruction of Jerusalem, which was to occur in 70 A.D., as the **desolation**. It is a fact that the Roman Empire fell and Rome was sacked in 476 A.D., but in its place arose Papal Rome, and it is this phase of Rome on which we need to fasten our vision!*

---

* Note: The Hebrew word for "abomination" is **Shigguts**. It was applied to unclean foods and that which was displeasing to God. This word was also applied to the heathen nations which worshiped idols and which were basically sun worshipers. These nations were known for their filthy practices and especially for their blood-thirsty religious rituals in which human sacrifices and all kinds of cruelty abounded. Papal Rome exalted and absorbed the Pagan (abomination) practices, and the prophet John saw her "drunken with the blood of the saints of Jesus," which was the "desolation" of God's people.

Part 5. WHAT IS THE "ABOMINATION OF DESOLATION" OF DANIEL 12?

The **abomination of desolation** is mentioned in Daniel 12 as follows:

> And from the time that the daily...shall be taken away, and the abomination that maketh desolate set up, there shall be a thousand two hundred and ninety days. Dan. 12:11.

Jesus interpreted this term found in Matthew 24:15, and defined in Luke 21:20, to refer to the **armies of ROME**. This interpretation should be sustained.

1. In the days of Christ, the abomination referred to Pagan Rome—the Roman Empire.
2. It must be remembered that the Roman Empire was succeeded by Papal Rome.
3. It is Papal Rome which fulfilled the prophecies of Daniel 8 and 11 in reference to the **abomination of desolation** from 538 to 1798.
4. Therefore, any endtime application must refer to Papal Rome.
5. It is Papal Rome which again fulfills the prophecy of Daniel 12:11 in the future.

The **abomination of desolation** describes Papal Rome in its persecutions, past, present and future. It was Rome which **desolated** Jerusalem in 70 A.D., it was Papal Rome which **desolated** the saints for 1260 years (Daniel 8) and it will be Papal Rome which will **desolate**—persecute God's people in the future as designated in Daniel 12.

Therefore, the term **abomination of desolation** is specifically, the Papacy involved in a persecution and described as a future threat in Daniel 12.

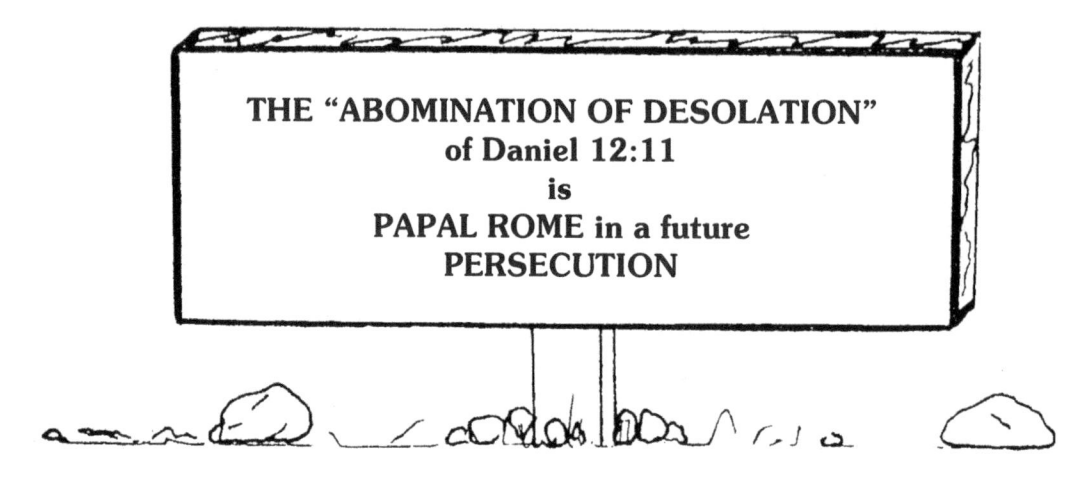

> THE "ABOMINATION OF DESOLATION"
> of Daniel 12:11
> is
> PAPAL ROME in a future
> PERSECUTION

If there is one truth which Satan would obscure, it is this. If there is one truth needed, to understand the three timelines of Daniel 12, it is this: that the **abomination of desolation** is Papal Rome since it will persecute the saints just before Jesus comes. It is the beast of Revelation 13, and the focus of the third angel's warning message of Revelation 14.

Part 6. WHAT IS A "DUAL APPLICATION"?

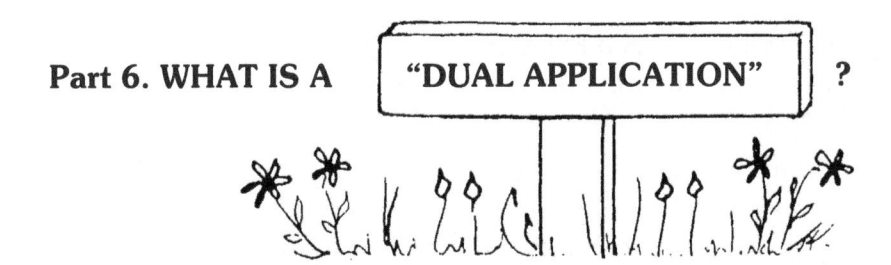

Definitions:

"Tell us," they said, "when shall these things be? and what shall be the sign of Thy coming, and of the end of the world?" Jesus did not answer His disciples by taking up separately the destruction of Jerusalem and the great day of His coming. He **MINGLED** the description of these **TWO** events. Had He opened to His disciples future events as He beheld them, they would have been unable to endure the sight. In mercy to them He **BLENDED** the description of the **TWO** great crises, leaving the disciples to study out the meaning for themselves. When He referred to the destruction of Jerusalem, His prophetic words reached beyond that event to the final conflagration in that day when the Lord shall rise out of His place to punish the world for their iniquity, when the earth shall disclose her blood, and shall no more cover her slain. This **ENTIRE** discourse [Matthew 24] was given, not for the disciples only, but for those who should live **IN THE LAST SCENES OF THIS EARTH'S HISTORY**. DA 628.

The prophecy which He uttered was **TWOFOLD** in its meaning: while foreshadowing the destruction of Jerusalem, it prefigured **also** the terrors of the last great day. DA 25.

The Saviour's prophecy concerning the visitation of judgments upon Jerusalem is to have **ANOTHER FULFILLMENT** [a dual application] of which that terrible desolation was but a faint shadow. In the fate of the chosen city we may behold the doom of a world that has rejected God's mercy and trampled upon His law. GC 36.

The disciples asked a **dual** question:

1. "When shall these things [destruction of Jerusalem] be?" Matt. 24:3.
2. "What shall be the sign of thy coming, and **the end** the world?" Matt. 24:3.

Jesus gave them a **dual** answer. Not until the prophetic expositor understands the dual application of Matthew 24:3 can he comprehend the **dual** reference to the "abomination of desolation spoken of by Daniel the prophet." Matthew 24:15.

The Matthew 24:15 prophecy has a dual application but the "abomination of desolation spoken of by Daniel the prophet" applies to **three** historical events!

"Three Historical Events"

1. Daniel 9:26,27   The 70 A.D. destruction of Jerusalem
2. Daniel 7;8; 11:31   The 538-1798 Papal Supremacy No. 1 persecutions in Europe

3. Daniel 12:7, 11;   The future endtime healed Papal Supremacy No. 2
over all the world, described in Revelation 13.

Valid applications have been made from Matthew 24:15 to the "abomination of desolation," referring to the 538-1798 Papal Supremacy. The early Advent pioneers and Ellen G. White, under inspiration of God, made this application. However, today we recognize that this was a **secondary** application because it was not yet a fulfillment of the "terrors of the last day" nor was it yet the final "doom of the world that has rejected God's mercy and trampled upon his law."

Definition: "Primary." Primary means first in **importance** and not necessarily in time or sequence. "Secondary" refers to that of lesser importance.

Today we recognize that the secondary application of Matthew 24:25 to the 538-1798 Papal Supremacy must give way to a future, endtime application of primary importance to the last generation who will surely see the "terrors of the last day." Therefore a future application of Matthew 24 and Daniel 12 now have become of primary importance. From the vantage viewpoint of the last generation, it is obvious that there are two primary applications to Matthew 24:15:

a. Destruction of Jerusalem, A.D. 70
b. The end of the world

The secondary application pertained to the 538-1798 Papal Supremacy. See the diagram below, as it is also combined with Daniel 12.

**The Primary Dual Application of
The Abomination of Desolation
of Matthew 24:15**

**Primary Application
No. (1)
Daniel 9:26,27
Jerusalem 70 A.D.**

**Primary Application
No. (2)
Daniel 12:7-11
The END**

**Secondary Application
538-1798 Papal
Supremacy**

The ruin of Jerusalem was a symbol of the final ruin that shall overwhelm the world. The prophecies that received a partial fulfillment in the overthrow of Jerusalem have a more direct application to the last days. We are now standing on the threshold of great and solemn events. A crisis is before us, such as the world has never witnessed. MB 120.

Part 7. WHAT WAS THE "FIRST APPLICATION" OF MATTHEW 24:15?

Not until the Bible student has a clear concept of the dual application of Matthew 24:15, and is knowledgeable of the first application, which is the historical record of the fall of Jerusalem in 66-70 A.D., can he comprehend the second application in its reference to "the abomination of desolation, spoken of by Daniel the prophet," as given in Daniel 12:11. Only as he gets a full view of both the first and second of these dual applications, can he understand the three timelines of Daniel 12 and the warning contained within.

Therefore, to get a clear picture of Matthew 24:15 it is necessary to:

a. understand the language or terminology used by Jesus
b. review the historical record of the fall of Jerusalem

1. **The Historical Setting**:
   When the revolt against Rome broke out in the spring of A.D. 66[*], Jerusalem saw much bloodshed. Under Gessius Florus, the last procurator of Judea, Jews began to massacre Gentiles, and Gentiles Jews, until all semblance of order and government was gone. Cestius Gallus, the legate of Syria, took command of Judea and in the autumn of A.D. 66 marched against Jerusalem. Although at one point he penetrated as far as the northern wall of the Temple he was repelled and for some unknown reason retreated, losing many of his soldiers on the march. The Christians, heeding the warning of Jesus (Matthew 24:15-20), took this opportunity to leave Jerusalem and found refuge at Pella in Perea. From late A.D. 66 until the spring of A.D. 70 Jerusalem did not suffer any direct attacks of the Romans. Vespasian, upon his arrival in the country in A.D. 67, followed the plan of reducing the country to submission, allowing the various political factions in Jerusalem to fight against, and weaken, one another. In A.D. 69, when Vespasian was proclaimed emperor, most of Palestine was in Roman hands, but had been converted into a wilderness. Titus, Vespasian's son, took over the command of the army and immediately made preparations to capture Jerusalem, the strong capital city of Judea. 8 BC 560.

2. **A Definition of "the holy place" of Matthew 24:15.**
   When ye therefore shall see the abomination of desolation, spoken of by Daniel the prophet, **stand in the holy place**, (whoso readeth, let him understand:) Then let them which be in Judea flee into the mountains: Matt.24:15,16.

What was the "holy place" in which the Roman armies, the abomination of desolation, were to stand? While it is true that in 66 A.D. Cestius Gallus "penetrated as far as the northern wall of

---

[*] Note: It is important to take note of the fact that the Christians left the city in 66 A.D., which was **three and a half years** before it fell in 70 A.D. This three and a half year period is a parallel of the timelines of Daniel 12.

the Temple" in Jerusalem, he did not enter into the Temple itself, not into the holy place nor the Most Holy place of its sanctuary. "He was repelled and for some unknown reason retreated." 8 BC 560. If the Roman armies did not at that time enter into the holy place of the Temple, what was the "holy place" on which they stood in fulfillment of Matthew 24:15?

In Luke 21:20 Jesus said, "And when ye shall see Jerusalem, **compassed** with armies...then...flee." The word "compassed" infers that these Romans would surround or be **outside** of Jerusalem. What "holy place" was **outside** of Jerusalem? The prophet explains it this way:

> When the idolatrous standards of the Romans should be set up in **the holy ground** [holy place], which extended some furlongs **outside** the city walls, then the followers of Christ were to find safety in flight. GC 26.

The question then follows: What exactly was this "holy ground" outside the walls of the city? What made it holy? What was its purpose?

Explanation:

The city fathers of Jerusalem were strict Sabbath keepers. They made certain that the gates of Jerusalem were locked at the beginning of the Sabbath so that no merchandising or vendors could carry on business within the city during the holy Sabbath hours. Not until the sun went down on Saturday night could traffic begin. Worldly vendors liked to camp up close to the walls, spread out their wares, attract attention of any on top of the wall or near the gates or of any who might need to enter or depart during the Sabbath hours. Therefore, to remove this distraction or infringement, for several furlongs beyond the walls there was established the "holy **Sabbath** ground" or "holy place" on which worldly vendors could not camp.

3. **How did the Roman armies "stand"** on that holy Sabbath ground? They placed their idolatrous standards, flags and banners and symbols, or jabbed them into that ground to announce the "takeover" by Rome!

The Roman standard, equivalent of our flag, was the **MARK** or symbol of the authority of Rome. Pagan Rome was a union of religious and civil power. Pagan Rome was a union of sun worship and civil authority so that the standards bore on them the symbols of the sun and other things.

Jesus explained to His followers in Matthew 24:15 that when they should see Rome place its **MARK** of authority, its symbol of sun worship on their holy Sabbath ground, they would know that it was time for them to flee from the city to the mountains.

Not until we understand this significant circumstance are we ready to comprehend the second application to the endtime prophecies in the dual application of Matthew 24:15.

A standard of Rome

Christ gave His disciples a sign of the ruin to come on Jerusalem, and He told them how to escape:....The Christians obeyed the warning, and **not a Christian perished** in the fall of the city. DA 630.*

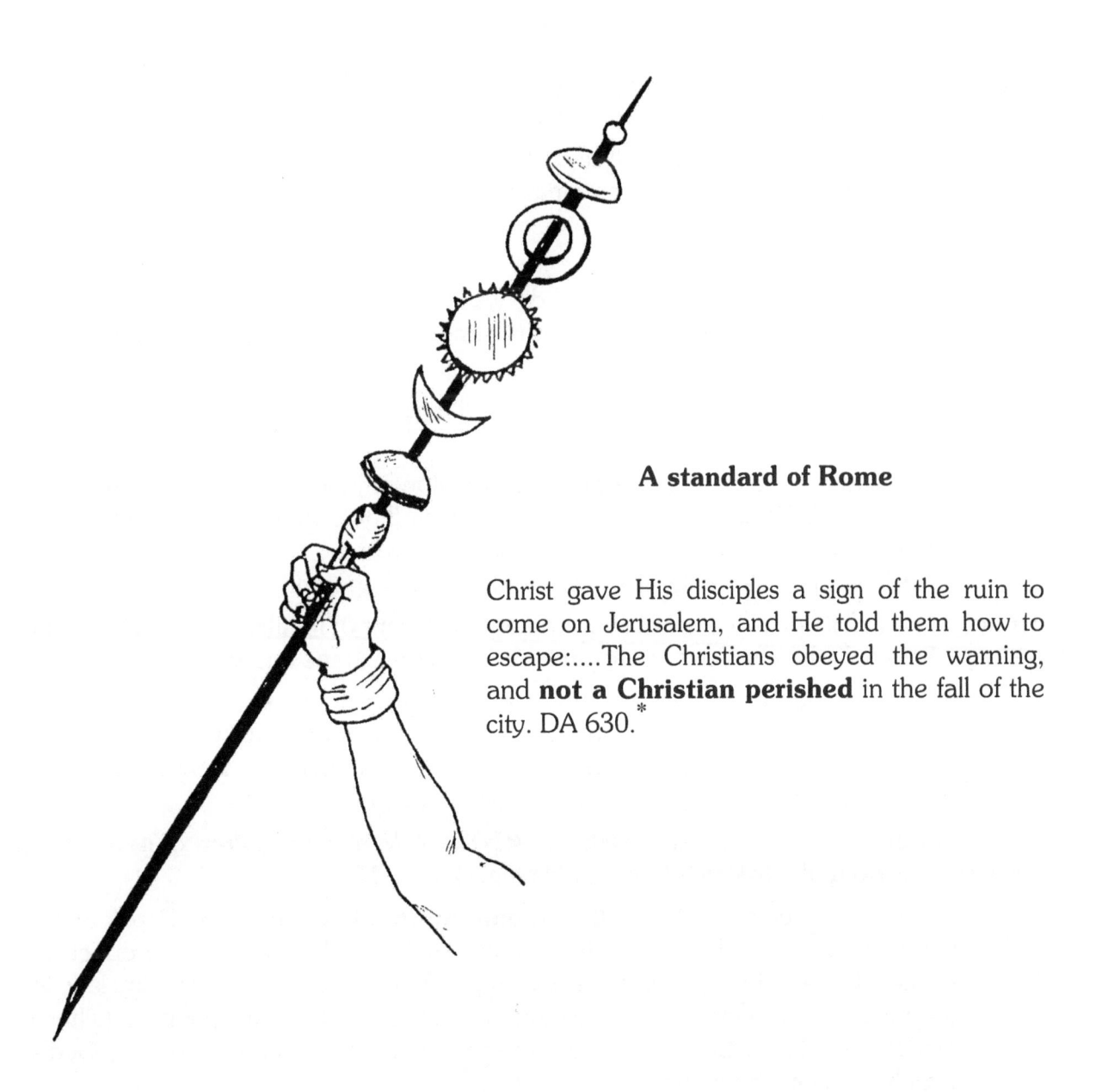

* Note: The book *God Cares*, by C. Mervyn Maxwell, Vol. 2, p.28, shows a picture of the Roman soldier's standard having on it the symbols of Roman sunworship—specifically the sun and tokens of sunworship.

Part 8. WHAT IS THE "SECOND OR ENDTIME APPLICATION" OF MATTHEW 24:15?

In Matthew 24:15 the disciples asked a dual question:

1. "When shall these things be?" (the destruction of Jerusalem)
2. "What shall be the **sign** of thy coming and of the **end** of the world?"

Jesus gave them a dual answer:

> The prophecy which He uttered was **twofold** in its meaning: while foreshadowing the destruction of Jerusalem, it prefigured also the terrors of the last great day. GC 25.

The first application was to occur in their day, but the **greater** fulfillment was to be at the end of the world.

> The Saviour's prophecy concerning the visitation of judgments upon Jerusalem is to have **ANOTHER FULFILLMENT**, of which that terrible **desolation** was but a faint shadow. In the fate of the chosen city we may behold the **doom of a world** that has rejected God's mercy and trampled upon his law. GC 36.

This endtime fulfillment is the **greater** or primary fulfillment of Matthew 24:15,16. But the same warning that applied to the Jews will apply to God's people in the endtime.

> As He warned his disciples of Jerusalem's destruction, giving them a sign of the approaching ruin, that they might make their escape; so He has warned the world of the **day of final destruction** and has given them tokens of its approach, that all who will may flee from the wrath to come. GC 37.

What **sign** did Jesus give? What is **THE WARNING**? What is the **token** of its approach? The **sign**, the **warning**, the **token** is found in Matthew 24:15, 16.

> When ye therefore shall see the **abomination of desolation** [Papal Rome trampling on God's holy Sabbath ground], spoken of by Daniel the prophet [in Daniel 12] stand in the holy place [placing its mark of authority, a Sunday law, in the very country which is the headquarters of God's remnant people], (whoso readeth let him understand:) Then let them which be in Judea [among God's people] flee into the mountains: Matt. 24:15, 16.

> As the siege of Jerusalem by the Roman armies was the signal for flight to Judean Christians, so the assumption of power on the part of our nation [the United States of America] in **the decree enforcing the Papal sabbath** will be a **WARNING** to us. It will then be time to leave the large cities, preparatory to leaving the smaller ones for retired homes in secluded places among the mountains. 5 T 464, 465.

Although many states in the United States have Sunday laws or "blue laws" on the books, the nation has never yet ventured to legislate a **National** Sunday Law. Other countries have local or even National Sunday Laws but the United States of America has not yet done so because the Constitution forbids it:

> **Congress shall make no law respecting an establishment of religion**. GC 442.

> Only in flagrant violation of these safeguards to the nation's liberty, can any religious observance be enforced by civil authority. GC 442.

> When...our country shall repudiate every principle of its Constitution...we may know, that ...**THE END** is near. 5 T 451.

By virtue of this religious freedom and prosperity, the United States has been the headquarters for the remnant people who keep the commandments of God and the faith of Jesus. It has been the means by which they could take the gospel with its three angel's messages to all the world over this last century. This fact brings the United States of America into the focus of endtime prophecy. (Revelation 13:11). Prophecy focuses on God's people all the way through history. The Jews were God's people in the Old Testament and today it is God's people upon whom prophecy focuses in Revelation 13 and Daniel 12!

As the Jews were the focus of the warning of Matthew 24:15, so again at the end of this world's history, it is the remnant people in the United States who shall also be warned by that same prophecy and its fulfillment as the **sign** or token for them to flee the **desolation** to come.

Therefore, a **National Sunday Law** in the United States of America is the primary endtime fulfillment of Matthew 24:15 and it is the beginning of the endtime scenario timelines of Daniel 12:7-12. The details will be developed in the following chapters.

A NATIONAL SUNDAY LAW in the USA Begins the END TIME scenario

Part 9. WHAT IS THE "WARNING"?

The "WARNING" is found in Matthew 24:15 **and** Daniel 12!

As the siege of Jerusalem by the Roman armies was the signal for flight to the Judean Christians, so the assumption of power on the part of our nation in the decree enforcing the Papal sabbath will be a **WARNING** to us. It will then be time to leave the large cities, preparatory to leaving the smaller ones for retired homes in secluded places among the mountains. 5 T 464, 465.

Let us read and study the 12th chapter of Daniel. It is a **WARNING** that we shall all need to understand before the time of the end. E.G. White Ltr. 161, 1903.

The same warning of Matthew 24:15 is amplified in Daniel 12. This warning begins the timelines of Daniel 12 and will be explained in the next four chapters. First **THE WARNING** must be examined in detail.

What exactly is **THE WARNING**? It is a **National Sunday Law in the United States of America (NSL-USA).** "...the assumption of power on the part of our nation in the decree enforcing the Papal sabbath."

Why must God's people leave the large cities? **How soon** must they leave after the National Sunday Law is passed? **Why the haste**? **What follows**? What did Jesus say?

> ...flee into the mountains: Let him which is on the housetop not come down to take anything out of his house: Neither let him which is in the field return back to take his clothes. And woe unto them that are with child, and to them that give suck in those days! But pray that your flight be not in the winter, neither on the sabbath day: For **then shall be great tribulation**,.... Matt. 24:16-21.

What is the **great tribulation** which follows the National Sunday Law in the United States of America?

> It is at the time of the national apostasy [legislation of a National Sunday Law], when, acting on the policy of Satan, the rulers of the land will rank themselves on the side of the man of sin [the Papacy], it is then the measure of guilt is full; the national apostasy [Sunday Law] is the signal for **NATIONAL RUIN**. 2 SM 373.

Apparently this **national ruin** follows so quickly after the NSL-USA that Jesus urged and warned His people to act **immediately** to leave the large cities. No time is to be taken to dispose of goods and properties or to prepare for the new life in the country. It is then **too late** to make preparations. Many of God's people have already acted by taking their families to the country. Not one believing Christian perished in Jerusalem and there is no need for any believing Christian to perish in the cities in the near future. Those who are still in the large cities, to save their lives, must then leave at once, by whatever medium of transportation they can get!

They need to be thinking now where they will go at that time.

What is **national ruin**? None of us have experienced it. Will it be a financial collapse? Will it be accompanied by judgments such as natural and man made disasters? Will it pertain to war? Will it be many things at once? We have never experienced the United States in **RUIN**. Can we imagine our country with its communication-transportation systems inoperative? Can we imagine a nation without food, transport, medicines, heating supplies, electricity, when there is such a strife and confusion that those in the cities will not be able to move out?

THE WARNING of Matthew 24:15 and Daniel 12 has many facets to help us save our lives. However, there is much more of spiritual significance!

The National Sunday Law in the United States of America not only initiates the beginning of God's judgments on the cities, but also begins a series of events in heaven and on earth which has to do with the eternal destiny of those who are living on the earth at that time. This brings us to Part 10.

Part 10. WHAT IS THE "FINAL TEST"?

THE WARNING, of Matthew 24:15 and the Daniel 12:7-11 timelines, is not merely to alert God's people that the time has come to leave the large cities! The **National Sunday Law** in the United States of America is the **alarm, the siren's shrill note** of prophetic fulfillment which **initiates** the following important actions in the closing of God's work on earth!:

1. The formation of "the image to the beast"
2. The Sabbath-Sunday controversy has become the **great** or **final test** to the last generation
3. The **final test** initiates the judgment of the living
4. The judgment of the living results in:
   a. The indelible **mark of the beast** placed on the wicked
   b. The **seal of God** placed upon the righteous
5. The formation of the **144,000**
6. The outpouring of the **Latter Rain**
7. The repeat of the Three Angel's Messages and amplification by the angel of Revelation 18 in the "Loud Cry"
8. The Third Angel's **WARNING** to the world
9. The **close of probation**
10. The outpouring of the **plagues** and final Death Decree
11. The final **deliverance** of the people of God

Part 11. WHAT IS THE FORMATION OF "THE IMAGE OF THE BEAST?"

Before the "image of the beast" can be identified, it is necessary to identify the "beast" himself. The "beast" of Revelation 13:1-10 refers to Papal Rome as it reigned from 538-1798 over Europe (the Old World). This "beast"—Papal power was a **persecutor**. However, the "beast"—Papacy could not persecute nor enforce its religious laws without a union of church and state. Then the "beast"—Papacy could use civil power to legislate religious laws, enforce them, and persecute dissenters. (See Revelation 13:7).

Revelation 13:11 brings to view another "beast"—a lamblike beast which suddenly speaks like a dragon. This "beast" represents Protestant America (the New World). When Protestantism in the United States of America brings about a union of church and state, so that it can legislate religious laws, use civil power to enforce them and persecute dissenters, it will "mirror" or form an image to the Papal "beast" before it.

When Protestantism legislates a National Sunday Law in the United States, with ensuing penalties and persecutions of dissenters, the "image of the beast" will have been formed.

> In order for the United States to form an image of the beast, the religious power must so control the civil government that the authority of the state will also be employed by the church to accomplish her own ends. GC 443.
>
> The Lord has shown me clearly that the image of the beast will be formed before probation closes; for it is to be the **great test** for the people of God, by which their eternal destiny will be decided...(Revelation 13:11-17 quoted)...This is **the test** that the people of God must have before they are sealed. 7 BC 976.*

---

* Note: The "beast" of Revelation 13 is the "abomination that maketh desolate" of Daniel 12:7 and 11. The National Sunday Law in the USA is the beginning of the endtime scenario as presented in the Daniel 12 timelines.

Part 12. WHAT IS THE SABBATH-SUNDAY CONTROVERSY THAT IS THE "GREAT TEST" TO THE LAST GENERATION?

> The Sabbath will be the **GREAT TEST** of loyalty; for it is the point of truth especially controverted. When the **FINAL TEST** shall be brought to bear upon men, then ... one class, by accepting the sign of submission to earthly powers, receive the mark of the beast, the other, choosing the token of allegiance to divine authority, receive the seal of God. GC 605.

Obviously, it is not the dead of past ages who are confronted by this **FINAL** test. It is the **LIVING**. It is the last generation remnant who will be tested, that is, brought into judgment by this test. Therefore, it is this test which will initiate the **Judgment of the Living**!

Part 13. WHAT IS "THE JUDGMENT OF THE LIVING"?

> As the books of record are opened in the judgment, the lives of all who have believed on Jesus come in review before God. Beginning with those who first lived upon the earth, our Advocate presents the cases of each successive generation, and **closes with the living**. GC 483.

> The judgment is now passing in the sanctuary above. For many years this work has been in progress. Soon, none know how soon, it will **pass to the cases of the living**. GC 490.

It is true that "none know how soon" the judgment will pass to the cases of the living, because now we do not know how soon a National Sunday Law will be passed in The United States of America. We can know for sure that **when** such a law is passed it will be the **FINAL TEST** by which the living shall be tested or judged!

> When the **decree** shall go forth enforcing the counterfeit Sabbath, and the loud cry of the third angel shall warn men against the worship of the beast and his image, the line will be clearly drawn between the false and the true. Then those who still continue in transgression will receive the **mark of the beast**. Ev 234,235.

> When the third angel's message closes,...An angel returning from the earth announces that his work is done; **THE FINAL TEST** has been brought upon the world, and all who have proved themselves loyal to the divine precepts have received the Seal of the living God. GC 613.

The last generation remnant, who see a National Sunday Law in the United States of America, will know that it is **THE FINAL TEST** by which they will be brought into the judgment of the living. Therefore, they give the first angel's message with specific emphasis in the Loud Cry which combines with the second and third angel:

> Saying with a loud voice [the Loud Cry], Fear God, and give glory to him; for the hour of his judgment [of the living] is come.... Rev. 14:7.[*]

---

[*] Note: "Judgments" which fall on man down here on earth as a result of their own wickedness or to other natural disasters should not be confused with the judgment process going on in heaven.

Part 14. WHAT IS "THE SHAKING"?

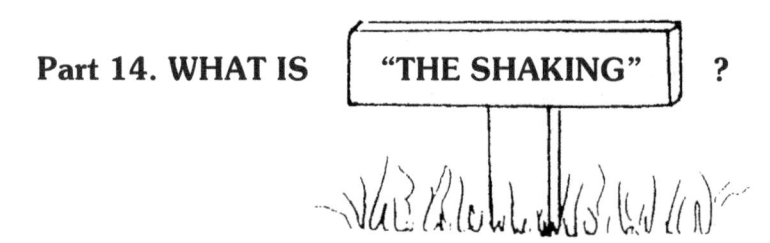

It is true that through the many ages of time, God's people have experienced a **shaking** of trials, persecutions, troubles, temptations, and many other things. However, the last generation, who face **THE FINAL TEST** know they are in the judgment of the living. They must be overcomers through the blood of Christ to receive the **Seal of the living God**. They are then empowered to live through the seven last plagues without a Mediator. This is a peculiar **SHAKING**. This shaking was viewed by the prophet and described:

> I saw some, with strong faith and agonizing cries, pleading with God. Their countenances were pale and marked with deep anxiety, expressive of their internal struggle. Firmness and great earnestness was expressed in their countenances; large drops of perspiration fell from their foreheads. Now and then their faces would light up with the marks of God's approbation, and again the same solemn, earnest, anxious look would settle upon them.
>
> Evil angels crowded around, pressing darkness upon them to shut out Jesus from their view, that their eyes might be drawn to the darkness that surrounded them, and thus they be led to distrust God and murmur against Him. Their only safety was in keeping their eyes directed upward. Angels of God had charge over His people, and as the poisonous atmosphere of evil angels was pressed around these anxious ones, the heavenly angels were continually wafting their wings over them to scatter the thick darkness.
>
> As the **praying ones** continued their earnest cries, at times a ray of light from Jesus came to them, to encourage their hearts and light up their countenances. Some, I saw, did not participate in this work of agonizing and pleading. They seemed indifferent and careless. They were not resisting the darkness around them, and it shut them in like a thick cloud. The angels of God left these and went to the aid of the earnest, praying ones. I saw angels of God hasten to the assistance of all who were struggling with all their power to resist the evil angels and trying to help themselves by calling upon God with perseverance. But His angels left those who made no effort to help themselves, and I lost sight of them.
>
> I asked the meaning of **the shaking** I had just seen....
>
> Said the angel, "List ye!" Soon I heard a voice like many musical instruments all sounding in perfect strains, sweet and harmonious. It surpassed any music I had ever heard, seeming to be full of mercy, compassion, and elevating, holy joy. It thrilled through my whole being. Said the angel, "Look ye!" My attention was then turned to the company I had seen, who were mightily **shaken**. I was shown those whom I had before seen weeping and praying in agony of spirit. The company of guardian angels around them had been doubled, and they were clothed with an armor from their head to their feet. They moved in exact order, like a company of soldiers. Their countenances expressed the severe conflict

which they had endured, the agonizing struggle they had passed through. Yet their features, marked with severe internal anguish, now shone with the light and glory of heaven. **THEY HAD OBTAINED THE VICTORY**, and it called forth from them the deepest gratitude and holy, sacred joy.

...Evil angels still pressed around them, but could have no power over them.

I heard those clothed with armor speak forth the truth with great power...I asked what had made this great change. An angel answered, "It is the latter rain, the refreshing from the presence of the Lord, the loud cry of the third angel." EW 269-271.

It is important in an understanding of endtime events to see the sequence. These events in their order are:

1. The National Sunday Law in the United States of America. This is the formation of the **image to the beast.** The Sunday law and its adherence becomes the **mark of the beast**. The decision for Sunday or for Sabbath is **THE FINAL TEST**.
2. The spiritual **shaking** occurs in which God's people make their decision. They obtain the victory (the Seal of God). Thus, they pass through the judgment of the living victoriously.
3. They receive the latter rain, the refreshing, to enable them to give the loud cry of the third angel to the entire world.

Not until God's people are thus prepared is the Loud Cry to be given in the power of the Latter Rain—outpouring of the Holy Spirit. **Judgment** begins **at the house of God** with the **ancient men** and **probation closes** for the people of God. They are then prepared to witness to the world in the power of the angel of Revelation 18 in the Latter Rain, after which the world is also brought to decision and **then probation closes for the world**.

Part 15. WHAT IS THE "SEAL OF GOD"?

> Those who are living upon the earth when the intercession of Christ shall cease in the sanctuary above, are to stand in the sight of a holy God without a Mediator. GC 425.

It is only the righteous of the last generation who shall stand **without a Mediator**. When "the intercession of Christ shall cease in the sanctuary above," the seven last plagues will be poured out! It is therefore clear that the last generation will "stand without a Mediator" all through the seven last plagues. How can this be?

> Those who receive the seal of the living God and are protected in the time of trouble [the seven last plagues] must reflect the image of Jesus fully. EW 71.

How can the last generation **reflect the image of Jesus fully** so that they will not need a Mediator? The answer is very simple. When in the shaking they gain the victory over self and sin, **they are sealed** in that condition to reflect the image of Jesus fully. They can do that only by having the Fathers' name (His character) sealed or imprinted in their foreheads (minds).

> I saw another angel ascending from the east, having the seal of the living God: and he cried with a loud voice to the four angels, to whom it was given to hurt the earth and the sea, Saying, Hurt not the earth, neither the sea, nor the trees, till we have **sealed** the servants of our God in their **foreheads**. Rev. 7:2, 3.

> ...a hundred forty and four thousand, having his Father's name written in their **foreheads**...the first fruits unto God and to the Lamb. And in their mouth was found no guile: for they are **without fault before the throne of God**. Rev. 14:1-5.

This process of sealing is described as follows:

> Zechariah's vision of Joshua and the Angel applies with peculiar force to the experience of God's people in the **closing up** of the great day of atonement [the judgment of the living]. The remnant church will be brought into great trial and distress [the **final test**, and the **shaking**]. ...Their **only hope** is in the mercy of God; their **only defense** will be prayer...They are fully conscious of the sinfulness of their lives, they see their weakness and unworthiness...their unlikeness to Christ,...[Satan] hopes to so destroy their faith that they will yield to his temptations, turn from their allegiance to God, and receive the mark of the beast.

> But while the followers of Christ have sinned, they have not given themselves to the control of evil. They have **put away their sins**,...Jesus will bring them forth as gold tried in the fire. Their earthliness must be removed that the image of Christ may be perfectly reflected;...the anguish and humiliation of God's people is unmistakable evidence that they are regaining the strength and nobility of character lost in consequence of sin....

> The spotless robe of **Christ's righteousness** is placed upon the tried, tempted,

yet faithful children of God. The despised remnant are clothed in glorious apparel, **nevermore to be defiled** by the corruptions of the world....

Now they are **eternally secure** from the tempter's devices...holy angels, unseen, were passing to and fro, placing upon them the seal of the living God.

...[These are] the hundred and forty and four thousand,....

Now is reached the complete fulfillment... Christ is revealed as the Redeemer and Deliverer of His people. 5 T 472-476.

It is imperative to understand that the **seal of the living God** occurs in the **forehead**—in the **MIND**! It is also important to understand its correct timing: that it **occurs in the judgment** of **the living** (also known as the **Day of Atonement**) as explained in the following statements:

> As in the final atonement the sins of the truly penitent are to be blotted from the records of heaven, **no more to be remembered or come into mind**, so in type they were borne away into the wilderness, forever separated from the congregation. PP 358.

> Their sins had gone beforehand to judgment, and pardon had been written. Their sins had been borne away into the land of **forgetfulness**.... 3 SG 135.

> Their sins have gone beforehand to judgment, and have been blotted out; and **they cannot bring them to remembrance**. GC 620.

These statements are absolutely necessary to an understanding of the meaning of the **seal of the living God** as it shall be given to the last generation who shall go through the judgment of the living under the **final test** of the National Sunday Law in the USA.*

---

* Note: The "seal of God" or seal of approval, called the "earnest" or down-payment of the Spirit, has been granted to God's people of every generation, but it must not be confused with the "seal of the living God" as given to the last generation, to carry them through the seven last plagues without a Mediator.

Part 16. WHAT IS THE "LOUD CRY" WARNING?

Although there are some who understand and proclaim the three angels' message today, it is a mute sound; but the Scriptures declare that these messages must go with a **Loud Cry**. There are millions in the world today who do not recognize the name of Jesus! Millions have never heard of Adventism. Thousands of Adventists are unable to explain the content of the three angels' messages. To such persons the third angel's message is an enigma! However, at the end of the world the prophet said that it would go with a "Loud Voice."

> And I saw another angel fly in the midst of heaven...Saying with a **LOUD VOICE**.... Rev. 14:6,7.

> And the third angel followed them, saying with a **LOUD VOICE**.... Rev. 14:9.

> And after these things I saw another angel come down from heaven, having great power; and the earth was lightened with his glory. An he **CRIED, MIGHTLY WITH A STRONG VOICE**,.... Rev. 18:1,2.

What is the content of these messages? Content is briefly listed below:
1.
   a. The everlasting gospel
   b. Fear God and give glory to Him
   c. The hour of His judgment is come (Judgment of the living)
   d. Worship the Creator by observance of the 7th-day Sabbath
2.
   a. Babylon (apostate religion) is fallen, morally
   b. All nations are corrupted by false religion
3.
   a. Do not worship the beast (ROME—the Papacy)
   b. Do not worship his image (Apostate Christendom)
   c. Do not receive the mark of the beast (Sunday observance)
   d. Do not **believe** or **conform** to it
   e. If you accept the mark of the beast you will suffer the seven last plagues
   f. The seven last plagues will be poured out without mixture of mercy
   g. All who worship the beast will find themselves in the lake of fire
   h. God's people keep His commandments and the faith of Jesus
4.
   a. Babylon (apostate religion) is completely fallen with the union of church and state to persecute the saints
   b. Apostate religion is degenerate: The churches have become the habitation of devils and every evil and unclean thing resides in the modern apostate churches
   c. All nations are contaminated with false religion
   d. Come out of her, my people
   e. **The time has come** for the plagues and retribution on Babylon.

The four angel's messages will be given as a combined unit to all the world in the power of the latter rain, with **Pentecostal** force and results. It will be given in the Loud Cry, with **tongues of fire**, and will reach all the people of the world.

Part 17 WHAT IS THE "THIRD ANGEL'S WARNING MESSAGE"?

And the third angel followed them, saying with a loud voice, **If any man worship the beast and his image**, and receive his mark in his forehead, or in his hand, The same shall drink of the wine of the wrath of God, which is poured out without mixture into the cup of his indignation; and he shall be tormented with fire and brimstone in the presence of the holy angels and in the presence of the Lamb:

And the smoke of their torment ascendeth up for ever and ever: and they have no rest day nor night, who worship the beast and his image, and whosoever receiveth the mark of his name.

Here is the patience of the saints: here are they that keep the commandments of God, and the faith of Jesus. Rev. 14:9-12.

The "faith of Jesus" and the "keeping of the commandments" are "the gospel" of the "righteousness of Christ," imputed and imparted—the glad news of salvation, through the keeping of God's Law! In this sense, the people of God have been giving the third angel's message since 1844. It includes all aspects of the Present Truth: health reform and every step higher and higher, to bring them back to reflect the image of Jesus. It is in the power of the early rain of the Holy Spirit that this work has been done for more than a century;

However, the first part of the third angel's message is specifically for the endtime because:

1. The **beast** is still in the healing stage of its wound of 1798
2. **ALL** the world does not yet worship the beast
3. At this date the **image of the beast** has not yet been formed
4. The **mark of the beast** has not yet been legislated

Therefore: The Third Angel's Message Warning will not be given in the power of the **Loud Cry—Latter Rain** until the image to the beast is formed by the National Sunday Law in the United States of America and the mark of the beast is set up as a **FINAL TEST** which initiates the judgment of the living. Then it will be the time in which to give the great warning regarding the seven last plagues from which there will be no escape except to receive the Seal of the **Living God**.

Therefore: The third angel of Revelation 14 is a counterpart of the **WARNING** given in Matthew 24:15 and the **WARNING** as given in Daniel 12, which we all need to understand **before** the time of the end!

SUMMARY OF CHAPTER II

WHAT IS "THE WARNING" IN DANIEL 12?

Chapter II is composed of a series of definitions. It would be impossible to study the endtime timelines of Daniel 12 until these basic terms and concepts have been clarified. A Summary of these definitions follows:

1. Daniel 12 and Matthew 24 ask the same question: "How long shall it be to the end?"
2. Daniel 12 and Matthew 24 contain related answers—both are warnings to focus on the "abomination of desolation"
3. The "abomination of desolation" is Rome: past and future
   a. Pagan Rome in 70 A.D. destruction of Jerusalem
   b. Papal Rome in the future as described in Revelation 13 and Daniel 12
4. Daniel 12 "abomination of desolation" is the counterpart of the Revelation 13 "beast"
5. Matthew 24 presents a dual question: It provides a dual answer application
   a. The first application pertains to the 70 A.D. destruction of Jerusalem
   b. The second application pertains to the end of the world—specifically to a National Sunday Law in the United States of America
6. The **WARNING** as given in Matthew 24:15 and Daniel 12 is the legislation of a National Sunday Law in the United States of America and is to God's people:
   a. A signal to flee the large cities for the mountains
   b. A signal that National Ruin is soon to follow
   c. A signal that the "Final Test" is in operation
   d. A signal that the Judgment of the Living has begun
   e. A signal that the final "shaking" will occur immediately
   f. A signal of the nearness of the close of probation (first for the church and then for the world)
   g. A signal that the Latter Rain is about to begin
   h. A signal that the Loud Cry—third angel's message is to go to all the world in the power of the fourth angel of Revelation 18
   i. A signal that persecution will soon begin
   j. A signal that the timelines of Daniel 12 have begun
7. The "Seal of the living God" takes place in the forehead or mind
8. The "Seal of the living God" prepares God's people to live through the seven last plagues without a Mediator
9. THE WARNING comes, not just from the book of Daniel and its three timelines, but is reinforced by Matthew 24 and Revelation 13-18
10. The fact that these prophecies are opened up to God's people at this time is a signal that these events will happen in the very near future.

In Conclusion: **THE WARNING** is not merely to provide for physical safety in leaving the large cities but is of greater importance **a signal for God's people to prepare spiritually** for the Seal of God and the shaking which precedes it. **THE WARNING** helps them to cooperate with God as they near the close of probation.

CHAPTER III

WHAT IS THE "1335 DAYS" TIMELINE?

INTRODUCTION

Question: What is the correct way to study the 1335 days timeline?

Answer: Knowing this first, that no prophecy of the scripture is of any private interpretation. 2 Peter 1:20.

Whom shall he teach knowledge?...line upon line...here a little, and there a little. Isa 28:9-13.

Most specifically, how shall the book of Daniel and its chapter 12 timelines be understood? The Lord has given instruction through His servant:

> The book of **Daniel is unsealed in the Revelation** to John, and carries us forward to the **last scenes** of this earth's history. TM 115.

> The study of the Revelation directs the mind to the prophecies of Daniel, and both present most important instruction, given of God to men, concerning events to take place **at the close** of this world's history. GC 341.

The Bible student should **expect** that when these hermeneutic rules are followed, that Matthew 24 (and other Scriptures) **especially from Revelation**, will identify the events which begin and end the three timelines of Daniel 12. **The Bible will be its own expositor**. The human agent merely locates and organizes the data so that it can be seen easily in its correct relationships.

The Bible student should look at the Daniel 12 and the Revelation 12-18 complex as he would view a rosebud ready to open. Each petal is tightly enfolded within others and cannot be forced open until its time has come! Daniel and Revelation are tightly enfolded together. As the Sun of Righteousness shines His light on them at the right end-time hour, they unfold all together as one flower.

Therefore, the Bible student should expect in this study that, as the Daniel 12 timelines come into focus, the Revelation 16-18 enigmas will also clarify!

When Daniel 12 is studied in the light of Revelation, it will soon become very evident that the **Daniel 12 timelines are simply fulfillments of specific prophecies of Revelation. And the beginning and endings of the timelines are simply the fulfillment of specific verses of prophecy in Revelation**.

It will also become evident that timelines of Daniel 12 do not deal with trivia! They set forth the legislative and judicial decrees of nations on earth and declarations of the court of heaven! They pertain to the **eternal verities** involving the plan of salvation as it reaches the close of its work on earth and those events which are warnings to God's people of their final crisis and deliverance.

A master key of prophetic interpretation will provide insights to the specific events which begin and end the three timelines of Daniel 12. That master key is found in the following quotation:

> ...the **"SPEAKING"** of the nation is the action of its legislative and judicial authorities. GC 442.

It is speaking voices of prophetic Scripture which will solve the enigma of the nature and purpose of these timelines.

This chapter is intended to answer the following questions:

1. What are the **Precedent Voices** of previous time lines?
2. What **Event Begins** the 1335 days timeline?
3. What is the **Voice** or **speaking** of a Nation?
4. What is the **Wait** of the Daniel 12:12 timeline?
5. What is the **Blessing** of the 1335 days timeline?
6. What is the **Voice of God**?
7. What are the **Precedents** in Daniel 4:17, 23, 31, 33 that begin and end timelines?
   a. Fulfilled prophecy
   b. Speaking voices
   c. Decrees

Part 1. WHAT ARE THE "PRECEDENT VOICES" OF TIMELINES?

Prophetic timelines begin and end with **VOICES**—legislative and judicial actions. This is a rule which can be observed in timelines which have been fulfilled in the past. The same rule can be applied consistently to the timelines of Daniel 12 which are in the future.

Example 1: The 2300 day-year timeline prophecy of Daniel 8:14 began with legislative action—the **speaking** of a nation.

> Know and understand this: From the issuing of the **decree** [law or legislative action]....Dan. 9:25 NIV.

The 2300 day-year timeline began with the **VOICE** or speaking or legislation which occurred in 457 B.C. The 2300 day-year timeline ended with **judicial action**, "the **judgment** was set, and the books were opened" (Daniel 7:10) in 1844.

The 2300 day-year timeline is a model for the beginning and ending of the 1335 day prophecy of Daniel 12:12. The 1335 day timeline begins with a **DECREE** (A National Sunday Law) legislative action—the **VOICE** or **speaking** of the nation. It ends, as will be seen shortly, also with a **VOICE**—the Voice of God.

Example 2: The 1260 day-year timeline spoken of in Daniel 7:25 and Revelation 13:5 began with a legislative **DECREE** and ended with a judicial action. This **legislative action** which began the timeline is described in *The Prophetic Faith of our Fathers*, Vol. I, p. 504-517 as follows:

> Justinian I, (527-565), greatest of all rulers of the Eastern Roman Empire...is perhaps best known to history as a **legislator**, and **codifier of law**. His intervention altered the entire status of the bishop of Rome.... Justinian's... more important achievement was the codification of ...Roman law...(Corpus Juris Civilis). Justinian's third great achievement was...crowned by the imperial **Decretal** Letter seating the bishop of Rome in the church as the "Head of all holy churches," thus laying the **legal** foundation for Papal ecclesiastical supremacy...his code,...confirm[s] and enlarge[s] the privileges of the clergy. Thus the pen that wrote the imperial letter gave **legal** sanction to...[Papal] Rome.

And it was by **judicial action** that the 1260 day-year timeline ended in 1798 when Napoleon of France, by his general, took the pope captive and ended the 1260 year Papal Supremacy over Europe.

These timelines are a model. The timelines of Daniel 12 also begin and end with legislative and judicial **VOICES** of fulfilled prophecy!

Example 3: The Mount Sinai Covenant timeline began at the **Voice of God** when He spoke the Ten Commandments (Exodus 20:1-17). It ended when the Jewish counsel (Sanhedrin) took legislative and judicial action to stone Stephen. This was the speaking or **voice of the nation** (Acts 6:12). This legal action ended the **seventy weeks timeline** of Daniel 9:24 in 34 A.D. This legal action on the part of the nation was registered in heaven's court records! The Mt. Sinai (First) Covenant had come to its end.

It is important to understand that the great controversy between Christ and Satan is a legal prosecution and defense **court case**! All aspects of the sin problem are handled according to **due process of law** and the rules of the court! The words and actions of individuals are recorded in heaven's books to be reviewed under judicial process in the Investigative Judgment. This very process is specified by the timeline of Daniel 8:14 and began on a specific date, October 22, 1844. Not only the decisions and acts of individuals, but also the actions of legislative and judicial authorities who **speak** for a nation, which they represent, are recorded as important markers in the great controversy. When these legislative bodies **speak** and these actions are recorded in heaven's court, they then become public proclamations to the world, and to the entire universe! These official decisions and proclamations are the important markers in the unrolling of the scroll.

The timelines of Scripture are not concerned with trivia; rather with the legal documents enacted by governments on earth and in heaven which concern God's people. This is true of all the major timelines:

1. The Everlasting Covenant met **ratification** in 31 A.D. according to the timeline of Daniel 9:27
2. The last seventy weeks timeline of the Mt. Sinai Covenant according to Daniel 9:24 was finished in 34 A.D.
3. The 2300 year-day timeline of Daniel 8:14 ended in 1844, initiating the Investigative Judgment.
4. The 1260 timelines of Daniel and Revelation regarding the Papal Reign was from 538 to 1798.
5. The 1335 timeline of Daniel 12 will be a waiting time.
6. The 1260 timeline of Daniel 12 will be a period of persecution.
7. The 1290 timeline of Daniel 12 will be a period of Papal Supremacy No. 2.

It is imperative that we understand that the timelines of Scripture, and those of Daniel 12 especially, are not like pieces of furniture to be shoved about the room to suit our personal preferences of application. It is our responsibility to find a set of hermeneutic principles which are consistent with timelines throughout the Scripture and apply them in the same consistent manner to Daniel 12.

The 1335 days timeline of Daniel 12:12 is the longest of the three timelines in that chapter, and reaches the farthest back to the beginning of the crisis. Further study in the next chapters of this book, also reveal that the context of the shorter timelines pertains to events which follow the National Sunday Law in the USA. This National Sunday Law is related to that sign or warning given in Matthew 24:15, which should alert God's people to the fact that the final crisis has begun. This enables them to make the necessary moves, physically and spiritually. The purpose of the timelines in Daniel 12 is to reinforce these concepts and to bring them into focus in a unified manner helpful to God's people.

We have been counseled:

> Let us read and study the 12th chapter of Daniel. It is **A WARNING** that we shall all need to understand before the time of the end. E. G. White Ltr. 161, 1903.

It is the beginning of the 1335 days timeline of Daniel 12 that reinforces that warning as reiterated by Jesus in Matthew 24:15.

Part 2. WHAT "EVENT BEGINS" THE 1335 DAYS OF DANIEL 12:12?

Blessed is he that waiteth, and cometh to the thousand three hundred and five and thirty days. Dan. 12:12.

The 1335 days timeline of Daniel 12:12 begins with a fulfillment of prophecy. The event which begins the timeline is found in the prophecy of Revelation 13:11,14.

> And I beheld another beast coming up out of the earth; and he had two horns like a lamb, and he **spake** as a dragon...that they should make an image to the beast.... Rev. 13;11,14.

This prophecy says when amplified:

> And I beheld another beast coming up out of the earth; [USA] and he had two horns like a lamb, and he **spake** as a dragon [legislated a National Sunday Law]...that they should make an image to the beast [Papal Rome].

A National Sunday Law in the United States of America initiates endtime crisis and God's people will "Wait" it out. The 1335 days timeline of the prophecy of Daniel 12:12 says: "Blessed is he that waits...." Therefore, the 1335 days timeline of Daniel 12:12 **begins** with a National Sunday Law in the United States of America, continues 1335 days, and **ends** on the 1335th. day with a "Blessing."

Part 3 WHAT IS THE "VOICE" OR "SPEAKING" OF A NATION?

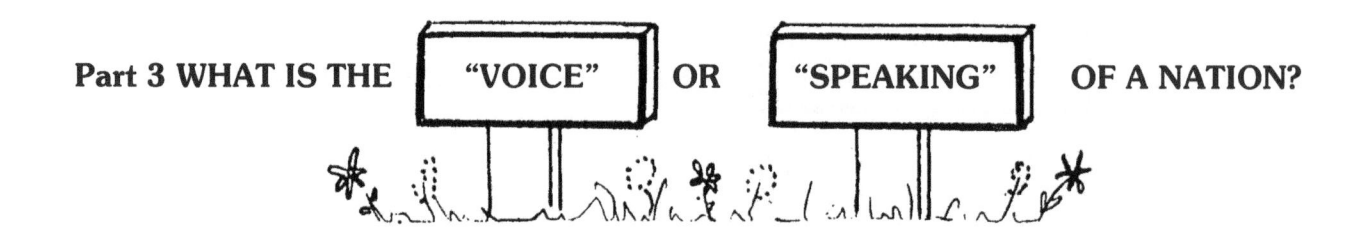

...**and he spake as a dragon**. Rev. 13:11

...The **speaking** of the nation is the action of its legislative and judicial authorities. GC 442.

The above definition cannot be overemphasized! It is a **KEY** to understanding all three of the timelines of Daniel 12! All three of the timelines **begin and end** with the **speaking** or **voice** of governments: government on earth or government in heaven. When the prophecy indicates that the two horned beast **spake** like a dragon it refers to its legislative action in passing a National Sunday Law in the United States of America. The **speaking** or **VOICE** of the nation thus initiates **the image to the beast** and fulfills Revelation 13:14. This speaking, or **VOICE** of the nation, enables God's people to know that the **endtime scenario** (timeline) has begun.

Part 4. WHAT IS "THE WAIT" OF DANIEL 12:12?

> Blessed is he that **waiteth**, and cometh to the thousand three hundred and five and thirty days. Dan. 12:12.

This 1335 days timeline is sometimes referred to as **the 1335 days WAIT**. It is evident from this statement that God's people will be **waiting** for something. It is self evident that if God's people are going to **wait** they must:

1. Know when they are to begin waiting
2. What they are waiting for
3. What will end the wait

The event which alerts God's people to the fact that they have begun the final crisis is the National Sunday Law in the United States of America. From that event they will **WAIT** it out until deliverance! Therefore, they will begin their 1335 days **WAIT** at the National Sunday Law in the United States and the prophetic timeline itself declares that they will wait for the 1335 days. They will be waiting for deliverance from the time of trouble first mentioned in Daniel 12:1.

> And it shall be said in that day, Lo, this is our God; we have **WAITED** for him, and he will save us: this is the Lord; we have **WAITED** for him, we will be glad and rejoice in his salvation. Isa. 25:9.

Part 5. WHAT IS "THE BLESSING" OF THE 1335 DAYS?

> **BLESSED** is he that waiteth, and cometh to the thousand three hundred and five and thirty days. Dan. 12:12.

It appears that the 1335 days wait will carry them through the **end time scenario**. But the question is: What is the **blessing** for which they are waiting? What is this **blessing** that will deliver them?

THE BLESSING has been described by the Lord through His servant as follows:

> The voice of God is heard from heaven, declaring the day and hour of Jesus' coming, and delivering **the everlasting covenant** to His people. Like peals of loudest thunder His words roll through the earth. The Israel of God stand listening, with their eyes fixed upward. Their countenances are lighted up with His glory, and shine as did the face of Moses when he came down from Sinai. The wicked cannot look upon them. And when **THE BLESSING** is pronounced on those who have honored God by keeping His Sabbath holy, there is a mighty shout of victory. GC 640.

THE BLESSING is the pronouncement of **THE EVERLASTING COVENANT** which will be spoken to Gods's true remnant people by The Voice of God which occurs under the 7th plague. (See Revelation 16:17).

From the time that **THE WARNING** is given to God's people in a National Sunday Law in the USA to indicate that the endtime scenario has begun they will **WAIT** 1335 literal days to hear the Voice of God pronounce the **BLESSING**. This everlasting covenant is pronounced as a **legal** statement—a **judicial declaration** of assurance of Eden restored and everlasting life to God's people.

"Blessed is he that waiteth"...the Bible student must recognize the fact that no one could wait 1335 years for some event. No one lives that long! This is one more evidence that this 1335 deals not with symbolic time but 1335 literal days!

From the National Sunday Law, all through the final crisis, God's people will **WAIT** it out, until under the 7th plague they are delivered by the Voice of God. Does the 1335 day timeline give the day and hour of the coming of Jesus? **NO**. It is the Voice of God which gives the day and hour of His coming! None of the three timelines give the day or hour of His coming.

But there is a great deal of information regarding the Voice of God which occurs under the 7th plague (Revelation 16:17). So much is given in the writings of Ellen G. White that the next few pages simply list what the Voice of God says and what events occur at that time, with the references listed as follows in Part 6.

Part 6. WHAT IS THE "VOICE OF GOD"?

What is the **Voice of God** that ends the 1335 days timeline of Daniel 12:12? The **Voice of God** is brought to view in Revelation 16:17. Its timing is extremely important. It occurs at the beginning of the seventh plague.

This **Voice of God** is **NOT** to be confused with the Second Coming of Jesus. In fact it is the **Voice of God** which declares the day and hour of His coming. (See the following quotations). God's people may know endtime events are **even at the door** (Matthew 24:33) but not the day and hour of His coming (Matthew 24:36) until it is spoken by the **Voice of God**! God's people will actually be able to count the 1335 days from a National Sunday Law in the USA to their **Voice of God** deliverance. They cannot know the **day and hour** until given that information by the Voice itself.

What does the **Voice of God** say?

1. "It is done." Rev. 16:17
2. It will give the day and hour of Jesus' coming EW 15
3. It delivers the everlasting covenant or "covenant blessing" to God's people EW 285,286

What happens at the **Voice of God**? Eighty inspired statements are made regarding the happenings which occur at the **Voice of God**. They are listed below:

From *Great Controversy*
1. It occurs at midnight .... GC 636
2. The sun appears
3. The streams cease to flow
4. Dark heavy clouds clash against each other
5. One clear space of indescribable glory is seen in the heavens
6. The **Voice of God** shakes the heavens and the earth
7. There is a mighty earthquake .... GC 637
8. The firmament appears to open and shut
9. Glory from God's throne flashes through
10. Mountains shake like a reed in the wind
11. Ragged rocks are scattered on every side
12. There is a roar of coming tempest
13. The shriek of a hurricane sounds like demon voices on a mission of destruction
14. Earth's surface heaves and swells
15. Earth's surface is breaking up
16. Earth's foundations are giving way
17. Mountain chains are sinking

18. Inhabited islands disappear
19. Seaports are swallowed up by water
20. Babylon (false religion) is identified
21. Hailstones destroy great cities
22. Beautiful palaces and homes are destroyed
23. Prison walls break open (God's people are set free)
24. Graves are opened in a special resurrection
25. All who died in faith in the 3rd angel's message come forth, glorified to hear the covenant blessing on those who kept His law
26. Those who pierced Jesus are resurrected
27. Persecutors of God's people of all ages are resurrected to see God's people glorified
28. Fierce lightning envelopes the earth in a sheet of flame..GC 638
29. Voices declare the doom of the wicked (understood by false shepherds)
30. The wails of the wicked are heard above the sound of the elements
31. Demons acknowledge the deity of Christ
32. Men grovel in terror and cry for mercy
33. The wicked seek to enter the caves, casting away gold and silver
34. A star, four fold in brilliance, brings hope and joy from heaven (The same star terrorizes the wicked)
35. The righteous are delivered from their enemies..................................... GC 639
36. The faces of the righteous are aglow with wonder, faith and love
37. God's people quote Psalms 46:1-3
38. The glory of the holy city, with gates ajar, streams from heaven
39. Two tables of stone (The Ten Commandments) appear in the sky folded together
40. A hand opens the tables of stone
41. The Ten Commandments are seen in the heavens as traced with a pen of fire
42. All men view the Ten Commandments—the standard of judgment (All superstition and heresy is swept away from their minds)
43. The wicked are in horror and despair
44. The wicked are condemned by The Ten Commandment Law
45. It is too late for repentance and change.. GC 640
46. The **Voice of God** declares the day and hour of Jesus' coming
47. The **Voice of God** delivers the everlasting covenant to his people
48. The covenant words are like peals of thunder
49. The covenant words, sentence after sentence, roll around the earth
50. God's people stand listening, eyes fixed upward
51. Their faces light up with glory (as did Moses as he came down from Mt. Sinai)
52. The wicked cannot look upon the glory of the righteous
53. The righteous give a mighty shout of victory
54. Soon after the Voice of God a sign is given of the coming of Jesus—a small black cloud in the East

From *Early Writings* additional concepts are given:

55. The "Voice of God" sounds like many waters
    EW 15
56. The living saints, 144,000 in number, knew and understood the voice
57. The wicked thought the voice was an earthquake
58. At the **Voice of God**, declaring the day and hour of Jesus' coming, God pours out the Holy Ghost so that the faces of the righteous light up and shine like Moses' as he came down from Mt. Sinai
59. The 144,000 were all sealed and perfectly united
60. The wicked rush violently to lay hands on God's people to thrust them into prison
61. The righteous stretch forth the hand in the name of the Lord and the wicked fall helpless to the ground
62. The wicked fall helpless to the ground and worship at the saint's feet

From *Testimonies*, Vol. 1 additional concepts emerge:

63. At the **Voice of God** buildings were shaken down.. 1 T 184
64. Their (God's people's) captivity was turned
65. A glorious light shone upon them
66. How beautiful they then looked
67. All weariness and marks of care were gone
68. Health and beauty were seen in every face
69. Their enemies fell like dead men
70. The wicked could not endure to look upon their glory
71. The light and glory shining on the delivered ones remained on them until Jesus was seen coming in the clouds of heaven
72. Buildings totter and fall with a terrible crash
73. The sea boils like a pot.. 1 T 354
74. The captivity of the righteous is turned
75. With sweet and solemn whisperings the righteous say to one another "We are delivered. It is the Voice of God."
76. The wicked fear and tremble while the saints rejoice
77. Satan and his angels and wicked men witness the glory conferred on God's people who have kept His Law and Sabbath
78. The faces of the righteous reflect the image of Jesus
79. Satan and his angels flee from the glorified saints
80. Their power to annoy them is gone forever

Great confusion has resulted by not distinguishing between the **Voice of God** events and the Second Coming of Jesus. The **Voice of God** which begins the 7th plague occurs before the Second Coming. It proclaims the day and hour of His coming. Although we may not know that day and hour until the Voice of God tells it, we can hold high the torch of prophecy of Daniel 12:7-12 and by those timelines know, step by step, where we are in the difficult events in the history of the world spoken of as the **final crisis**.

SUMMARY OF CHAPTER III

WHAT IS THE 1335 DAY TIMELINE?

THE 1335 DAY TIMELINE:

1. Cannot be understood by **private** applications of conjecture and assumption.
2. Must be understood by use of correct hermeneutic principles.
3. Must be understood by Biblical cross reference (Isaiah 28)
4. Must be unsealed by a study of Revelation.
5. Is entwined with the enigmas of Revelation 16-18 and they unfold together.
6. Begins and ends with fulfilled prophecies of Revelation 13:11 and 16:17.
7. Is consistent in structure with other timelines of Daniel and Revelation.
8. Begins with the "speaking" or "voice" of the nation spoken of in Revelation 13:11.
9. Ends with the speaking or "Voice of God" Revelation 16:17.
10. Begins with a National Sunday Law in the United States of America.
11. Begins with the same "warning" that is given in Matthew 24:15.
12. Is a "wait" from the NSL in the USA to the Voice of God deliverance.
13. Is a "wait" for the "Blessing" which proclaims the everlasting covenant.
14. Is a proclamation of legislative and judicial actions of governments.
15. Is the longest of the three timelines and begins the Endtime Scenario.
16. Does **not** give the day nor hour of the Second Coming of Jesus, Latter Rain or Close of Probation.
17. Prepares and assists God's people to understand endtime events.
18. Gives courage to God's people to live through the final crisis.

THE 1335 DAYS TIMELINE OF DANIEL 12:12

Blessed is he that waiteth, and cometh to the thousand three hundred and five and thirty days. Dan. 12:12.

| Rev. 13:11-14
Fulfilled
The **VOICE**—USA
"speaking"
NSL in the USA | Rev. 16:17
Fulfilled
The **VOICE of God**
"speaking" the
Everlasting Covenant |

The 1335 days

WAIT (for the) BLESSING

CHAPTER IV

WHAT IS THE "1260 DAYS" TIMELINE OF DANIEL 12:7?

And I heard the man clothed in linen, which was upon the waters of the river, when he held up his right hand and his left hand unto heaven, and sware by him that liveth for ever that it shall be for a time, times, and an half; and when he shall have accomplished to scatter the power of the holy people, all these things shall be finished. Dan. 12:7.

INTRODUCTION

The Daniel 12:7 timeline of the 1260 days is one more brilliant facet of the Great Controversy story, which gleams with light on the closing scenes of the final conflict. In this one verse of Daniel 12:7, the two main characters of the Great Controversy are brought to view: **Christ** and **antichrist**! Christ is "the man clothed in linen," and antichrist is "**he** (that) shall have accomplished to scatter the power of the holy people." (He is also known as the "**abomination of desolation**" in Daniel 12:11 and Matthew 24:15 and as the **beast** in Revelation 13.) The "holy people" of Daniel 12:7 are the last generation which are caught in the middle of the Great Controversy!

The events which begin and end the 1260 days timeline are of the greatest importance in the closing scenes of the Great Controversy: not only to God's people and the wicked down here on earth, but also to the court of heaven, where all things in the Great Controversy struggle are witnessed and **legally** processed!

It is through God's people, by their demonstration of the redeeming power and restoration of God's love, that the Creator is vindicated before the universe. At the same time, a complete demonstration of the malignity of sin will have run its course. Wickedness will have been completely demonstrated by the antichrist persecution of the "holy people." By legislation of a Universal Death Decree to destroy all of God's people from the earth, the ultimate of sin is revealed. By the end of the 1260 day timeline, "all these things [which the wicked can do] shall be finished." Daniel 12:7. By this decree the wicked seal their own doom, and the action begins by which the righteous may be delivered!

The Bible student should understand that these timelines are the **Torch of Prophecy** which will light the path of the last generation with hope and joy as they enter and travel through the final conflict.

Surely the Lord God will do nothing, but he revealeth his secrets unto his servants the prophets. Amos 3:7.

The timeline was revealed to the prophet more than two millennia ago, but it is to be understood at the time when needed. Before the 1260 days timeline of Daniel 12:7 can come clearly into focus, it is necessary to continue with a scholarly procedure: (a) There must be a study of the original language in which the text was written. (b) Definitions must be clearly stated. Linkage with other prophetic texts, especially with those of Revelation, will reveal the unified nature of prophecy and give clear meaning.

The following questions need answers:
1. Who is "the man clothed in linen, which was upon the waters of the river"?
2. Who are the "holy people"?
3. What is "to scatter the power of" the holy people?
4. Who is "he" that shall have accomplished to scatter the power of the holy people?
5. What is "The Historicist View" of Daniel 12?
6. What is "a time, times, and an half" of Daniel 12:7?
   a. What is "Prophetic Terminology"?
   b. What is "Prophetic Time"?
   c. What is "Literal Time"?
   d. What is "Time"?
   e. What is "time, times, and an half"?
7. What is Revelation 13: Past or Future?
   a. What is a "Primary Application"?
   b. What is a "Secondary Application"?
8. What is "Papal Supremacy No. 2"?
9. What are the "Voices" which begin and end the 1260 day timeline?
10. What event begins the 1260 day timeline?
11. What event ends the 1260 day timeline"?
12. What is the "Universal Death Decree"?
13. What is "The One Hour" of Revelation 17:12,13?
14. What is "The Year-day Computation Principle" of Prophetic Interpretation?
15. What is the relationship between the 1335 day timeline and the 1260 day timeline of Daniel 12?
16. What is "The Time of Jacob's Trouble"?
17. What are "all these things" that "shall be finished" in Daniel 12:7?

Part 1. WHO IS "THE MAN" CLOTHED IN LINEN?

Jesus is known as **The Man** in prophecy as follows:

> Behold **the man** whose name is the **BRANCH**; and he shall grow up out of his place, and he shall build the temple of the Lord: Even he shall build the temple of the Lord; and he shall bear the glory, and shall sit and rule upon his throne; and he shall be a **priest** upon his throne:.... Zech. 6:12,13.

In contrast, the antichrist is known as **the man of sin** (See 2 Thessalonians 2:3). In the quotation of Zechariah 6:12,13, **the man**, Jesus Christ, "shall be a **priest** upon his throne." In the book of Hebrews 1:14-18 the point is made that it is the **humanity** of Jesus "made like unto his brethren" that qualified Him to be our priest in heaven. The fact that he is **the man, clothed in linen** also points to His work as our **high priest**:

> And the priest shall put on his linen garment. Lev. 6:10.

> After completing the morning service the high priest laid aside his "golden robes" and put on the clothes of an ordinary priest, to signal the surrender of his honored position and his assumption of the role of a servant. His act depicted the "self-emptying of our intercessor, who laid "aside his royal robe and kingly crown, [and] clothed his divinity with humanity," (EGW RH, June 15, 1905) and "taking the form of a servant...offered sacrifice, Himself the priest, Himself the victim (DA 25). Israel's high priest wore his "golden garments" for all the "daily" services which he performed during the Day, and changed into the uniform of an ordinary priest only for the unique rites of the Day of Atonement. Leslie Hardinge, *Christ Is All* (Boise, Idaho: Pacific Press Publishing Association, 1988), pp. 37,38.

The priests of Israel, who were types of Christ, were clothed in linen. In Daniel 12:7 Christ is brought to view as our high priest making atonement for His people.[*] Daniel also saw him **standing upon the waters**. There is One in Scripture who was able to stand and walk upon the waters—Jesus!

> And in the fourth watch of the night Jesus went unto them, walking on the sea. Matt. 14:25.

What does Jesus, our high priest, do in Daniel 12:7?

> ...held up his right hand, and his left hand unto heaven, and sware by him that liveth for ever.... Dan. 12:7.

---

[*] It should be understood, that Christ began his work as our high priest wearing the "linen garment" in 1844. (The high priest in Israel wore the linen garment on the Day of Atonement **only**). Therefore, this description of Christ places these events of Daniel 12 **after** 1844—as endtime prophecy.

It is in court that men hold up the right hand to take an oath to tell the truth.* By holding up both hands it is a **double promise**—a solemn oath to His people. He thereby gives them hope and courage. He makes this solemn oath to His people that it will be "**time, times and an half**...until all these things shall be finished." He assures the last generation that the final crises will not be dragged out indefinitely. They will need this promise to give them hope in the darkest hour! As they suffer through the time of trouble and the seven last plagues they can pin their faith in this promise in the Word of God. It is a message of Jesus to His beloved 144,000!

---

*   Also, the fact that Jesus holds up His hands, as in taking an oath in court provides a judgment **court** scene **after** 1844.

Part 2. WHO ARE THE "HOLY PEOPLE" OF DANIEL 12:7?

...it shall be for a time, times, and an half; and when he shall have accomplished to scatter the power of the **holy people**, all these things shall be finished. Dan. 12:7.

Daniel 12:7 and Matthew 24:34 appear similar:

...the **HOLY PEOPLE**,	...**THIS GENERATION** shall not pass,
all **these things** shall be **finished**. Dan. 12:7.	till all **these things** be **fulfilled** Matt. 24:34.

The prophet, Daniel, called the last generation the "**holy people**," and Jesus simply referred to them as "**this generation**." Obviously, it is the last generation which "**shall not pass**" off the scene of action, as they will still be alive when Jesus comes! It is they who will see "**all these things**" "**finished**" (Daniel 12:7) or "**fulfilled**" (Matthew 24:34).

When Jesus uttered these words, to His disciples on the Mount of Olives, "this generation shall not pass, till all these things be fulfilled," it became evident, with the death of John, the Revelator, that Jesus was not referring to them! Nor was it in reference to those who saw the destruction of Jerusalem in 70 A.D.

Neither was it those many generations who were martyred in Europe from 538 to 1798. It was not those who experienced the Lisbon earthquake in 1755! Nor those who saw the dark day of 1780 and the blood red moon! Nor the falling of the stars in 1833 over one hundred and fifty years ago! They saw the "**time of the end**" ushered in, but they were not the generation who should see **all** things fulfilled! It is not the generation who suffered the 1844 disappointment of whom Jesus spoke. It should not be necessary to find someone who is over one hundred fifty years old to fulfill this prophecy!

It is not **the generation** who proclaimed the Present Truth for their day, that the Investigative Judgment **began** in 1844 who live to see "**all things fulfilled**"! It is **the last generation** who proclaims the Present Truth for their day, that the Investigative Judgment is about to **end** which will "**not pass**" until all things are fulfilled.

The **last generation** is that "**holy people**" who will see that "all these things shall be finished" and they will do the following:

The Characteristics of the Last Generation "Holy People" of Daniel 12:7
1. They will proclaim, by fulfilled prophecy, the beginning of the Investigative Judgment of the Living according to Revelation 14:6,7,14-18.
2. They will pass through the Judgment of the Living and have their sins blotted out (Acts 3:19).

3. They will be "without fault" and "reflect the image of Jesus fully." Revelation 14:5.
4. They will be sealed with the Father's name (character) written in their foreheads (minds). Revelation 14:1-7.
5. They will receive the "Latter Rain." Joel 2:23.
6. They will give the "Loud Cry"—third angel's warning to the world. Rev. 14:9-18.
7. They will warn the world against the beast, his image and his mark. Rev. 13.
8. They will live through the reign of the "beast" and his persecutions as described in Revelation 13, and Daniel 12:7.
9. They will live through the time of trouble and the seven last plagues without a Mediator.
10. They will be delivered by the Voice of God. Rev.16:17.
11. They will live through the final Universal Death Decree. Rev. 13:15.
12. They will see Jesus coming in the clouds of heaven.
13. They will see the final fall of Babylon or false religion. Rev. 18.
14. They will be translated—not seeing death.
15. They will be "gathered from the four winds." Matt. 24:31.
16. They will be the 144,000.

This is "the holy people" of Daniel 12:7 who will live through the timeline of "time, times, and an half" (1260 days). This is the "generation" which will not pass till **all these things be fulfilled** or finished!

Part 3. WHAT IS "TO SCATTER THE POWER" OF THE HOLY PEOPLE?

...it shall be for a time, times, and an half; and when he shall have accomplished to **scatter the power** of the holy people, all these things shall be finished. Dan. 12:7.

Definition:

> "Scatter" as in Daniel 12:7. No. 5310 Strong's Exhaustive Concordance. (Hebrew and Chaldee Dictionary) "naphats," (pronounced naw-fats), a primitive root: to dash in pieces; be beaten in sunder, break in pieces, broken, dash (in pieces), caused to be discharged, dispersed, be overspread, scatter.

The above definition indicates that the last generation of "holy people" will be "scattered" or "dashed in pieces"! "dispersed"! "overspread"! or "beaten in sunder"! What word could be more expressive of fierce persecution?

Definition:

> "power" as in Daniel 12:7, as in "scatter the power of" the holy people. No. 3027 *Strong's Exhaustive Concordance* (Hebrew and Chaldee Dictionary) "yad" (pronounced yawd) a primitive word; a hand (the open one [indicating power, means, direction, etc.]...) in a great variety of applications, both literal and figurative,...dominion...service...ministry....

To "scatter the power" of the holy people means that they will be persecuted to the extent that their "hands will be tied" or broken. The mission program to all the world will eventually cease.

The mark of the beast will be received in the forehead or in the hand (Revelation 14:9). The seal of the living God will be placed in the forehead (Revelation 14:1). The seal of God is not mentioned in Revelation as being placed in the hand. It is evident that God's people will not be able to display with the hand their work for God, as it is revealed in Daniel 12:7 that the "hand" will be broken or prevented from functioning in the usual manner because of the persecution or martyrdom.

> ...prior to the last closing conflict, many will be imprisoned, many will flee for their lives from cities and towns, and many will be martyrs for Christ's sake in standing in defense of the truth.... You will not be tempted above what you are able to bear. 3 SM 397.

> ...I saw the souls of them that were beheaded for the witness of Jesus...which had not worshiped the beast, neither his image, neither had received his mark upon their foreheads, or in their hand; and they lived and reigned with Christ a thousand years. Rev. 20:4.

Part 4. WHO IS "HE" THAT SHALL HAVE ACCOMPLISHED TO SCATTER THE POWER OF THE HOLY PEOPLE? IN DANIEL 12:7?

"**He**" is a pronoun and refers to someone elsewhere mentioned. "**He**" is mentioned several times previously in the book of Daniel and is mentioned by name again almost immediately in Daniel 12:11 as follows:

> And from the time that the daily sacrifice shall be taken away, and the **abomination** that maketh desolate set up, there shall be a thousand two hundred and ninety days. Dan. 12:11.

It should be noticed that in Daniel 12:7 "He" is **doing the same thing** that the "**abomination**" is doing in Daniel 12:11. He is **persecuting** God's people! In Daniel 12:11 He, the abomination, "maketh **desolate**" or **persecutes**. In Daniel 12:7 "He...scatters the...holy people"—persecutes. In plain language "He" is the persecuting power that "**scatters**" or makes "desolate" God's people. This is illustrated below:

HE shall... **SCATTER** [persecutes] the holy people. Dan. 12:7.	...the **ABOMINATION MAKETH DESOLATE**.... [persecutes] Dan. 12:11

In Chapter II Parts 3-5 "The Abomination of Desolation" was fully identified as ROME:

1. Pagan Rome in 70 A.D. **persecuting** the Jews and early Christians.
2. Papal Rome in 538-1798 **persecuting** the people of God in Europe.
3. Papal Rome, will in the endtime, persecute again as foretold in Revelation 13 and 14, with added detail in the timelines of Daniel 12.

Papal Rome is identified by many prophetic symbols as follows:

Papal Rome Identified by Prophetic Symbolism as the Persecutor, Desolator:

Dan. 7:25	"The Little Horn"	"shall wear out the saints" "think to change times and laws" "saints...given to his hand"
Dan. 8:10	"The Little Horn"	"cast down ... the host" "stamped upon them"

Dan. 11:31	"The abomination"	"that maketh desolate"
Dan. 11:44	"The king of the north"	"shall go forth with great fury to destroy" "and utterly to make away many"
Dan. 12:7	"He"	"to scatter the power of the holy people"
Dan. 12:11	"The abomination"	"that maketh desolate"
2 Thess. 2:3	"The man of sin" "The son of perdition"	"sitteth in the temple of God."
Rev. 12:3,4	"The Dragon" [working through Rome]	"to devour her child" [Jesus]
Rev. 12:13	"The Dragon" [working through Papal Rome]	"persecuted the woman"
Rev. 12:15	The Dragon"	"that he might cause her to be carried away by the flood [of persecution]"
Rev. 12:17	"The Dragon" [working through Papal Rome]	"was wroth with the woman" "went to make war with the remnant"
Rev. 13:1-10	"The beast"	"to make war with the saints" "to overcome them" "leadeth into captivity" "killeth with the sword"
Rev. 14:9-11	"The beast"	
Rev. 17:11-14	"The beast" and "kings"	"shall make war with the chosen and faithful"
Rev. 19:19	"The beast"	"gathered together to make war... against the Lamb ...and His armies"

In view of the fact that this antichrist persecutor is so often mentioned in the prophecies of Scripture, it is not surprising that Jesus, when mentioning this power in Daniel 12:7, simply referred to it as "He" and it is expected that those who study the prophecies shall understand it!

> Many shall be purified, and made white, and tried; but the wicked shall do wickedly: and none of the wicked shall understand; but the wise shall understand. Dan. 12:10.

Part 5. WHAT IS THE "HISTORICIST VIEW" OF DANIEL 12:7?

Satan leads apostate Christendom into confusion and darkness by mixing truth with error. It is also his purpose that when God's people reject gross errors, that they shall also reject truths which are important for their time in history. In this manner, Satan has clouded the issue of the future reign of the "beast" power or antichrist of Revelation 13,14.

Apostate Christendom, with its rapture theory and many other errors, has also declared that a future antichrist will reign for three and a half years during a great "tribulation." It is Satan's plan that the remnant shall reject, not only the error of the rapture theory, but also those prophetic Scriptures, which pertain to the final crisis described in Revelation 13 and the attending timelines of Daniel 12!

Centuries ago, apostate Christendom rejected the historicist principles of interpretation, which identified the antichrist-beast of Scripture as being fulfilled in Papal Rome. In order to remove the accusing finger from Papal Rome, the false prophetic expositors, known as "Futurists," declared that all such prophecies pointed to a mysterious, **unidentified** antichrist which would arise in endtime for a three and a half year period of "tribulation." This idea, along with many errors, is "Futurism." Its primary purpose is to remove the accusing finger from the Papacy in the past when it reigned over Europe from 538-1798, and in the future when it will reign again.

The Futurists discarded the "Year-day Computation Principle" by which the prophetic times of Daniel and Revelation could be interpreted. Papal Rome could not then be identified in the past. It is only by bringing such blindness upon the apostate churches that Papal Rome can return to power in the near future.

Therefore, it is only a true historicist who continues to "decode" all prophetic symbolism by Biblical cross reference and uses the "Year-day Computation Principle" to decode symbolic time. The historicist today may use literal prophecy and **literal time correctly, to identify Papal Rome** and see its future reign according to Revelation 13 and 14 as linked to Daniel 12. It is only a true historicist who can give the third angel's message of Revelation 14 or be among the "wise" [who] shall understand. Daniel 12!*

---

* Note: An application of Daniel 12:7-13, which uses the time-honored "Literal Approach," recognizes the literal language, and applies the literal "days" timelines to the future is **NOT** promoting "Futurism." Neither is such an application giving Daniel 7,8 and 9 a "Dual Application." Rather, it simply **extends** the Historicist principles of prophetic interpretation, merely adding the **final segment** of fulfilling prophecy!

An application of the three timelines of Daniel 12, which places the fulfillment in the future, links the past persecutions of Papal Reign (538-1798) to that which is predicted in Revelation 13 and which are still future.

Whereas "Futurism" seeks to remove the finger from Papal Rome, a future application of Daniel 12:7-13 points directly to Papal Rome, adding the future persecution to that of the past.

Part 6. WHAT IS "TIME, TIMES, AND AN HALF" OF DANIEL 12:7?

> ...it shall be for a **time, times, and an half**; and when he shall have accomplished to scatter the power of the holy people, all these things shall be finished. Dan. 12:7.

Before a question can be answered there must be a clear definition of terms as follows:

1. What is "prophetic terminology"?
2. What is "prophetic time"?
3. What is "literal time"?
4. What is "time"?
5. What is "time, times, and an half"?

1. What is "prophetic terminology"?

The prophet, Daniel, used "prophetic terminology" when he made a prophecy to king Nebuchadnezzar as follows:

> Let his heart be changed from a man's, and let a beast's heart be given him; and let seven **times** [prophetic terminology] pass over him. Dan. 4:16.

This prediction was indeed prophecy. For Nebuchadnezzar, it was a future event. In this prophetic setting, Daniel used prophetic terminology—"times." It was "prophetic time" but not **symbolic** time to be interpreted by the Year-day Computation Principle! Nebuchadnezzar understood this prophetic terminology to refer to a **LITERAL SEVEN YEARS**.

Remember that Daniel 11 and 12 are not couched in symbolism. Therefore the phrase "time, times, and a half" are simply "prophetic terminology," not symbolic time, and should not be considered "prophetic time" to be computed or decoded by the Year-day Computation Principle.

2. What is "prophetic time"?

As mentioned above, "prophetic time" must be decoded only when the time is couched in a context of prophetic **symbolism**.

3. What is "literal time"?

If, in the literal setting of Daniel 12, the prophet had not used the prophetic terminology, "times", but had simply said, "three and a half years" it would be necessary to understand that literal time is that in which a year contains 365 1/4 days, and when added up would equal just over 1278 plus days! To prevent this error, Daniel used prophetic terminology, "time, times, and an half." Prophetic terminology is readily recognized by experienced expositors. It is so linked with the 1260 days and the 42 months of related Scripture that there is an instinctive perception that, even in a literal setting, it refers to a period of 1260 days.

4. **What is a "time"?**

   Because of the fact that the prophetic terminology of a "time, times, and an half" is equated in several texts of Scripture to 42 months, or 1260 days, it is generally understood that a "time" represents a "Bible year" of 360 days. See the following explanation:

   > A comparison with parallel prophecies, ...by other designations [of time], enables us to calculate the length of time involved [in a "time, times, and a half"]. In Revelation 12:14 the period is...referred to earlier in the chapter by the designation "a thousand two hundred and threescore days" (Revelation 12:6). In Revelation 11:2,3 the expression "a thousand two hundred and threescore days" is equated with "forty and two months." Thus it is clear that a period of three and a half times equals 42 months, ...equals 1260 days, and that a "time" represents 12 months, or 360 days. 4 BC 833.

Therefore, to avoid confusion, it is better to speak of the "time, times, and an half" as being 1260 days or 42 months rather than "three and a half years."

In conclusion, it can be established that Daniel 12:7 asserts that God's holy people will be persecuted by Papal Rome for a period of 1260 days. It should also be understood from previous chapters that Daniel 12:12 asserts that those who "wait it out" for 1335 days will be blessed at the Voice of God deliverance from the wicked.

Note: The word, "time," as used by Daniel in prophecy comes from the Biblical records of Noah's flood wherein 5 months are equated to 150 days (see Genesis 7 and 8). Each month was therefore 30 days. When the word "time" is used in a prophetic timeline in the book of Daniel, each "time" should be counted as 360 days, not 365 1/4 days.

Part 7. WHAT IS "REVELATION 13" PAST? OR FUTURE?

If only Revelation 12 and 13 were not separated by chapter headings! Revelation 12 is an introduction-preview to chapter 13. It states plainly:

> And the dragon was wroth with the woman, and went to make **war with the remnant** [the last generation] of her seed, which keep the commandments of God, and have the testimony of Jesus Christ. Rev. 12:17.

Much of Revelation 13 fulfillment is yet future. Beginning at verse 3, the following statements have not yet been fulfilled:

> ...and ALL the world wondered after the beast. (verse 3)

> ...power was given him over ALL kindred, and tongues, and nations. (verse 7)
> And ALL that dwell upon the earth shall worship him, whose names are not written in the book of life.... (verse 8)

> ...and he spake as a dragon. (verse 11)

Nearly all prophetic expositors admit that Revelation 13:11-17 has not yet met fulfillment. Even in verse 3, "ALL" the world has not yet fulfilled this prophecy! This preponderance of unfulfilled prophecy in this chapter places the passage in the general area of **FUTURE PRIMARY APPLICATION**! The beginning verses give sufficient information so that the main characters can be identified with historic linkage to the past. There is sufficient information to understand that this chapter deals with Papal Rome (past, present and future) and with the United States of America. But other than this, the chapter is one which outlines future events.

In Revelation 12:17 the drama is plainly introduced as it pertains to the "remnant" or "last generation." It is to this generation that **PRIMARY** FULFILLMENT will take place. Other past applications have been "secondary."

Definition: "Secondary" 1. Next below the first in importance. 2. Immediately derived from or dependent on that which is original or primary. *Webster's Dictionary*.

Peter's use of Joel 2:28-32 is an excellent example of a "secondary application" (See Acts 2:14-21). The pioneers of Adventism used many endtime prophecies giving them a "secondary application." But these secondary applications must not prohibit or sweep away the primary applications to endtime, last generation fulfillment. Note that the words "primary" and "secondary" are based on "importance," **not necessarily in sequence**!

With these concepts clearly in mind, it is important to determine what is the primary fulfillment of Revelation 13. Look carefully at the action which pertains to the future, keeping the entire passage connected and in context! Because of the fact that the verses of Revelation are connected with "And," it appears to be a "running (sequential) account" of future events:

REVELATION 13:3-8

And I saw one of his heads wounded to death [1798] and his deadly wound was healed [happening now] and **ALL** the world wondered after the beast [future] and...and...and.... And it was given him to continue **forty and two** months...and...and...and.... And it was given him to make war with the saints, and to overcome them: and power was given him over **ALL** kindreds, and tongues, and nations. And ALL that dwell on the earth **shall** worship him, whose names are not written in the book of life....

The above passage takes the reader from 1798, to the present and into the **FUTURE.** The word "ALL" (the world) qualifies the times specified because of the fact that "all" the world was not under the European Papal Supremacy. It may therefore be understood that the forty two months of Revelation 13 is a parallel of the 1260 day timeline of Daniel 12:7.

...and power was given him to continue **forty** and two months.... And it was given unto him to make **war** with the saints, and to overcome them.... Rev. 13:5,7.

it shall be for a **time, times, and an half**: and... shall have accomplished to **scatter** the power of the holy people,.... Dan. 12:7.

Part 8. WHAT IS **"PAPAL SUPREMACY NO. 2"** ?

Prophecy predicts two Papal Supremacies. The first was "Papal Supremacy No. 1" which reigned over Europe from 538-1798 A.D. The second is "Papal Supremacy No. 2" which **will reign** over "**ALL**" the world, for "power was given him over **all** kindreds, and tongues, and nations." Revelation 13:7. The first Papal Supremacy is given in the context of prophetic symbolism in Daniel 7:25 in which the prophetic "days" represent 1260 **years**. But the second Papal Supremacy is given in **literal context of literal days** (1260 days of persecution) in Daniel 12:7.

TWO PAPAL SUPREMACIES

Papal Supremacy No. 1 Daniel 7:25; 11:31; Revelation 12:6 538 1260 years 1798 over Europe	Papal Supremacy no. 2 Daniel 12:7, 11; Revelation 12:17;13-18 1260 days over ALL the world

We are standing on the threshold of great and solemn events. Many of the prophecies are about to be fulfilled in quick succession. Every element of power is about to be set to work. **Past history will be repeated**: old controversies will arouse to new life, and peril will beset God's people on every side. Intensity is taking hold of the human family. It is permeating everything upon the earth.... Study Revelation in connection with Daniel, for **history will be repeated**.... We, with all our religious advantages, ought to know far more today than we do know. TM 116.*

Should the 2300 year-day prophecy of Daniel 8:14 be given a dual application and applied to endtime fulfillments? At least at the present time the answer would be "No" for the following reasons:

1. Daniel 12 does not mention in its timelines 2300 days. That timeline is not mentioned in

---

* Note: "When the time shall come, in the providence of God, for the world to be tested upon the truth for that time, minds will be exercised by His Spirit to search the Scriptures, even with fasting and prayer, until link after link is searched out and united in a perfect chain.... They [preceding generations] had the Bible, as we have; but **the time for the unfolding of special truth in relation to the closing scenes of the earth's history is during the last generation that shall live upon the earth.**" 2 T 692,693.

Revelation. Therefore there is no cross reference in regard to time as there is in the three timelines of Daniel 12.

2. The book of Daniel is progressive. It moves steadily forward, chapter by chapter, continually enlarging or advancing historical movements among nations and powers until at last, chapter 12 moves into endtime events. It is probably unwise to go back to chapters 8 and 9 to lift the 2300 year timeline out of its historical setting of past history.

3. Whereas the timelines of Daniel 12, with reference to the "abomination of desolation" were mentioned specifically by Jesus in Matthew 24:15 in a prophecy of endtime (verse 3) and verified of its endtime fulfillment by the Spirit of Prophecy statements, there is no such linkage provided by Jesus or the Spirit of Prophecy for a dual application of the 2300 days.

4. The 2300 day prophecy deals mainly with heavenly drama in the sanctuary and with the judgment **which is still in process**. Many expositors feel that it is unwise to attempt to give a prophecy a second application while the first process or application is still not yet completely fulfilled.

5. Those who have attempted to give the 2300 year-day prophecy a dual application have not fulfilled the hermeneutic requirements and rules which permit the Bible to be its own expositor. Unfortunate attempts have been made to fit various endtime events into the picture by their own subjective conjectures. This leads only to confusion and division of opinions.

6. Prophetic exposition in its true perspective is an attempt to find the meaning (primary application) of specific verses of the Bible.

Part 9. WHAT ARE THE "VOICES" WHICH BEGIN AND END THE 1260 DAYS?

If the prophetic exposition is correct, the same hermeneutic principles and the same procedures should be applied not only to the 1335 day timeline but also to the 1260 day timeline of Daniel 12:7.

The 1335 day timeline of Daniel 12:12 began and ended with "Voices." It begins with the "voice" of a nation (USA) and ends with the "Voice of God." It begins with the "speaking" of a nation in legislative action (A National Sunday Law in the United States of America) and ends with the "speaking" of God as He pronounces the Blessing of the Everlasting Covenant. It begins with a fulfillment of prophecy (Revelation 13:11) and ends with a fulfillment of prophecy (Revelation 16:17).

In like manner, the 1260 day timeline begins and ends with "Voices." It begins with the "Voices" of ALL nations united with the voice of the "beast" power (Revelation 13:5) and ends with the "Voices" of ALL nations united with the "image to the beast." (Revelation 13:15).

These "**Voices**" are the "speaking" of the nations which are **legislative decrees**. The 1260 day timeline begins and ends with the fulfillment of prophetic Scripture. Both in hermeneutic principle and in application the 1335 day timeline and the 1260 day timeline are identical!

The 1260 day timeline begins with a fulfillment of Revelation 13:5. It ends with the fulfillment of Revelation 13:15. Both of these verses are the "speaking" or Voices of prophetic fulfillment:

The 1260 Day Timeline of Daniel 12:7

BEGINS | ENDS

| And there was given unto him a mouth ***SPEAKING***... and power was given him to continue forty and two months.
Rev. 13:5 | ...the image of the beast should both ***SPEAK***, and cause that as many as would not worship the image of the beast should be killed.
Rev. 13:15 |

1260

Part 10. WHAT "EVENT" BEGINS THE 1260 DAY TIMELINE?

> And there was given unto him a mouth speaking great things and blasphemies; and power was given unto him to continue forty and two months. Rev. 13:5.

> The "speaking" of a nation[s] is the action of its legislative and judicial authorities. GC 442.

The "speaking" or legislative action which takes place in Revelation 13:5 is done, not by the USA, but by the "beast" himself! Papal Rome will legislate and the nations of the world will take judicial action! This represents a union of church and state on a worldwide basis. The prophecy continues:

> And ALL that dwell upon the earth shall worship him,... power was given him over **all** kindreds, and tongues, and nations... **power was given unto him** to continue forty and two months [1260 days!].... Rev. 13:8,7,5.

What kind of legislation or what kind of law would cause all nations to **worship** him? What is the **mark** of his authority? By what legislation could Papal Rome claim the **worship** of all nations?

> As the sign of the authority of the Catholic Church, papist writers cite "the very act of changing the Sabbath into Sunday, which Protestants allow of;...because by keeping Sunday, they acknowledge the church's power...." Henry Tuberville, *An Abridgement of the Christian Doctrine*, p.58. GC 448.

> The enforcement of Sunday-keeping on the part of Protestant churches is an enforcement of the worship of the papacy—of the beast. GC 448.

Therefore it is Sunday keeping which is the "mark" of authority of the Papacy "beast" of Revelation 13:5. And **the "speaking" of the beast is the legislation of a Sunday Law on a world wide basis**. The 1335 day timeline begins with a National Sunday Law in the USA, and the 1260 day timeline begins with a Universal Sunday Law over the whole world so that "ALL" shall worship him. Such a Universal Sunday Law is described as follows:

> Fearful is the issue to which the world is to be brought. The **powers of the earth, UNITING** to war against the commandments of God, will decree that "all, both small and great, rich and poor, free and bond" (Rev. 13:16), shall conform to the customs of the church by the observance of the false sabbath [Sunday]. GC 604.

A National Sunday Law in the United States of America begins the 1335 days timeline	A Universal Sunday Law over the whole world begins the 1260 days timeline

A Review of the Sequence of Events:

1. A National Sunday Law in the USA begins the endtime scenario of the 1335 days.
2. This is the sign to leave the large cities, preparatory for flight to the mountains.
3. A National Sunday Law in the USA is followed shortly by National Ruin.
4. A Universal Sunday Law over the whole world begins the 1260 day timeline.
5. The persecution or "scattering" of God's people begins as described below: "And to the woman were given two wings of a great eagle, that she might fly into the wilderness, into her place, where she is nourished for a time, and times, and half a time, from the face of the serpent." Rev. 12:14.[*]
6. The righteous experience the "shaking" and receive the Seal of God.
7. The righteous give the Loud Cry in the power of the Latter Rain.
8. The wicked receive the mark of the beast.

With the issue thus clearly brought before him, whoever shall trample upon God's law to obey a human enactment receives the mark of the beast; he accepts the sign of allegiance to the power which he chooses to obey instead of God. The warning from heaven is: "If any man worship the beast and his image, and receive his mark in his forehead, or in his hand. The same shall drink of the wine of the wrath of God, which is poured out without mixture into the cup of His indignation" Rev. 14:9,10.

The Sabbath will be the great test of loyalty.... When the final test shall be brought to bear upon men, then the line of distinction will be drawn between those who serve God and those who serve Him not....While one class, by accepting the sign of submission to earthly powers, receive the mark of the beast, the other, choosing the token of allegiance, to divine authority, receive the seal of God. GC 605.

---

[*] Note: Revelation 12:14 has been applied by some to Papal Supremacy 538-1798. However, the **primary application** of verses 14-17 refer to the "remnant" or last generation against whom the "dragon went to make war" at the very end of time. Those who assumed that Revelation 12:14 applied to the persecutions of the past should remember that "history will be repeated" in regard to Papal Supremacy and persecution. The "woman" which takes flight into the wilderness in the future will refer not merely to Europe, but to the most remote and desolate regions all over the world.

The timelines of Daniel 12 deal with the most climactic events in the history of the world by which the final destiny of man shall be decided!

Part 11. WHAT "EVENT" ENDS THE 1260 DAY TIMELINE?

The event which ends the 1260 DAY TIMELINE is again fulfillment of prophecy as found in Revelation 13:15. It is the "Voice" or "speaking" of the image of the beast and the nations. It is legislation of a "decree":

> And he had power to give life unto the image of the beast that the image of the beast should both **SPEAK**, and cause that as many as would not worship the image of the beast **SHOULD BE KILLED**. Rev. 13:15.

The event which ends the 1260 day timeline is a Universal Death Decree, intended to exterminate all the people of God from the earth. Who are the characters in this drama who attempt to do this? They are: 1. The "beast" which is the Papacy in the Old World—Roman Catholicism, and 2. The "image to the beast" which is Protestantism in the New World—the United States of America. They both seek to accomplish the same goal and that is why they are known as the "beast" and the "image to the beast"—one mirrors the other.

In Revelation 13:15 it declares that it is the "beast"—Rome, (backed by ALL nations) which will have the "power" to give life unto the "image to the beast"—the United States, that it should "speak" or legislate the Universal Death Decree, that "as many as would not worship the image of the beast should be **killed**." The United States leads out in this, but the rest of the world follows as expressed in the paragraph below. The manner in which this Death Decree is legislated is described:

> As the Sabbath has become the special point of controversy throughout Christendom, and religious and secular authorities have combined to enforce the observance of the Sunday, the persistent refusal of a small minority to yield to the popular demand will make them objects of universal execration. It will be urged that the few who stand in opposition to an institution of the church and a law of the state ought not to be tolerated; that it is better for them to suffer than for whole nations to be thrown into confusion and lawlessness. The same argument eighteen hundred years ago was brought against Christ by the "rulers of the people." "It is expedient for us," said the wily Caiaphas, "that one man should die for the people, and that the whole nation should perish not." John 11:50. This argument will appear conclusive; and a decree will finally be issued against those who hallow the Sabbath of the fourth commandment, denouncing them as deserving of the severest punishment and giving the people liberty, after a certain time, **to put them to death**. Romanism in the Old World and apostate Protestantism in the New will pursue a similar course toward those who honor all the divine precepts. GC 615,616.

Although the USA "speaks" it becomes a **universal** Death Decree in both the Old World and the New World—all over the world. It becomes the "Voices" of "ALL" nations which worship the beast. (Revelation 13:3,7,8,11).

Do not confuse "death penalties" which attend Sunday legislation with the final "Universal

Death Decree." Whereas death "penalties" occur before the seven last plagues begin, the final Universal Death Decree occurs under the 6th plague! This concept will be dealt with in detail in a chapter to come. This confusion between penalties and the final Universal Death Decree has caused some to get endtime events completely out of order. They have attempted to place the final Universal Death Decree before the seven last plagues begin. This is error. As will be seen later, the last generation are delivered from the final Universal Death Decree by the Voice of God which occurs under the 7th plague (See Revelation 16:17). The "gathering of the kings of the earth to legislate a final Death Decree occurs under the 6th plague. The Voice of God deliverance from the final Death Decree is the stroke of action which divides the 6th and 7th plagues in this final crisis.

> When the protection of human laws shall be withdrawn from those who honor the law of God, there will be, in different lands, a simultaneous movement for their destruction. As the time appointed in **the decree** draws near, the people will conspire to root out the hated sect. It will be determined to strike in one night a decisive blow, which shall utterly silence the voice of dissent and reproof. GC 635.

> As the decree issued by the various rulers of Christendom against commandment keepers shall withdraw the protection of government and abandon them to those who desire their destruction, the people of God will flee from the cities and villages and associate together in companies dwelling in the most desolate and solitary places. Many will find refuge in the strongholds of the mountains. Like the Christians of the Piedmont valleys, they will make the high places of the earth their sanctuaries and will thank God for "the munitions of rocks" Isaiah 33:16. But many of all nations and of all classes, high and low, rich and poor, black and white, will be cast into the most unjust and cruel bondage. The beloved of God pass weary days, bound in chains, shut in prison bars, sentenced to be slain, some apparently left to die of starvation in dark and loathsome dungeons. No human ear is open to hear their moans; no human hand is ready to lend them help. GC 626.

Let us keep in mind that the 1260 day timeline deals with the "scattering" or persecuting of God's people! It is the "scattering" which is **the subject** of the timeline! This "scattering" climaxes when the wicked determine to pass a final Universal Death Decree to wipe them out!

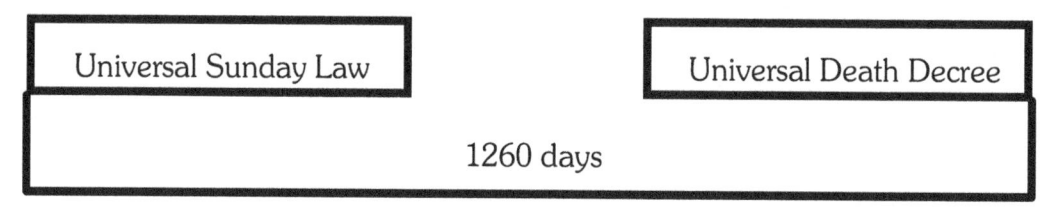

Universal Sunday Law		Universal Death Decree
	1260 days	

time, times, and an half" of "scattering"
[persecuting] of the "Holy People."
Dan. 12:7

Part 12. WHAT IS THE "UNIVERSAL DEATH DECREE"?

The Universal Death Decree is so important that it is a major event spoken of in Revelation 13:15 and it is a "marker" in the 1260 day timeline of Daniel 12:7. It is vital, not only to the climax of the drama down here on earth, but is the pivot of action in the court of heaven for God's deliverance of His people! God never runs ahead of the action and interaction of the demonstration of the great controversy between Christ and Satan. Before any action is taken by God; first evil must be unmasked and reveal itself completely before the universe. This principle of interaction has been demonstrated again and again in the Old Testament. First, wicked Pharaoh put to death the Hebrew babes, then God permitted the death of the Egyptian firstborn. Not until the Egyptian army vowed to destroy utterly the Hebrews, did God permit them to be destroyed at the Red Sea. Not until wicked Haman instigated a universal death decree against the Jews, did God permit the destruction of those who planned their death. And at the end of the great controversy, as demonstrated in this earth's history, not until the wicked have fully demonstrated their determination to rid the earth of God's people by "speaking" (audibly and legally)—by legislation and by ALL nations uniting their Voices in a Universal Death Decree, will God move to deliver His saints.

A study of the seven heads of the great red dragon of Revelation 12 reveals how Satan has attempted seven times to establish a universal kingdom. He attempts to do this in the Universal Death Decree:

> As Satan influenced Esau to march against Jacob, so he will stir up the wicked to destroy God's people in the time of trouble.... If he could blot them from the earth, his triumph would be complete. GC 618.

Satan assumes that if he could just once get all the inhabitants on this planet to follow him, without any voice of dissent, he could "legally" claim it before the universe. God has never permitted this to happen, and His people will come through the persecution triumphant, 144,000 in number.

> Ye shall have a song, as in the night when a holy solemnity is kept; and GLADNESS OF HEART, as when one goeth with a pipe [trumpet or flute] to come into the mountain of the Lord, to the mighty One of Israel. And the Lord shall cause his glorious VOICE to be heard.... Isa. 30:29,30.

Those who understand the timelines of Daniel 12 will see the Universal Death Decree as one more sign of their near deliverance!

Part 13. WHAT IS THE "ONE HOUR" OF REVELATION 17:12,13?

> And the ten horns which thou sawest are ten kings, which have received no kingdom as yet; but receive power as kings **one hour** with the beast. These have one mind, and shall give their power and strength unto the beast. Rev. 17:12,13.

How can this portion of prophecy which also deals with endtime events be understood?

> In view of the testimony of Inspiration, how dare men teach that the Revelation is a mystery beyond the reach of human understanding? It is a mystery revealed, a book opened. The study of the Revelation **directs the mind to the prophecies of Daniel**, and both present most **important instruction**, given of God to men, **concerning events to take place at the CLOSE OF THIS WORLD'S HISTORY**. GC 341.

Revelation 17 cannot be understood until the timelines of Daniel 12 are open to study. The timelines of Daniel 12 will not be completely unfolded until combined with a study of Revelation 17! The events which Daniel saw in Daniel 12:7,11 are exactly the same events which John saw when he wrote Revelation 17! They both describe the final events which occur just before the coming of Jesus.

Revelation 17 throws great light on the timelines of Daniel 12 as follows:

1. The first important concept which should be recognized is the fact that: There is an interval of time between the legislation (enactment) of a law and the date when it shall go into effect (effective date). There is an interval of time between the Universal Death Decree and the date when it goes into effect. This is clearly stated as follows:

   > ...a decree will finally be issued against those who hallow the Sabbath of the fourth commandment denouncing them as deserving of the severest punishment and giving the people liberty, **AFTER A CERTAIN TIME**, to put them to death. GC 615,616.

   > Though a general decree **has fixed the time** when commandment keepers may be put to death, their enemies in some cases may anticipate the decree, and before **the time specified**, will endeavor to take their lives. GC 631.

2. The second point of consideration is the fact that a law goes into effect at midnight. The Universal Death Decree goes into effect at midnight at "the time specified," the decree has "fixed the time," and "after a certain time" they are to be put to death. **Midnight is the hour**!

3. The "Voice of God" deliverance occurs at **midnight**. It delivers them from the Universal Death Decree, which goes into effect at **midnight**. This is clearly stated:

> As the time appointed in the decree draws near....It will be determined to strike in one **night** a decisive blow,.... GC 635.
>
> It is at **MIDNIGHT** that God manifests His power for the **deliverance** of His People.... In the midst of the angry heavens is one clear space of indescribable glory, whence comes the **voice of God** like the sound of many waters, saying: "It is done" Rev. 16:17. GC 636.

4. The legislation of the Universal Death Decree is to take place at a certain time: the end of the 1260 day timeline. And the date when it goes into effect is at "the time specified," a "**fixed**" time, a "**certain**" time. None of this is **indefinite**!

    "One hour" spoken of in Revelation 17:12 is **NOT INDEFINITE**! "One hour" is a specified unit of time, a fixed unit and a certain unit! Let no one assume that "One hour" is an "indefinite or just a short space of time."

5. The "One hour" of Revelation 17:12 is a time when the kings of the earth are united in purpose with the "beast," and it is a time when "these have one mind, and shall give their power and strength unto the beast," to enforce the Universal Death Decree. This fact is further reinforced in the next verse which declares that they are united for the purpose to make "war" with the Lamb (in the person of His people), for they that are "with him are called, and chosen, and faithful"!

6. This "one hour" of Revelation 17:12-14 describes the "reign" or triumph of the beast when he is able to get the kings of the earth to support his Universal Death Decree. From the time that the decree is enacted (legislated) until it is enforced is "one hour" of exultation. But for God's people it is described as the "time of Jacob's trouble."

    > The people of God will then be plunged into those scenes of affliction and distress described by the prophet as the time of Jacob's trouble. GC 616.

7. On a certain date at midnight the Universal Death Decree goes in effect. It would appear that one literal hour is too short an interval between legislation and enforcement. Therefore the "one hour" of Revelation 17:12, which is written in the context of symbolism of a "beast" and "horns" is also symbolic time. It needs to be decoded!

Part 14. WHAT IS THE "YEAR-DAY COMPUTATION PRINCIPLE" OF PROPHETIC INTERPRETATION?

The "Year-day Computation Principle" is a standard of conversion. It is, in a way, similar to a yardstick, which makes it possible to convert inches to feet, feet to yards, or inches to yards and vice versa. This "Year-day Computation Principle" makes it possible to convert "prophetic time" (symbolic time) to literal time. It, like the rule of measurement, is essential when decoding prophetic time and in matching symbolic-prophetic time prophecies to literal historical events or to prophecies which are written in literal language.

It is self-evident that Daniel 12 deals with time (timelines) written in literal language. But Revelation is couched in symbolism and the time which is within such context is also symbolic time. If Daniel and Revelation are to be studied together then it is necessary to use the "Year-day Computation Principle" of conversion to link the times of literal Daniel to the times specified in symbolic Revelation.

In order to decode the "one hour" of Revelation 17:12, we shall need to get out the old yardstick (Year-day Computation Principle) to see what "one hour" of prophetic time equals in literal time.

$$\begin{aligned}
1 \text{ prophetic day} &= 1 \text{ literal year} \\
1/24 \text{ of a prophetic day (one hour)} &= 1/24 \text{ of a literal year} \\
1/12 \text{ of a literal year} &= 30 \text{ days} \\
1/24 \text{ of a literal year} &= 15 \text{ days}
\end{aligned}$$

Therefore "one hour" of Prophetic time in Revelation 17:12 is **fifteen literal days**.

We may therefore conclude that from the time that the Universal Death Decree is enacted by legislation it will be fifteen days until the decree is to be enforced. These fifteen days are very important to the total structure of the entire three timelines of Daniel 12.

The "Year-day Computation Principle" is the special object of Satanic attack! By discarding it, the Futurists were able to remove the finger of accusation from Papal Rome. By discarding it they were able to place the whole book of Daniel in confusion and darkness where apostate Protestantism resides today. This "Year-day Computation Principle" has been under attack even in Adventism in the past decade. It is still under attack and there are some who protest its use to give light to the Revelation 17:12 verse declaring it better to remain in darkness than to use this profitable tool! Although there is no Spirit of Prophecy statement to declare that this rule has been removed, there are many who assume that it disappeared in 1844. For a full discussion of this problem see page 14 "What Prophetic Time Shall Be No Longer."

Part 15. WHAT IS THE "RELATIONSHIP" BETWEEN THE 1335 AND THE 1260 DAYS?

The relationship between the two timelines is illustrated below:

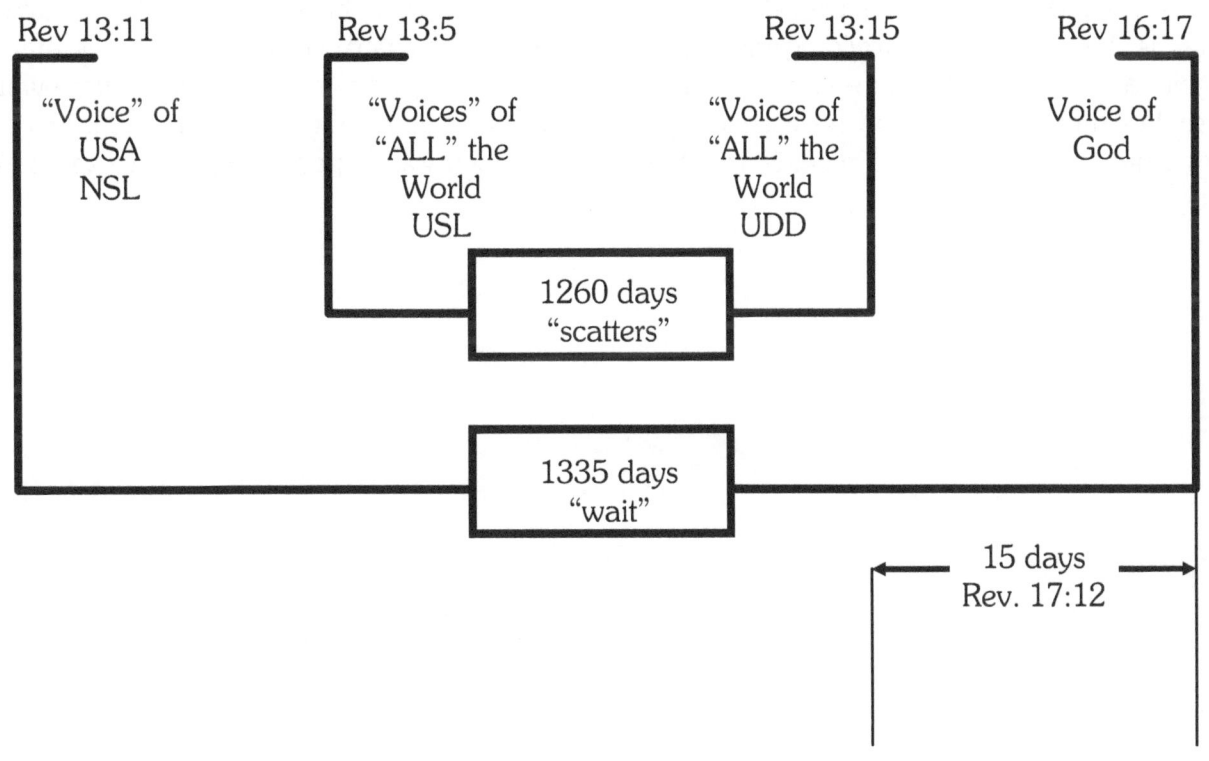

```
Rev 13:11            Rev 13:5              Rev 13:15             Rev 16:17

 "Voice" of          "Voices" of           "Voices of            Voice of
   USA                "ALL" the             "ALL" the              God
   NSL                 World                 World
                        USL                   UDD

                              ┌──────────────┐
                              │  1260 days   │
                              │  "scatters"  │
                              └──────────────┘

                      ┌──────────────────────┐
                      │      1335 days       │
                      │        "wait"        │
                      └──────────────────────┘
                                              ←─── 15 days ───→
                                                   Rev. 17:12
```

1. The timelines do not begin at the same time.
2. The timelines do not end together.
3. The 1260 day timeline resides within the 1335 day timeline.
4. Both timelines begin and end with "Voices" or Legislation or "speaking" of governments.
5. Both timelines begin and end with fulfilled prophecy from Revelation.
6. The 1260 days is that of persecution.
7. The 1335 days is a "Wait" for the Voice of God.
8. The legislation of the Universal Death Decree begins a "one hour" interim to effective date.
9. The "one hour" is fifteen literal days.
10. The fifteen literal days plus the 1260 days equals 1275 days.
11. The 1275 days subtracted from the 1335 days leaves a sixty day interval between the USA-NSL and the USL over ALL the world. (If there is not a 60 day interval the student of prophecy would know that this computation is incorrect.) But if there is a sixty day interval, he would gain confidence in the entire study of the three timelines and their relationship to each other.

QUESTION

Why does the 1260 days of "scattering" end at the Universal Death Decree legislation, rather than at the Voice of God deliverance of God's people?

ANSWER

In the 1260 day timeline of Daniel 12:7 **HE** (the persecutor) is the **subject** of the sentence. "He" is the one who is providing the action. This action, the verb of the sentence, is that he "shall have accomplished to scatter" (persecute). The 1260 days is a measurement of time which describes the persecutor and his ascending action of persecution to its very climax. He goes as far as he can go! It is not a measurement of time in which God's people are under stress and distress.

Part 16. WHAT IS "THE TIME OF JACOB'S TROUBLE"?

From the legislation of a Universal Death Decree to its effective date, (One symbolic "hour" of Revelation 17:12 or fifteen literal days), God's people endure **"the time of Jacob's trouble."**

> A decree went forth to slay the saints, which caused them to cry day and night for deliverance. This was the time of Jacobs's trouble. EW 36,37.

> ... a decree will finally be issued against those who hallow the Sabbath of the fourth commandment,... giving the people liberty, after a certain time to put them to death.... The people of God will then be plunged into those scenes of affliction and distress described by the prophet as the time of Jacob's trouble. GC 615,616.

> As Satan influenced Esau to march against Jacob, so he will stir up the wicked to destroy God's people in the time of trouble. And as he accused Jacob, he will urge his accusations against the people of God. He numbers the world as his subjects; but the little company who keep the commandments of God are resisting his supremacy. If he could blot them from the earth, his triumph would be complete. GC 618.

Although Satan is seeking to "blot them from the earth" through legislation and the actions of the wicked, yet guardian angels have them fully protected.

> He sees that holy angels are guarding them.... GC 618.

> The heavenly sentinels, faithful to their trust, continue their watch. Though a general decree has fixed the time when commandment keepers may be put to death, their enemies will in some cases anticipate the decree, and before the time specified, will endeavor to take their lives. But **none can pass the mighty** guardians stationed about every faithful soul. Some are assailed in their flight from the cities and villages; but the swords raised against them break and fall as powerless as a straw. **Others are defended by angels in the form of men of war**. GC 631.

The "affliction and distress" in the time of Jacob's trouble, is caused by Satan as he tries them in mental anguish. There is no visible evidence that they will be delivered from the wicked and they must live by faith in the Word of God. They have no tangible evidence that God will deliver them, and "They afflict their souls before God, pointing to their past repentance of their sins." GC 619.

> But while they have a deep sense of their unworthiness, they have no concealed wrongs to reveal. Their sins have gone beforehand to judgment and have been blotted out, and they cannot bring them to remembrance. GC 620.

A DIAGRAM OF THE TIME OF JACOB'S TROUBLE

```
┌─────────────────────────────────────────────────────────────────┐
│ BEGINS                                              ENDS        │
│                                                                 │
│                                                                 │
│ Universal Death Decree                      The Voice of God    │
│ Revelation 13:15                            Revelation 16:17    │
└─────────────────────────────────────────────────────────────────┘
```

THE TIME OF JACOB'S TROUBLE
One symbolic "Hour" of Revelation 17:12 or 15 literal days

A List of Events Which Begin and End and Occur During the Time of Jacob's Trouble as given in *Early Writings* and *The Great Controversy*:

1. "A writing" [Universal Death Decree] begins the time of Jacob's trouble ....EW 282, 283
2. The saints were calm and composed, trusting God 283
3. Satan desires to destroy them 283
4. The wicked rush in, but angels protect the saints 283
5. The saints cry day and night for deliverance from the wicked 283
6. Saints leave cities and villages 283
7. The wicked pursue—swords fall powerless as straw 284, 285
8. The saints suffer mental anguish—wrestling with God to help 283
9. At midnight the saints are delivered 285
10. The Voice of God speaks the day and hour of the coming of Jesus 285
11. The Voice of God delivers them from the time of Jacob's trouble 285

1. Legislation of a Universal Death Decree begins the time of Jacob's trouble. ....GC 616
2. As Esau marched aginst Jacob, the wicked surround the saints 616
3. Satan has an accurate knowledge of past sins of the saints 618
4. Satan presents their sins before God 618
5. The Lord permits Satan to try them to the uttermost 618
6. The saints see little good in their past lives 619
7. The saints are conscious of their weakness and unworthiness 619
8. Satan tells them their cases are hopeless 619
9. The saints afflict their souls: "Has every sin been repented of?" 619
10. The saints plead the righteousness of Christ 619
11. The saints desire wickedness to end 619
12. The saint's sins have been blotted out beforehand 620
13. The saints cannot remember the sins which have been blotted out 620

14. The saints endure weariness, delay, and hunger 621
15. Satan personates Christ (this may not be the first time) 624
16. The saints flee cities and villages 626
17. The saints associate together in companies 626
18. The saints retreat to the mountains 626
19. Some of the saints are imprisoned 627
20. The saints are defended against attack by angels as men of war 631
21. The saints are delivered from the time of Jacob's trouble by the Voice of God. Revelation 16:17. .... 635, 636

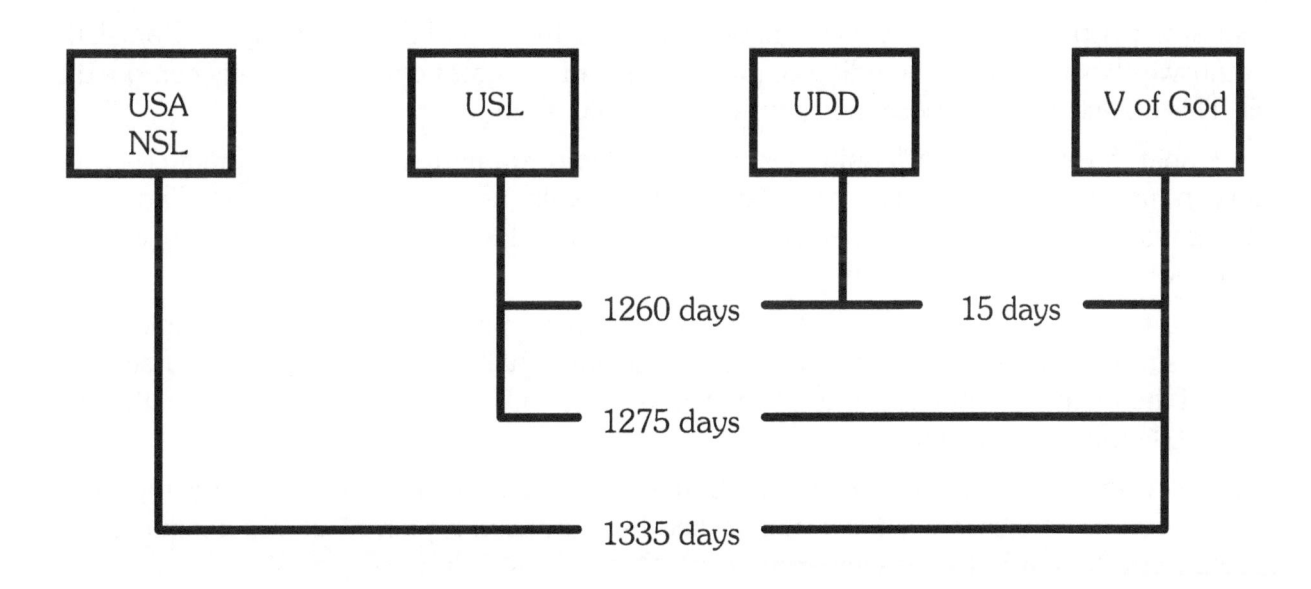

```
┌──────┐      ┌──────┐      ┌──────┐      ┌──────────┐
│ USA  │      │ USL  │      │ UDD  │      │ V of God │
│ NSL  │      │      │      │      │      │          │
└──┬───┘      └──┬───┘      └──┬───┘      └────┬─────┘
   │             │             │               │
   │             └── 1260 days ──┴── 15 days ──┤
   │             │                             │
   │             └────── 1275 days ────────────┤
   │                                           │
   └──────────────── 1335 days ────────────────┘
```

Part 17. WHAT ARE "ALL THESE THINGS" THAT "SHALL BE FINISHED" IN DANIEL 12:7?

> ...it shall be for a time, times, and an half; and when he shall have accomplished to scatter the power of the holy people, **ALL THESE THINGS** shall be finished. Dan. 12:7.

What are "**all these things**" which will be finished at the end of the 1260 days of Daniel 12:7? The answer lies in an understanding of the objective of the great controversy between good and evil. This objective is to expose the complete malignity of sin.

This planet, for nearly six millennia, has been the demonstration arena for the great controversy between good and evil. Satan has claimed this world as a proving ground. The unfallen inhabitants of the universe, as spectators, have watched this great struggle. God's people have borne the brunt of this confrontation.

From the time that Cain murdered Abel, the wicked have persecuted the "holy people." Daniel 12:7 is simply a statement that "He" the persecutor "shall have accomplished to scatter"-or reached the ultimate in persecutions by the legislation of a Universal Death Decree by the end of the 1260 literal days timeline.

The Universal Death Decree, which ends the 1260 days, culminates and encompasses all persecutions of all the ages. At last, the wicked have devised a plan to utterly annihilate God's people from the earth. In this Universal Death Decree they will have gone their limit! They can go no further. By this decree they will also have "spoken" or legislated their own condemnation in heaven's court!

When ALL the world wonders after the beast (Revelation 13), and when ALL their kings are gathered together by evil spirits under the sixth plague (Revelation 16:14) to legislate a Universal Death Decree, to rid the earth of the people of God, this action will be the culmination of all persecutions.

"ALL THESE THINGS" which the wicked have done against God's people **will be finished**." The universe will have seen enough. Satan and ALL his wicked hosts will have openly exposed their malignity in legal action. They will have **sealed** their doom.

While it is true that the Universal Death Decree is similar to Esau marching against Jacob, and that God's people will cry day and night for deliverance from their enemies in that interim between legislation and effective date (known as the "time of Jacob's trouble), yet they will be protected and "all these things" in the display of persecution will be finished.

"ALL THESE THINGS" that "shall be finished" at the end of the 1260 days, do not refer to the day and hour of the coming of Jesus! They do not refer to the Voice of God deliverance, nor the fall of Babylon described under the 7th plague. They do not refer to the millennium nor the destruction of sin and sinner in the lake of fire. They do not refer to the end of the distress and discomfort of God's people.

"All these things" refer only to that which is brought to view in the verse itself (Daniel 12:7) when "he shall scatter the power of the holy people"—persecution and the climax of all persecuting action of the wicked in the great controversy!

See the diagram below:

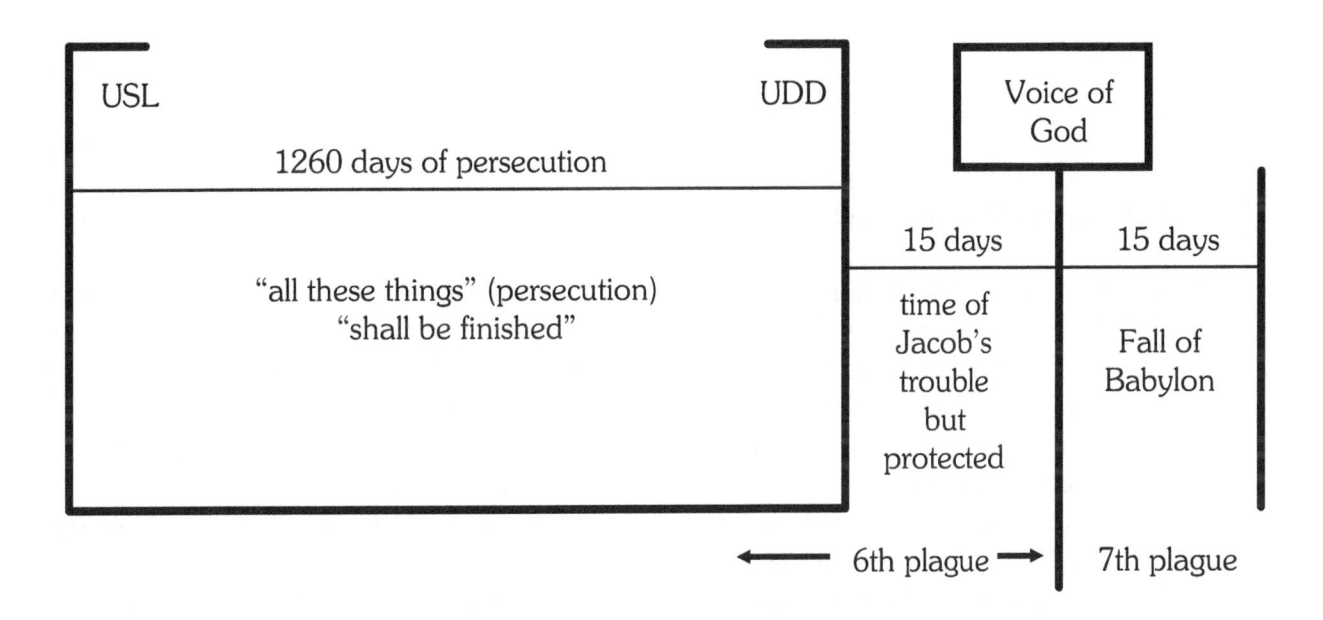

USL		UDD	Voice of God	
1260 days of persecution			15 days	15 days
"all these things" (persecution) "shall be finished"			time of Jacob's trouble but protected	Fall of Babylon
			← 6th plague →	7th plague

SUMMARY OF CHAPTER IV

WHAT IS THE "1260 DAYS" TIMELINE OF DANIEL 12:7?

The 1260 day timeline of Daniel 12:7 reveals the following:

1. Jesus, the man "clothed in linen," as high priest, places Daniel 12:7 in a time frame after 1844, within the "Day of Atonement" and at the "end" of earth's history.
2. Jesus, Himself, The Great High Priest in the Atonement, has taken an oath that the final "scattering" of the last generation shall not extend beyond 1260 literal days!
3. Not many generations, but the **last** generation shall see "all these things" (persecuting action attending the demonstration of the Great Controversy) "finished."
4. Papal Rome is "He" which will "scatter" or persecute the last generation for 1260 literal days in "Papal Supremacy No. 2."
5. Papal Supremacy No. 2 will reign, not merely over Europe, but over **ALL** kindreds, and tongues, and nations and people.
6. Not a Futurist, but a true Historicist identifies the endtime antichrist as Papal Rome.
7. The "time, times, and an half" of Daniel 12:7 are 1260 literal days.
8. The 1260 day timeline is consistent with the 1335 day timeline in that it begins and ends with "Voices."
9. The Daniel 12 timelines and Revelation 13 are parallel prophetic Scriptures.
10. The "Voices" are governments, "speaking" in Legislation.
11. The Event which begins the 1260 day timeline is a Universal Sunday Law.
12. The Event which ends the 1260 day timeline is a Universal Death Decree.
13. The Universal Death Decree is the climax of all persecuting action.
14. The Universal Death Decree is the end of the 1260 days of "scattering." God's people will be fully protected.
15. There is a time interval between legislation of a decree and its effective date.
16. There is a fifteen day interval between the Universal Death Decree and its effective date of enforcement, spoken of as "one [symbolic] hour" in Revelation 17:12.
17. The fifteen day interim is a "reign" of the wicked in exultation.
18. The fifteen day interim is "the time of Jacob's trouble" for the saints.
19. The "Year-day Computation Principle" is still valid and by it the "one hour" of Revelation 17:12 may be converted to fifteen days of literal time.
20. There is a relationship between the 1260 and the 1335 day timelines of Daniel 12. They neither begin nor end at the same time but are interlocking in their delineation of sequential events.

21. After the passing of the Universal Death Decree, God's people are protected from the wicked. The demonstration of the MALIGNITY of SIN ends at the Universal Death Decree.
22. The 1260 day timeline does not end the discomfort or distress of God's "holy people." Daniel 12:7 focuses on the **wicked** when "**He**" "shall have accomplished to scatter" or reached the climax of his "scattering" action in legislation of a Universal Death Decree when "all these things" (persecuting action) "shall be finished."
23. The righteous wait 1335 days for the "Voice of God" deliverance.
24. The righteous wait fifteen days from the Universal Death Decree to the Voice of God.
25. This delineation of events does not predict the day and the hour of Jesus' coming. It does give hope and joy to the last generation that they can survive the final crisis.
26. The timelines are not given as an exercise in counting, but to give firm support to God's people.

CHAPTER V

WHAT IS "THE DAILY" OF THE 1290 DAYS OF DANIEL 12:11?

And from the time that the daily sacrifice shall be taken away, and the abomination that maketh desolate set up, shall be a thousand two hundred and ninety days. Dan. 12:11.

INTRODUCTION

The prophet, Daniel, was told to "shut up the **words**, and seal the book, even to the time of the end." (Daniel 12:4) One of the "words" which was "shut up" and could not be understood was the "daily."

Not until "the time of the END," the last generation; was Daniel 12 to be understood, and not until ENDtime was the "daily" in the context of Daniel 12 to be "unsealed!"

Some parts of Daniel have always been understood. Some aspects of prophecy have always been at least partially comprehended. The European Reformers recognized the "little horn" of Daniel 7 to be Papal Rome and this brought about the separation between Rome and Protestantism. By 1798, when the Pope was taken captive, Protestants recognized the 1260 year-days of Daniel 7:25 to have begun in 538, and ended in 1798. The book of Daniel was further unsealed by the Great Advent Movement which began the emphasis on Daniel 8:14 and the 2300 year-day prophecy. After 1844 the Advent Pioneers opened further, Daniel 8 and 9, in an understanding of the Investigative Judgment. Looking at history from a 6,000 year perspective, it was correct that the Advent Pioneers did live in the "the time of the end" and great light shown on them regarding the meaning of Daniel 7, 8, and 9. However, they did not live in the ENDtime of the last generation which would finally bring Daniel 12 and the "daily" into focus!

> When the time shall come, in the providence of God, for the world to be tested upon the truth for that time, minds will be exercised by His Spirit to search the Scriptures, even with fasting and prayer, until link after link is searched out and united in a perfect chain.... They [the preceding generations] had the Bible, as we have; but the time for the unfolding of special truth in relation to the closing

scenes of the earth's history is **during the last generation** that shall live upon the earth. 2 T 692,693.

The "daily" could be likened to a time-lock on a bank vault which will not open until the time occurs for which it was set. Prophecy is "history written in advance," —"the unrolling of the scroll," and it cannot be pried open before it is about to happen. Only then, as God permits, can the prophetic expositor open the door of the prophetic vault to discover the treasure therein.

The "daily" has been so securely locked away until the end of time, that the efforts to discern its meaning have ended in uncertainty and frustration. For more than 2,000 years great men of the Word have wrestled with this enigma. For example:

1. The Jews believed the "daily" was the daily ritual and **sacrificial system,** and that it was "taken away" by Pagans who destroyed their temple and stopped the **daily sacrifices**.
2. Some early Christians believed the "daily" had been **Christ's ministry** here on earth which was "taken away" at the crucifixion.
3. Later, after the apostasy of the third and fourth centuries, some Christians believed the "daily" referred to the **true gospel** which had been "taken away" by the apostasy.
4. European reformers continued to understand the "daily" to refer to **Christ's priesthood and heavenly ministry** as presented in the **true gospel**, the **knowledge** of which had been "taken away" from the common people by Papal Rome.
5. Papal Rome declared the "daily" to be the **daily mass** and the **eucharist** which had been "taken away" by the European Reformers in the Protestant separation from Rome.
6. The pioneers of Adventism understood the "daily" to be **Paganism**, or Pagan Rome whose **seat and authority was taken away by Papal Rome**. Other early Adventists differed believing that the "daily" referred to Christ's continual ministry which has been taken away by Papal reign from the minds of the people.
7. Contemporary prophetic expositors vary: some believe that the "daily" refers to **Christ's heavenly ministry** which will be taken away at the close of probation. Others reason that the "daily" is the perpetual Sabbath (**the freedom to worship on the true Sabbath**) "taken away" by Sunday Laws. Still others have taught that the "daily" is the Everlasting Covenant which will be "taken away" from the wicked at the close of probation.

It is possible to find serious objections to every one of the above listed views. All of these views cannot be correct. Much could be classed as conjecture or at best the "wisdom of man" which usually leads to darkness and confusion. It is unprofitable, in regard to the "daily" to seek enlightenment from the mass of past and current confusion. We need to clear our minds and begin with a clean slate!*

Therefore, it is time to put away all preconceived ideas, and to approach the "daily" of Daniel

---

* Note: The various views of the past can be traced in the four volumes of *The Prophetic Faith of Our Fathers* by L. E. Froom. In these books there is a chart on the "daily" in which the various great expositors are listed with their views on the subject. Additional information is available on the chart. For Chart resume see: Vol. IV, p. 1118, 1119. Also see *A WARNING* Appendix.

12:11 with a clear mind. The study of this important subject should be accomplished with a scholarly approach and with utmost care to observe hermeneutic principles as follows:

1. The original language must be consulted according to primitive root meaning, not secondary meanings, nor attributive use! *It must be grammatically correct.
2. Spirit of Prophecy admonition and guidance should be observed.
3. The Isaiah principle of Biblical cross reference should be followed.
4. Contextual meaning of the chapter and the book must be observed.
5. The theme of the great controversy, as brought to view in the book of Daniel, must be considered.
6. Prophetic exposition is a "science" in which one concept is built upon another (see Isaiah 28:9-13 "Precept must be upon precept") and it must be reasoned through.
7. The conclusion must fit appropriately into the subject of the timelines, in regard to all aspects of final crisis and deliverance in harmony with other endtime prophecies of Revelation.

If the study is correct, the reader should be able to exclaim without reservation: "That is so clear, it is amazing that we haven't seen it before!"

This chapter gives answer to the following questions:

1. What is the "daily" "Sacrifice"?
2. What is the "daily" "tamiyd"?*
3. What is the context of the "daily"?
4. What is the "daily" Continuum?
5. What is the "daily" Cycle Continuum?
6. What is the "daily" Scepter?
7. How **was** the "daily" taken away"?
8. How **will** the "daily" be taken away?
9. What were the Advent Pioneers?
10. What did the prophet say about the "daily"?

---

*   Grammar. The Hebrew word, "tamiyd," as used in Leviticus and Numbers, is translated into English as "daily" or "continual." But in the book of Daniel, it shuld be translated as "**continuum**" for the following reasons: In Leviticus and Nubers the Hebrew word, "tamiyd" was translated into English as "daily" and was used as an adjective or adverb. When describing a sacrifice (which is a noun), the word, "tamiyd" is used as an adjective. When describing the action of making a sacrifice (which is a verb), the word, "tamiyd" is used as an adverb. In each case, the word, "sacrifice" was in the original text, and the word "tamiyd" was translated in English as "daily" meaning "continual." But in the book of Daniel, the word, "tamiyd" is used as a noun because the word, "sacrifice" was **not** in the original text. In the book of Daniel it is "**the daily**" and should be translated in English, not as "continual" but as "**continuum**."

Part 1. WHAT IS THE DAILY "SACRIFICE"?

In most Bibles, in the book of Daniel, the word "daily" is attached to the word "sacrifice" as follows:

Daniel 8:11	"The daily sacrifice was taken away"
Daniel 8:12	"given him against the daily sacrifice"
Daniel 8:13	"vision concerning the daily sacrifice"
Daniel 11:31	"shall take away the daily sacrifice"
Daniel 12:11	"daily sacrifice shall be taken away"

In most King James Versions (and others), in the book of Daniel, the word "sacrifice" is in italics, when connected to the word, "daily." This means that it was not in the original Hebrew language in which the book was written. The word "sacrifice" was supplied by the translators.

Why did the translators do this? Because they did not understand that the "tamiyd" - "daily" was being used in the book of Daniel as a noun. They *assumed* that it was to be used in the same way that it had been used in Leviticus and Numbers. They *assumed* that a word was missing in Daniel and did not recognize the grammatical difference between the book of Daniel from that of Leviticus and Numbers.

The translators of the Bible (KJV) tried to the best of their knowledge, to supply a noun, so they inserted the word "sacrifice." It seemed somehow to be appropriate, especially as the Jews had understood it to refer to the temple sacrifices and the Christians understood it to refer to the sacrifice or ministry of Christ.

The Lord revealed through His prophet to the remnant people, that this word "sacrifice" was incorrect and would lead God's people into error, darkness and confusion. She wrote:

> Then I saw in relation to the "daily" (Daniel 8:12) that the word "sacrifice" was supplied by man's wisdom, and does not belong to the text... darkness and confusion have followed. EW 74, 75.

The first thing the Bible student should do is to take a pen or pencil and put a line through the word "sacrifice" in all five references, as given above, in his own Bible, and put that idea completely out of his mind. We must understand that the "daily" has nothing to do with the types: ceremonial, sacrificial system (of burnt offerings of the earthly sanctuary as translated in the RSV). Neither has it anything to do with Christ's antitypical sacrifice on Calvary. All arguments which lead back to the sanctuary "daily" sacrifices and rituals or to Christ's sacrifice are incorrect.

There are some who assume that the "daily" refers to Christ's priestly role and heavenly ministry. They explain that His ministry is much greater than His sacrifice. However, the fact is that almost the entire book of Hebrews is an argument to prove that Christ's total ministry, as high priest and Mediator of the New Covenant, is valid only by virtue of His incarnation and sacrifice on Calvary. Paul explains that all priests officiated with blood and that Christ has entered into heaven and appears for us with the sacrifice of His own blood! It is impossible to separate the heavenly ministry of Christ from His sacrifice, for it is the central act of the entire process of the atonement!

Therefore, if the prophet stated clearly that the word "sacrifice" does not belong in the text and the concept of "sacrifice" is not to be associated with the "daily" of Daniel, then there is strong objection to the idea that the "daily" refers to Christ's continual heavenly ministry. It is probably this line of reasoning, among others, which caused the Advent pioneers to look in another direction for the meaning of the "daily" in the book of Daniel.[*]

---

[*] Note: See Appendix on "the Wider Ministry of Christ NOT the 'daily' of Daniel."

Part 2. WHAT IS THE "DAILY" "TAMIYD"?

Definition: "Daily" Word Number 8548.
"tamiyd" (pronounced taw-meed) from an unused **root** meaning **TO STRETCH**; prop. continuance (as **INDEFINITE EXTENSION**):
but used only attributively as continual...daily...even (more) perpetual.
Strong's Exhaustive Concordance Hebrew and Chaldee Dictionary p. 125.

The word "daily" has been translated from the original language, "tamiyd." This root is apparently no longer in use, but it originally had the meaning **"TO STRETCH—AN INDEFINITE EXTENSION"**—a **CONTINUUM**.

It is most unfortunate that it has been translated "daily" in Daniel giving the reader the idea of something that occurs over and over again. It is this troublesome problem which has caused so many, over the years, to immediately associate it with the sanctuary services with all the daily rituals, of the ceremonial law and especially with the daily or continual sacrifices there offered. This is entirely misleading. The root word, "tamiyd" has to do with a continuum, stretching out in an indefinite length, as from eternity to eternity,—everlasting to everlasting—rather than the idea of something happening over and over as in a continual repetition.

If we can now shift our thinking from something which happens over and over again, to an understanding of the "daily" as a CONTINUUM stretching out with unlimited boundaries at either end, we shall be able to make headway in discovering the true identity of this endtime concept as used in Daniel 12.

Part 3. WHAT IS THE "CONTEXT" OF THE "DAILY"?

When the noun is missing, and only the adjective is available, which denotes the subject to be something which "stretches out with indefinite extension," it is necessary to go beyond linguistic study to examine the context and theme. The prophetic expositor must examine:

1. The nature and purpose of the entire **book** of Daniel
2. The theme of the 12th **chapter** of Daniel
3. The concept presented in the 11th **verse** of Daniel 12
4. The major theme of the **entire Bible**

First, the entire book of Daniel should be examined for its theme. From chapter 1-12, it focuses on the rise and fall of nations. It traces the scepter of power from Babylon to Medo-Persia, to Greece, to Rome, to the nations of Europe, from Pagan Rome to Papal Rome, and at last to the great stone kingdom. One prophetic expositor said it nicely:

> Daniel wrote the history of the world from the standpoint of nations. ...he deals primarily with nations. *The Story of the Seer of Patmos*, S. N. Haskell. p. 289. 1905. Nashville, TN.

A contemporary prophetic expositor, in a discussion of the book of Daniel as a literary chiasm, has stated it this way:

> ...this literary structure conveys a theological thrust. That theological thrust revolves around the question of Who has "dominion"? That is a word that occurs frequently in chapter 7, thus it is a key theological term for understanding the vision. In chapter 7 each of the earthly kingdoms rise and fall, receiving dominion for a time and passing it on to a successor. These successive dominions are described in the first half of the chiasm. At the apex of the chiasm stands the scene of judgment in the heavenly court. As a result of the decision of this heavenly tribunal, there comes in the destruction of all earthly powers, as is described in the second half of the chiasm. The pattern then is one of dominion finally taken away. The vision then concludes with the giving of final, eternal, and all-inclusive dominion to the Son of man. (vss 13-14). William H. Shea, *Symposium on Daniel*, ed. Frank B. Holbrook (Washington: Bible Research Institute, 1986), D & R Committee Series, Vol. 2. pp. 176, 177.

The action of the book of Daniel is that which transfers the **SCEPTER OF POWER** from nation to nation, until in the last chapter, it is grasped by the "abomination that maketh desolate" in an unprecedented establishment of a one-world-system of control and persecutes the people of God until their final deliverance at the Voice of God. It is this concept which links Daniel 12:11 with Revelation 13. The establishment of the "beast" in which he holds the scepter of power in the endtime, is described as follows:

> ...and his deadly wound was healed: and all the world wondered after the

beast...and **POWER** [the scepter of power] was given unto him to continue [to reign] forty and two months....and **POWER** [the scepter of power] was given him over all kindreds, and tongues, and nations. Rev. 13:3,5,7.

The **book** of Daniel focuses on the scepter of power as it is transferred from nation to nation. **Verse** 11 of chapter 12 provides exactly the same focus. It simply says:

And from the time that the daily [scepter of power] shall be taken away [from all kindreds and tongues and nations] [and given to the Papacy] and the abomination that maketh desolate set up [established] there shall be a thousand two hundred and ninety days. Dan. 12:11.

The context of the book and the verse are synonymous!

Part 4. WHAT IS THE "DAILY"—"TAMIYD"—CONTINUUM?

Let the reader remember that the "tamiyd"—"daily" primitive root meaning is "to stretch, of indefinite extension."

The "daily"—"tamiyd" from everlasting to everlasting

What is the context of the "tamiyd"—"daily" in regard to **the whole Bible**? If, in the book of Daniel, the theme is that of a transfer of the scepter of power from nation to nation until it is finally restored to the saints and to Christ in God's new kingdom, is that not also the theme of the whole Bible, the entire plan of salvation—the idea of Eden restored?

The scepter of power originated in the eternal throne of God. It was delegated to Adam when he was given dominion (the scepter of power) over this earth.

> And God said, Let us make man in our image, after our likeness: and let them have dominion [the scepter of power].... Gen. 1:26.

At the fall of man, the devil usurped that dominion (scepter of power) and has delegated it, as far as God permits, to those nations whom he seeks to control and by whom he harasses and attempts to destroy the people of God. Immediately after Noah's flood, Nimrod grasped the scepter of power and built Babel which developed into the kingdom of Babylon with its counterfeit system of worship of the sun. It was the fully developed empire of Babylon in which Daniel lived. Therefore, the book of Daniel begins and traces this scepter of power from nation to nation until, at the end of time, it will revert back to Christ's throne kingdom.

Like a great circle, this scepter of power is from everlasting to everlasting. The scepter of power is the great "tamiyd"—"daily" continuum which stretches from eternity to eternity. It is "taken away" only in the sense that it passes from one hand to the next! In this sense it is the "tamiyd" continuum that is so obvious that Daniel neglected to name it. It is the subject not only of the book of Daniel but of the entire Bible!

The following illustration makes clear the "Cycle of the Scepter of Power" as traced in Scripture and specifically in the book of Daniel. This cycle is brought to its concluding action and final climax in Daniel 12:11.

THE CYCLE OF THE SCEPTER OF POWER
(The "tamyid" Continuum—"daily")

- God's throne
- Adam's dominion
- Usurped by Satan
- Nimrod Babel
- Babylon
- Medo-Persia Cyrus Darius Artexerxes
- Grecia Alexander the Great
- Rome Caesars
- Papal Rome Supremacy No.1 538-1798 Europe
- Napoleon 1798
- The kings
- (Ten) "ALL" kings
- Daniel 12:11 Papal Supremacy No. 2

119

Part 5. WHAT IS THE "SCEPTER" "TAMIYD"—"DAILY"?

> Thy throne, O God, is for ever and ever: the scepter of thy kingdom is a right scepter. Ps. 45:6.

The "scepter"—emblem of authority, may be seen in the hand of a king or a baton in the hand of a music instructor; or a rod in the hand of Moses as he parted the Red Sea and defeated the enemy; or as a walking stick in the hand of a tribal chief. It was the rod or "branch" of Aaron, the symbol of his priesthood, which flowered, budded and bore almonds.

Such a rod or staff was often formed from the "**branch**" of a tree. From antiquity, in many cultures such as ancient Babylon, the concept of rulership was connected to a **branch**. The scepter of power and rulership originated in the throne of God. Christ on His throne, in His role as Priest and King, is referred to as THE BRANCH or THE MAN WHOSE NAME IS THE BRANCH.

> Behold the man whose name is THE BRANCH;...[he] shall **sit** and **RULE** upon his throne; and he shall be a priest upon his throne. Zech. 6:12,13.

Not just the book of Daniel, but the entire Bible is a library, all books telling the story in one way or another of the lost **dominion** (lost scepter) and its restoration! The great controversy ends at the coming of Jesus when God's saints "shall be priests of God and of Christ, and shall **reign** with him a thousand years" Revelation 20:6. The whole book of Daniel is this story of the scepter passing from nation to nation until at last:*

> ...the saints of the most High shall take the kingdom, and possess the kingdom for ever, even for ever and ever. Dan. 7:18.

---

* Note: Daniel, chapter 11, is a reiteration of the rise and fall of kings from the days of Daniel until the end of time. In this chapter, each time the scepter of power is transferred from one king to the next, it says that the new king shall **STAND UP**—that is, he takes the scepter of power in hand. Twelve times in chapter 11, this phrase is used, beginning in verse 3:

And a mighty king shall **stand up**, that shall rule with great dominion and do according to his will. Dan. 11:3.

According to Strong's Exhaustive Concordance, the phrase "stand up" comes from the Hebrew word, "amad" (No. 5975). "Amad" is derived from an unused Hebrew root, "MD" (pronounced "meed"—as in "tamiyd" pronounced "taw-meed")

"Tamiyd"—the "daily" of Daniel 12, is simply a continuation of the reiteration of the rise and fall of kings in chapter 11. The scepter of power which is transferred from king to king in chapter 11, finally is "the daily taken away" from the kings of the earth in chapter 12 and placed in the hands to "set up" or establish the "abomination that maketh desolate," the Papacy, for 1290 literal days at the end of time. The Hebrew "MD" has derivations—"amad, tamiyd," similar in sound all of which refer to the transfer of the scepter of power, to grasp it or lose it, in the course of history. See Wigram's Englishman's Hebrew Chaldee Concordance of the Old Testament Numerically Coded to Strong's Exhaustive Concordance 1843, 5th edition, on "MD."

>...the Son of man came with clouds of heaven,.... And there was given him **dominion**, and glory, and a kingdom, [the scepter of power, seat, and authority] that all people, nations, and languages, should serve him: his dominion is an everlasting dominion, which shall not pass away, and his kingdom that which shall not be destroyed. Dan. 7:13,14.

This restoration is also the theme of Revelation 3:21; 5:9-14; 11:15-17; 19:16; 20:3-6; 21:10-27; and 22:3. It is the basic concept of the whole Bible, and it is the "daily" in the book of Daniel. By closing up and sealing the words (Daniel 12:4), especially the word, "daily" the Lord insured that the "wise shall understand," but kept secret until the time needed by the last generation!

Part 6. HOW IS THE "DAILY"—"TAMIYD"—"SCEPTER OF POWER" "TAKEN AWAY"?

Definitions:

7311	"Taken away" RUWM	as used in Daniel 8:11,12,13, pronounced, "room" means: "to exalt, to absorb"
5493	"Taken away" CUWR	as used in Daniel 11 and 12. pronounced, "soor" means: "to turn aside, to remove, leave undone, lay away..." *Strong's Exhaustive Concordance* Hebrew, Chaldee Dictionary

There is a difference as to how the "daily" (scepter of power) **was** taken away by the Papacy from the Roman Empire and how it **will be** taken away from the kings of the earth by the Papacy in its future reign. In Daniel 8, the Hebrew word "RUWM," translated as "taken away," has the meaning of absorption or to be exalted, but in Daniel 12:11 the Hebrew word "CUWR" is used to mean "lay away," so that the kings of the earth will "lay away" their scepters and give them willingly to the Papacy in its future reign.

Look at Daniel 8:11:

> Yea, he [the little horn Papacy] magnified himself [exalted himself]...and by him the daily [scepter of power] was taken away [absorbed and exalted, from the Roman Empire or Pagan Rome]....

In the book, *God Cares*, Vol. 1, the contemporary author, Maxwell, explains it this way:

> In the West, the Church took over the defenses of Roman civilization. The emperor gave up the [Pagan] title of Pontifex Maximus [high priest] because the Roman gods were no longer worshiped. The bishop of Rome assumed these priestly functions, [a process of absorption], and this is why the Pope today is sometimes referred to as the Pontiff.... [I]t was the Pope and not the emperor which stood at the gates of Rome. The Roman Empire had become the Christian church. *God Cares* Vol. I, p. 154 (from Harry A. Dawe, *Ancient Greece and Rome*, World Cultures in Perspective. Columbus, Ohio: Charles E. Merrill Pub. Co., 1970 p. 188)

> ...when Rome through the neglect of the Western emperors was left to the mercy of the barbarous hordes, the Romans turned to one figure for aid and protection and asked him to rule them; and thus...commenced the temporal sovereignty of the popes. And meekly stepping to the throne of Caesar, the vicar of Christ **TOOK UP THE SCEPTER**.... American Catholic Quarterly Review. April 1911.

The author, Maxwell, recognizes the transfer of the scepter of power, seat and authority from Pagan Rome to Papal Rome as a continuum, the very essence of an identification of the meaning of the "daily." He wrote:

> The true fulfillment of the little horn of Daniel 8 can only be the Roman Empire and its successor, the Roman Church.... [I]n their **beastlike** aspects, Pagan and Christian Rome constituted a **continuum**. The Roman bishop was successor to the Roman emperor. C. Mervyn Maxwell, *God Cares* (Boise:Pacific Press Publishing Association, 1981) Vol. I, p. 154.

Of course, the succession from Pagan Rome to Papal Rome was just one step in the continuum which is illustrated below:

Babylon — Medo-Persia — Greece — Pagan Rome — Papal Rome — Napoleon

It is important to understand that the Roman Empire was a church-state union of political and religious power. Its religion was Paganism or sun worship. Therefore, when the scepter of state power was transferred, Paganism was a part of the transaction! It was by the absorption of Pagan worship and an exaltation of it that the Papacy gained favor in the Roman Empire and thereby acquired the scepter of power!

Therefore the "daily"—scepter of power, seat, and authority (with its Pagan culture and religion) was **absorbed and exalted** by Papal Rome. It was all one package! Therefore, in Daniel 8:11 the word, RUWM, is used to indicate that the "daily"—scepter of power was "taken away" from Pagan Rome by **absorption and exaltation** of the Pagan culture and worship into Papal Rome. Therefore, Roman Catholicism has been called "Baptised Paganism."

In regard to the future Papal Supremacy, as described in Daniel 12 and Revelation 13, the "daily"—scepter of power will be "taken away" (using a different Hebrew word, CUWR). In a different kind of process, the scepter now held by many "kings"—governments of earth, will be willingly laid aside. They will then place the Papal king upon his throne and the scepter in his hand! The scepter is "taken away" from the kings of the earth, from governments, kindreds, tongues, and nations, and given to the "abomination that maketh desolate" (Daniel 12:11).

It was in this framework that the pioneers of Adventism viewed Daniel 8. They understood the "daily" to refer to the transfer of the scepter of power, seat, and authority from Pagan Rome to Papal Rome. They also understood the interlacing of Paganism (sun worship) with the state religion of Pagan Rome. They knew that it was the absorption and exaltation of sun worship-paganism that brought Papal Rome into a position to grasp the scepter. They "abbreviated" all this into such statements as:

> ...the "daily"...was Paganism.... Uriah Smith, *Daniel and the Revelation* (Nashville: Southern Publishing Association, 1944), pp. 176, 177, 282, 285.

> Paganism—the "daily" of Daniel 8:12 was taken away.... S.N. Haskell. *The Story*

of Daniel the Prophet, (Lancaster, Mass: The Bible Training School, 1908), p. 112. Facsimile reproduction by Southern Publishing Assn., Nashville, TN. 1977.

Regrettably, the pioneers did not express their full knowledge of these concepts in written form and the lack of their statement of rationale has been a source of perplexity ever since.

However, it is necessary to get this perspective on Daniel 8 before the "daily" of Daniel 12 can be correctly understood and aligned with it. A true understanding of the "daily" opens to view the relationship between Daniel 8 and Daniel 12. It also reveals the relationship between Daniel 12 and Revelation 13 on ENDtime events.

The following is a paraphrasing of Daniel 12:11 and Revelation 13:

Daniel 12:11	**Revelation 13:2,3,7,10**
And from the time that the daily—scepter of power, seat and authority shall be taken away or laid aside by the kings of the earth, so that Papal Reign No. 2 can begin or so that "the abomination that maketh desolate" will be set up or established, there shall be a thousand, two hundred and ninety days, after which the Papacy will be destroyed.	And the dragon—Satan, gave him (the Papacy, the daily)—scepter of power, and his seat, and great authority,...and all the world wondered after the beast...and power (the scepter) was given him over all kindreds, and tongues, and nations....and it was given him to make war with the saints (to desolate them)...he that killeth with the sword must be killed with sword.

Daniel 8:9-14

Daniel 8:9-14 has been difficult for most readers to comprehend. Not until there is a good understanding of the "daily" as the scepter of power, seat, and authority, is it possible to make sense of this passage. Not until the phrase "taken away" is perceived in both meanings can it be applied correctly. At this point, liberty is taken to paraphrase Daniel 8:9-14 into everyday English.

Daniel 8:9 And out of them came forth a little horn—Papal Rome. It became very great, extending itself in every direction.

Daniel 8:10 It (Papal Rome) became so great that it even oppressed and persecuted God's true people. It put to death a host—millions, of them, even the greatest of the Christian faith. It stomped on them in a persecution intended to utterly destroy them.

Daniel 8:11 The Papacy, established to exalt the Popes, magnified itself even to the extent of usurping the roles and offices of the Prince—Christ Himself! (The popes are called by the titles of: Lord God, the Pope; The Holy Father; Prince of peace; Vicar of Christ; The Highest Priest and Pontiff.) By the Papacy, the "daily"—scepter of power, seat and authority was taken away from Pagan Rome by the process of absorption and exaltation of sunworship. The place of Christ's sanctuary—the Christian Church on earth, was cast down.

Daniel 8:12 A host of God's people—millions of them, were given over to persecution at the hand of the Papacy. This was possible because the Papacy was full of transgression and sin, and because the Papacy held the scepter of power—the "daily" in its hand, thus giving it power of state to persecute. The Papacy cast down the truth to the ground. It practiced and prospered and extended itself all over the world.

Daniel 8:13 Then I heard one saint speaking, and another saint said unto that certain saint which spake, How long will this vision extend which deals with the "daily"—scepter of power, as it resides in the hand of the Papacy which desolates and destroys God's people? That is, how long will this host of God's people be persecuted? How long will the records of these terrible persecutions continue to be recorded on heaven's books? Heaven is defiled by such records of atrocities. When will the heavenly sanctuary which contains all these records of evil be cleansed?

Daniel 8:14 And he said unto me: There will be 2300 evening-mornings (days of atonement) until the sanctuary will begin the process of the Investigative Judgment. All these atrocities will be brought to judgment. The records of these sins will be removed from the sanctuary and it will therefore be cleansed of that defilement.

Part 7. WHAT WERE THE "ADVENT PIONEERS"?

The pioneers of Adventism were extremely skillful prophetic expositors of the Historicist "school" of Prophetic Interpretation! They understood Daniel 7-9, in its historicist setting of rising and falling empires. They put aside centuries of tentative speculation in regard to the meaning of the "daily." By historicist context and cross reference study, Daniel was connected with Revelation. They arrived at an understanding that the "daily" was related to the concept of a transfer of power, seat, and authority. By this kind of study they identified Papal Rome as the "beast" of the third angel's message and began to give that warning from Revelation 14.

Today we have no record of their many studies and dissertations and interactions which brought this understanding of the "daily" to the front, reiterated by the pioneers such as S.N. Haskell and Uriah Smith. Perhaps, in the providence of God, they never did state their rationale as has been done in this chapter of this book. Their ultimate conclusion on the "daily" was correct, in as much as its application involved the transfer of power from Pagan to Papal Rome.

Unfortunately, Uriah Smith and Haskell, and others did not distinguish—at least to us—between Paganism and the scepter of power of the state government. They did not explain the difference between the scepter of power and the hand which held the scepter, as illustrated below:

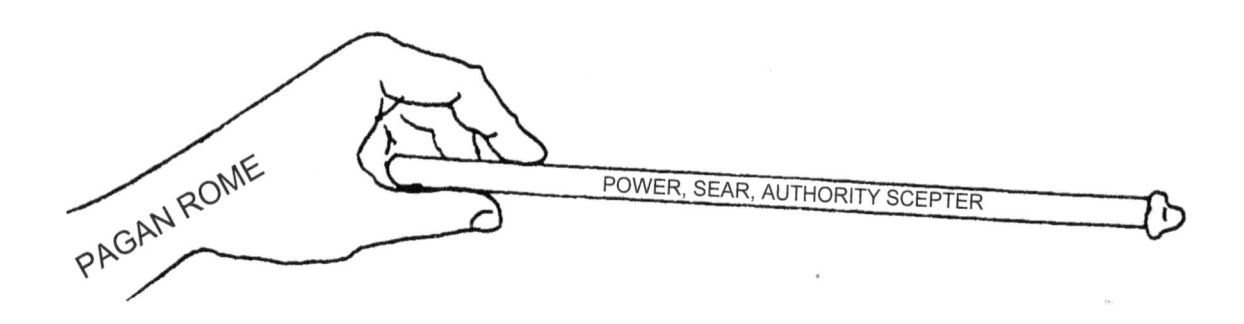

The following statements reveal this lack of clarity:

> ...the "daily"...was Paganism.... Uriah Smith, *Daniel and the Revelation* (Nashville, TN: Southern Publishing Association, 1944), pp. 270, 273.

> Paganism—the "daily" of Daniel 8:12—was taken away.... S.N. Haskell, *The Story of Daniel the Prophet.* (Nashville, TN: Southern Publishing Association, 1977), p. 112.

However, it is self-evident that these pioneers understood the basic concept as may be seen in Haskell's explanation. He wrote:

> This transfer from Paganism [the Roman Empire] to the papacy is represented as **a transfer of power**....[Rev. 13:7]. Ibid. 129.

The clarification between "Pagan Rome" and "paganism" is the answer to the objection which many have voiced, that Paganism has never been taken away! They reason that if the "daily" was Paganism and the "daily" was taken away (Daniel 8:11), then this world should be free from Paganism at this time. However, it is evident today that Paganism is very much with us and that the final conflict will be over the "mark of the beast" which is a false Sabbath directly derived from Paganism. Therefore, it is imperative that this clarification be made between Pagan Rome and its state religion which was "paganism" or sun worship. The pioneers could not express these things clearly because the "daily" was "closed up" until the end time.

Let us beware of an attitude of derision toward the Advent pioneers who constructed the platform of doctrine and prophetic understandings on which we have securely rested for more than a century. Those who have such an attitude would dispose of the Historicist "School" of Prophetic Interpretation, for new views.

The Scriptures describe those Advent pioneer prophetic expositors as paraphrased below:

> ...men of war; they marched every one on his ways, and they did not break ranks: Neither did one thrust another, they walked every one in his path: and when they fell upon the sword, the Word, they were not wounded. Joel 2:7-10.

> ...valiant men...the valiant of Israel, they all held swords (the Word of God), being expert in war: every man had his sword upon his thigh because of fear in the night. Song of Solomon 3:7,8.

The Advent pioneers were the great men who had an understanding of their times as they needed it regarding an interpretation of Daniel 7,8,9. They lived nearly two centuries ago as "prisoners of history." We will not improve on that which was commissioned to them for their time. They could not improvise an application for our day and could not be expected to understand Daniel 12. That remained for **our generation**.

The Advent pioneers, like many prophetic expositors, through the centuries before them, tried to understand Daniel 12. They tried to fit the timelines into the events which marked their day, but these ideas have been dormant through the years, seldom used by pastors or evangelists. Therefore, Daniel 12 appeared to be a superfluous "tacked on" addition, to what they already knew. Their efforts on Daniel 12 were out of timing and were not a primary fulfillment. Therefore, the manner in which they treated Daniel 12, we understand to have been a secondary application which was useful to them at that time. Today the last generation seeks an ENDtime or primary application. Our final application of Daniel 12 must be consistent with that of the pioneers in the basic interpretation of the "daily," but applicable to final events in the great crisis.

Part 8. WHAT DID THE PROPHET SAY ABOUT THE "DAILY"?

Very little! Ellen G. White was a prophetess, not primarily a prophetic expositor. She did not seek to extend her ministry into the realm in which God has given responsibility to His people to "search the Scriptures" for themselves to find light and present truth for each age. In a case where there was contention and difficulty which would have weakened the church, she was given a minimum amount of information to prevent disaster. Her comment on the "daily" is as follows:

> Then I saw in relation to the "daily" (Daniel 8:12) that the word "sacrifice" was supplied by man's wisdom, and does not belong to the text, and that the Lord gave the correct view of it to those who gave the judgment hour cry. When union existed, before 1844, nearly all were united on the correct view of the "daily"; but in the confusion since 1844, other views have been embraced, and darkness and confusion have followed. Time has not been a test since 1844, and it will never again be a test. EW 74,75.

The Prophetic Faith of Our Fathers Vol. 4 by L. E. Froom gives the interpretations of the principal Millerite leaders, and it is readily seen that the consensus was that the "daily" represented Roman Paganism. Here it is seen that the "daily" was understood to represent the transfer of power from Roman Paganism (The Roman Empire) to Papal Rome, See the Appendix: Letter from the Ellen G. White Estate, Inc.

It is apparent that, after 1844, "other views" brought in "darkness and confusion" which has existed until the present time. It is also important to consider the idea that the knowledge of the "daily" was withdrawn from God's people after 1844, so that Daniel 12 might not be understood before its due date! It is apparent in the following quotation that it was not to be clarified at the **time** the quotation was written:

> I have words to speak to my brethren east and west, north and south. I request that my writings shall not be used as the leading argument to settle questions over which there is **NOW** so much controversy. I entreat Elders H, I, J, and others of our leading brethren, that they make no reference to my writings to sustain views of "the daily".... I cannot consent that any of my writings shall be taken as settling this matter. The true meaning of "the daily" is not to be made a test question.
>
> I **NOW** ask that my ministering brethren shall not make use of my writings in their arguments regarding this question, for I have had no instruction on the point under discussion, and I see no need for the controversy. Regarding this matter under **PRESENT CONDITIONS**, silence is eloquence...this is not a test question. 1 SM 164,165.

Again the element of correct timing for the understanding of "the daily" is emphasized in the following quotation:

> There are many subjects upon which we can speak—sacred, testing truths, beautiful in their simplicity. On these you may dwell with intense earnestness. But

let not "the daily," or any other subject that will arouse controversy among brethren be brought in at **THIS TIME**; for this will delay and hinder the work that the Lord would have the minds of our brethren centered upon **JUST NOW**. 1 SM 167.

While **THE PRESENT CONDITION** of difference of opinion regarding this subject exists let it not be made prominent. Let all contention cease. **AT SUCH A TIME** silence is eloquence. 1 SM 168 (Ltr. 62, 1910).

The year 1910 was not the time to pursue the "daily" but today this subject is pertinent to the impending crisis. If the brethren had full understanding on "the daily" and used it in regard to Daniel 12:11 there would have been an excitement nearly 80 years premature! The "daily" has been under time-lock, and the fact that it is opening up in regard to Daniel 12 is a sure sign that we are coming to the ENDtime final crisis within the very near future. In answer to the question, What did the prophet say? Very little! What she **did say** has set apart from the world, all those whom Daniel described as "the wise" who shall understand. They can know that the word "sacrifice" and all concepts pertaining to sacrifice (including Christ's ministry) do not belong to the text of the "daily." They may also know that concepts involving "sacrifice" are of man's wisdom and lead to darkness and confusion! These tiny keys open the door to a correct exposition of Daniel 12 and give meaning to the three timelines therein.

Part 9. WHAT IS THE IMPORTANCE OF THE "DAILY"?

What difference does it make how we view the "daily"? Much! Let us consider the following:

1. The "daily" is an integral foundation stone in the third angel's warning message yet to be given in the power of the Loud Cry.

The "daily," when correctly understood, in Daniel 8, explains how the "little horn"—Papacy acquired the scepter of power, seat, and authority from Pagan Rome, so that it could persecute the saints for 1260 years in "Papal Supremacy No. 1" over Europe. The "daily," taken away from Pagan Rome and given to Papal Rome, reinforces the decretal letter by Justinian in 538 A.D. as the beginning of the 1260 day-years of Daniel and Revelation. The "daily," when understood to refer to a transfer of power, seat and authority, identifies Papal Rome as the persecuting BEAST of Revelation 13 and 14—against whom the third angel's warning is directed.

The "daily" not only calls attention to Papal Rome in Daniel 8 as the BEAST of the third angel's message, but observing the hermeneutic rule of first mention, consistently follows into Daniel 12 to refer to the same transfer of power, seat and authority from the kings of the earth to "Papal Supremacy No. 2" over **all** nations in the near future. It is this transfer of the scepter, which will enable the Papacy to persecute (make desolate, Daniel 12:11) in the future, and it is against such power that the third angel gives warning.

Therefore, a correct understanding of the "daily" is vital to the proclamation of the Loud Cry of the third angel of Revelation 14. It is also vital to an understanding of the three timelines of Daniel 12. A correct understanding of the "daily" gives contemporary expositors a consistent position with the Advent pioneers who provided the historical and theological foundations of our church today.

2. The "daily" requires consistent definition with hermeneutic precision. There are those who believe the "daily" to refer to the ministry of Christ. They are aware of the fact that the Spirit of Prophecy has warned that the word "sacrifice" does not belong to the text, but they explain that Christ's ministry includes much more than sacrifice.

Those who hold this position believe that when the "daily" is "taken away" in Daniel 12:11, it refers to the close of probation and closing of the investigative judgment.

This definition of the "daily" initiates problems as follows:

While it is true that the close of probation brings an end to Christ's role as the Sin-bearer, and He no longer pleads His blood **sacrifice** as an atonement for sin, leaving His people without a Mediator for sin, His MINISTRY (which is much more than sacrifice) **continues** for His saints. As He led Israel in the wilderness, He will provide the 144,000 with food and water, and will protect them all through the seven last plagues, and from their enemies.

His sacrificial ministry and atonement cease at the close of the investigative judgment and close of probation. But His ministry "which includes more than sacrifice" never ceases. It is therefore obvious that by the very definition of those who believe the "daily" to be Christ's ministry—"much more than sacrifice" cannot say that it is taken away at the close of probation.

In conclusion, if the "daily" is defined as the "blood sacrifice—Mediatorial atonement for sinners which continues in the Investigative Judgment" and ends at the close of probation, it violates the caution given by Ellen G. White, that the word (or concept) of "sacrifice" leads to darkness and confusion. And if the "daily" is defined as Christ's ministry (much more than sacrifice), which is never taken away from Christ's people, then neither definition applies to the "daily" taken away in Daniel 12:11. Both concepts are self-contradictory.

3. The "daily" must be defined by hermeneutic precision.

Linguistics.

The position that the "daily" refers to Christ's ministry is derived from "attributive" use, not ROOT meaning in the Hebrew. The attributive use leads the Bible student to the Levitical system of daily sacrifices and daily rituals. This diversion distracts the mind away from:

    a. The theme of the entire book of Daniel—the rise and fall of nations, and Eden restored, the scepter returned to the throne of Christ's kingdom and to His saints.
    b. The "warning" of coming persecution by the establishment of "Papal Supremacy No. 2"—fulfillment of Revelation 13.

4. The "daily" viewed in the light of the nature and purpose of prophecy.

If prophecy is "HISTORY written in advance" it deals primarily with events of history, past, present and future, **which occur down here on earth**. Prophetic timelines, if they are to be of use to God's people must be **observable** markers of events connected with the welfare of God's people. Even the 1844 beginning of the investigative judgment in heaven was attended by signs observable to men and the great disappointment which **happened down here on earth**.

The "daily" "taken away" in the Daniel 12:11 timeline should be an **observable** event down here on earth. If the "daily" is a transfer of the scepter of power from the kings of the earth to Papal Rome to establish Papal Supremacy No. 2, this will be an historical event which all men can see and recognize. That will also be a fulfillment plainly visible in regard to the prophecy of Revelation 13 and 14.

The close of probation is quite the opposite. We are told by Inspiration that we will not know the time of the close of probation. It will occur in heaven and men on earth cannot use it as a marker of events as outlined in the Daniel 12 timeline.

5. The "daily" preserved in logic and sequence.

The Daniel 12:11 timeline specifies first, the "daily, taken away" and then the establishment of the "abomination that maketh desolate"—or Papal Supremacy No. 2." **There is sequence here to be observed**.

It is common knowledge that the Papacy cannot enforce its mark or its number until it has in hand the scepter of power, seat and authority. The "daily"—scepter must be taken from the kings of the earth and placed in the hand of the Pope of Rome, before it can "desolate" or persecute God's people. **There is sequence here to be observed.**

It is the establishment of the "abomination that maketh desolate"—the Papacy of Daniel 12:11 which brings the "mark of the beast" into full force. It is this issue which brings upon all men the "great test" or "FINAL TEST" by which their eternal destiny is decided. Their decision determines whether they shall have the "mark of the beast" or the "Seal of God." This must occur **BEFORE** the close of probation.

To assume that the ministry of Christ (the "daily") is taken away before the "abomination that maketh desolate" is established is to get "the cart before the horse." Since the close of probation, for the church and for the world, cannot be known it would be a "non-event" down here on earth and hold no prophetic significance as far as a TIMELINE is concerned with definite markers of beginning and ending for the enlightenment of God's people.

IN CONCLUSION: The "daily," in its definition, should not distract the mind away from the theme of the Bible, the book of Daniel, the great controversy, away from the role of the Papacy in final events or violate the sequence of endtime events.

SUMMARY OF CHAPTER V

WHAT IS "THE DAILY" OF THE 1290 DAYS OF DANIEL 12:11?

1. The "daily" is a word that was "shut up and sealed" until the end.
2. The "daily" may be correctly understood by use of hermeneutic principles.
3. The word "sacrifice" does not belong to the text of the "daily."
4. The concept of "sacrifice" leads to darkness and confusion.
5. The "daily"—"tamiyd" linguistic should be obtained from the Hebrew root.
6. The "daily"—"tamiyd" root means "to stretch in indefinite extension."
7. The "daily" "taken away" relates to a succession of nations, as the scepter of power, seat, and authority is "taken away" and given to another.
8. The "daily" is the scepter of power, seat, and authority.
9. The "daily"—scepter of power, seat, and authority of indefinite extension originated at God's throne, was given to Adam, usurped by Satan, handed from nation to nation, until it returns to God's throne and the saints of Christ's kingdom.
10. The "daily"—"tamiyd" is of indefinite extension because it is the scepter which is from everlasting to everlasting.
11. The "daily"—"tamiyd" scepter of power, seat, and authority is "taken away," only in the sense that it is taken away from one nation and given to the next.
12. The "daily" scepter was "taken away" (RUWM) from the Roman Empire and given to Papal Rome through the process of absorption and exaltation of Paganism. (See Daniel 8:9-11).
13. The "daily" scepter will be "taken away" (CUWR) from the kings of the earth who willingly lay it aside and place it in the hands of Papal Rome in the future. (See Daniel 12:11).
14. Daniel 12:11 says, when paraphrased: And from the time that the "daily" scepter of power, seat, and authority is taken away or laid aside by the kings of the earth and placed in the hands of the Papacy so that the abomination that maketh desolate (Papal Supremacy No. 2) can be set up or established over all kindreds, tongues, and nations, there shall be a thousand two hundred and ninety literal days until its reign is ended.
15. Daniel 8:9-13 also needs to be paraphrased in everyday English.
16. The Advent pioneers cast aside all concepts pertaining to "sacrifice"—the interpretations of 2,000 years, in a study of the "daily" to establish the unique historicist application to Pagan and Papal Rome.
17. The Advent pioneers understood that the "daily" pertained to the transfer of the scepter of power, seat and authority from Pagan Rome to Papal Rome.
18. The Advent pioneers did not explain their rationale clearly to us.

19. The Advent pioneers did not perceive or state clearly the difference between the scepter "daily" and the hand which held it.
20. The Advent pioneers were united on the "daily" pre-1844.
21. The prophet verified the pre-1844 perception of the "daily" as it focused on the fall of Papal Rome in 1798 and the identification of Papal Rome in Daniel 7,8,9.
22. The subject of the "daily" was not to be discussed a century ago. It was then premature to fulfillment.
23. The "daily" and its meaning is imperative to the last generation in their study of Daniel 12 timelines.
24. The "daily" must be clearly defined, fit into the sequence of endtime events, and conform to hermeneutic rules.
25. Daniel 11, a reiteration of the rise and fall of kings and transfer of the scepter of power from one to the next, is simply continued in Daniel 12:11 where that scepter is at last taken away from the kings of the earth and placed with Papal Rome.
26. The "daily" scepter of power at last returns to God, to Christ and His saints.

CHAPTER VI

WHAT IS THE "1290 DAY TIMELINE" OF DANIEL 12:11?

And from the time that the daily...shall be taken away, and the abomination that maketh desolate set up, there shall be a thousand two hundred and ninety days. Dan. 12:11.

INTRODUCTION

The 1290 day timeline of Daniel 12:11, when correctly understood, provides a fantastic insight into the closing events of this world's history! The three timelines of Daniel stand independent of each other. When they are viewed as one unit they are **interlocking** and give the student of prophecy an understanding of the complex actions of the very last scenes of the final conflict—final deliverance and end of evil in this world!

The 1290 day timeline is to be understood in exactly the same manner as the 1260 and 1335 timelines: as fulfillments of specific texts in Revelation. Likewise, the 1290 day timeline is bounded (begins and ends) with "Voices" speaking in legal action on earth and in heaven. The same hermeneutic principles and procedures apply to all three timelines.

Once again, the meaning of this section of Daniel is to be understood by reference to the closing chapters of Revelation. In turn, these chapters will take on new emphasis as the meaning of the 1290 day timeline takes its place.

Once more, let it be said, that none of the three timelines give a date for the day and hour of the coming of Jesus. Not until the Voice of God under the 7th plague gives the day and hour, will God's saints know this. But we may know "when it is near even, at the door." The torch of prophecy will light the path of God's people all the way through the dark night of the final tribulation! The last generation will not stumble their way to the kingdom through the most trying time in earth's history, but will go as with a song in the night as to a happy celebration, waiting for the soon coming of the Bridegroom! (Isaiah 30:29).

Part 1. WHY IS THE "DAILY" SCEPTER OF POWER TAKEN AWAY?

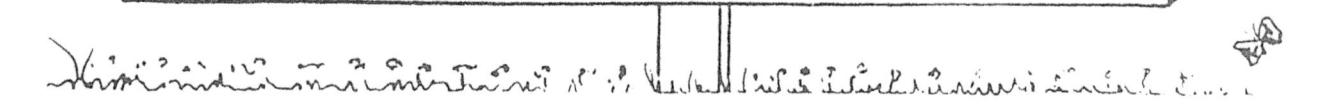

> And from the time that the daily...shall be taken away, and the abomination that maketh desolate set up.... Dan. 12:11.

A comment in the Seventh-day Adventist Bible Commentary clarifies the meaning of this text as follows:

> The clause may be translated literally, "and from the time of the taking away of the continual (sic) [continuum scepter of power and authority] **EVEN IN ORDER TO SET UP** the abomination." This would indicate that the "taking away" was done with the direct intent of setting up the abomination. 4 BC 880.

From a political standpoint, Revelation 13 cannot be fulfilled so that the "beast-papacy can have the scepter of "power...over **all** kindreds, and tongues, and nations" until the kings or governments of the earth "lay aside" that scepter and place it in his hand! We may understand that the Lord permits Satan to accomplish this so that in the great controversy the struggle between good and evil may come to a head. Satan brings all the world under his control through the medium of the one man who sits as "Lord God The Pope." Not until this man has the scepter of power and authority in his hand will he be able to "make war with the saints" and overcome them or "make desolate." (Daniel 12:11).

From a spiritual point of view, why does Satan seek to accomplish this? If only Satan could once bring the entire world under his control, without a dissenting voice, he could stand before this universe and claim this planet as legally his by common consent! It will be his purpose at the end of time to bring about a world government which will, by common consent, determine to annihilate God's people. This very crisis is the focus of all three timelines of Daniel 12.

This very concept of Satan's endtime strategy brings Daniel 12:11 and Revelation 13-19 into an interlocking unit. Satan not only gets the scepter of power, seat and authority into the hands of the "abomination that maketh desolate" and carries on a 1260 day persecution, but he also devises a final Death Decree and this leads directly into a study of the seven last plagues. In particular, it is the 6th plague in which the kings of the earth are **gathered together**, not against each other, but to legislate the final Universal Death Decree. And it is under the 7th plague that the saints are delivered from the Universal Death Decree by the "Voice of God." Revelation 16:17.

It is not possible at this point in time to pinpoint the exact situation which will cause the kings of the earth to place the scepter in the hand of the Pope, but current events point in that direction and we will soon be informed! The United States of America has led the way by placing its military under the United Nation forces. It is laying aside its sovereighnty to come under the New World Order.

Part 2. WHAT "EVENT" BEGINS THE 1290 DAY TIMELINE?

Daniel 12:7 focuses on God's people who will be "scattered" or persecuted.

Daniel 12:11 focuses on the "abomination" which accomplishes the persecution.

These two verses and these two timelines are simply "two sides of the same coin"!

The same event which gives the "abomination that maketh desolate" the scepter of power, seat and authority by which it can persecute is the very same event by which God's people's persecution begins!

In Papal Supremacy No. 1 over Europe, the Pope received power in 538 A.D. and it was at that very same date that the "woman fled into the wilderness" for 1260 years. (Revelation 12:6).

Whereas Daniel 7:25 describes the "little horn" persecutor, Revelation 12:6 described the "woman" who was persecuted. In similar manner, Daniel 12:11 describes the persecutor, while Daniel 12:7 describes the "woman"—"holy people" to be persecuted.

Just as 538 A.D. was the beginning date for **both** the persecutor to come to power and also the date for the church to flee into the wilderness, so also **the same event begins both the timelines of Daniel 12:7 and 12:11.**

The **event** which begins the 1260 day timeline of Daniel 12:7 will be **a Universal Sunday Law. The same event begins the 1290 day timeline**. Just to refresh the memory the following quotation is given again:

> The powers of earth, **uniting** to war against the commandments of God, will decree that "all, both small and great, rich and poor, free and bond" (Revelation 13:16), shall conform to the customs of the church by observance of the false sabbath. GC 604.

The false sabbath is the "mark" of authority, seat and power of the beast! When such a law is passed it begins the Papal Supremacy No. 2 over all "kindreds, tongues, and nations" (Revelation 13:7). A one world government system of control over which the Pope will be the head, is the beginning of the reign of the "abomination of desolation" of Daniel 12:11.*

The following diagram illustrates the beginning of all three of the timelines of Daniel 12:7, 11, 12—the 1260 days, the 1290 days, and the 1335 days.

---

* Note: The "speaking" or legal action by which legislation occurs is described in Revelation 13:5. It is this "speaking" which begins the Papal Supremacy No. 2—the "abomination which maketh desolate" of Daniel 12:11.

And there was given unto him a mouth SPEAKING great things and blasphemies; and the [scepter of] power was given him.... Rev 13:5.

THE BEGINNING OF THE THREE TIMELINES
OF DANIEL 12

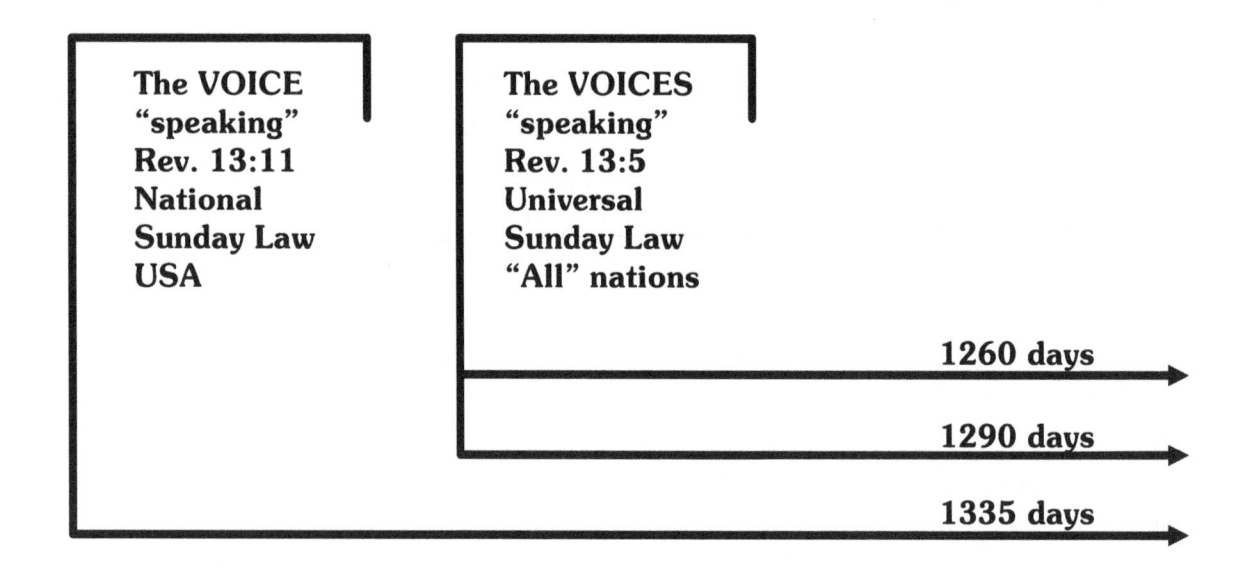

The VOICE
"speaking"
Rev. 13:11
National
Sunday Law
USA

The VOICES
"speaking"
Rev. 13:5
Universal
Sunday Law
"All" nations

1260 days →

1290 days →

1335 days →

Part 3. WHAT "EVENT" ENDS THE 1290 TIMELINE OF DANIEL 12:11 ?

> And the seventh angel poured out his vial into the air; and there came a great voice out of the temple of heaven, from the throne, saying, It is done. And there were **VOICES** and thunders, and lightnings;.... Rev. 16:17,18.

The 1290 day timeline of Daniel 12:11 begins and ends like the other timelines in Daniel 12, with VOICES! These voices are speaking legislative and judicial actions! What are these VOICES saying which follow the Voice of God deliverance?

> It is at midnight that God manifests His power for the deliverance of His people.... In the midst of the angry heavens in one clear space of indescribable glory, whence comes the voice of God like the sound of many waters, saying: "It is done." Revelation 16:17. That voice shakes the heavens and the earth. There is a mighty earthquake.... Graves are opened.... All who have died in the faith of the third angel's message come forth from the tomb glorified, to hear God's covenant of peace with those who have kept His law.... Fierce lightnings leap from the heavens, enveloping the earth in a sheet of flame. Above the terrific roar of thunder, **VOICES**, mysterious and awful, **declare the doom of the wicked**. The words spoken are not comprehended by all; but they are distinctly understood by the false teachers. Those who a little before were so reckless, so boastful and defiant, so exultant in their cruelty to God's commandment-keeping people, are now overwhelmed with consternation and shuddering in fear. Their wails are heard above the sound of the elements. Demons acknowledge the deity of Christ and tremble before His power, while men are supplicating for mercy and groveling in abject terror. GC 636-638.

These VOICES follow the "Voice of God." These VOICES "**declare the doom of the wicked**." These are voices from the court of heaven. They are declaring with legal finality a statement of legislative and judicial action—an executive order! In the court of heaven, these witnesses and judges have declared the legality of the fall and execution of Babylon—all the wicked! It is these VOICES of judgment, both in proclamation and execution, which bring to an end the 1290 day timeline of Daniel 12:11.

Part 4. WHAT IS "THE FALL OF BABYLON"?

Ancient Babylon fell before the Medo-Persians. From this historical root the prophetic symbolism of Revelation describes the final fall and destruction of wicked Babylon. This fall of spiritual Babylon at the end of time is described in Revelation 16:17-21. It is known as the 7th plague. It begins with the "Voice of God" and ends with a great hail. Between the "Voice of God" and the hail there are a number of other things which occur as listed below:

> And the seventh angel poured out his vial into the air; and there came a great voice [The Voice of God] out of the temple of heaven saying, It is done. Rev. 16:17.
>
> 1. And there were voices, [declaring the doom the wicked]
> 2. and thunders, and lightnings
> 3. and there was a great earthquake, such as was not since men were upon the earth, so mighty an earthquake, and so great
> 4. And the great city [Babylon] was divided into three parts
> 5. and the cities of the nations fell
> 6. and great Babylon came in rememberance before God
> 7. to give unto her the cup of the wine of the fierceness of his wrath
> 8. And every island fled away
> 9. and the mountains were not found
> 10. And there fell upon men a great hail out of heaven, every stone about the weight of a talent: and men blasphemed God because of the plague of the hail; for the plague thereof was exceeding great. Rev. 16:17-21.

Between the "Voice of God" deliverance, of God's people, and the coming of Jesus there is an **interim of time** which pertains to the fall of Babylon and the judgment which falls on the wicked—the "Voice of God" brings the "abomination that maketh desolate" to its final end.

An entire chapter in *The Great Controversy* is devoted to an explanation of "The Fall of Babylon" under the 7th plague. The reader should take the time to read that entire chapter. It is most important to understand that events occur during that 7th plague which require a **span of time** before the wicked are completely destroyed. Notice the events as they occur as described below:

> The voice of God is heard from heaven, declaring the day and hour of Jesus' coming,.... Soon there appears in the east a small black cloud,.... [this is] the sign of the Son of man.... Jesus rides forth as a mighty conqueror. GC 640,641.

The word "soon" as used above has led some to conclude that it means immediately! But the following chapter entitled "Desolation of the Earth" actually uses more than the first half of that chapter to describe the fall of Babylon. These events transpire after the "Voice of God." The chapter begins by quoting Revelation 18, which is a description of the fall of Babylon. Notice what occurs during that **span of time**:

> When the voice of God turns the captivity of His people, there is a terrible awakening of those who have lost all in the great conflict of life.... The rich bemoan the destruction of their grand houses, the scattering of their gold and silver.... The wicked are filled with regret.... The minister who has sacrificed truth to gain the favor of men now discerns the character and influence of his teachings.... Ministers and people see that they have not sustained the right relation to God.
>
> The people see that they have been deluded. They accuse one another of having led them to destruction; but all unite in heaping their bitterest condemnation upon the ministers.*
>
> ...these teachers confess before the world their work of deception.*
>
> The multitudes are filled with fury*...they turn upon the false shepherds.*
>
> The swords which were to slay God's people are now employed to destroy their enemies. Everywhere there is strife and bloodshed....*
>
> Now the angel of death goes forth, represented in Ezekiel's vision by the men with their slaughtering weapons,.... "Slay utterly old and young, both maidens and little children, and women! ...begin at My sanctuary...." The false watchmen are the first to fall....*
>
> ..."And the slain of the Lord shall be at that day from one end of the earth even unto the other end of the earth:...." Jeremiah 35:33. GC 654-657.

---

* The actions described here take **time**. They occur after the "Voice of God" deliverance. The question occurs: How much time? Revelation gives us an exact, definite answer! Three times it specifies exactly how much time it will take for Babylon to fall.

Part 5. WHAT IS THE "ONE HOUR" OF REVELATION 18?

Three times, just to make sure we don't miss it, the Bible tells the prophetic expositor exactly how long it takes for the fall of Babylon:

1. ...Alas, alas that great city Babylon, that mighty city! for in **one hour** is thy judgment come! Rev. 18:10.
2. For in **one hour** so great riches is come to naught. Rev. 18:17.
3. ...for in **one hour** is she made desolate Rev. 18:19.

"One hour" is a specific unit of time. It most certainly is not "indefinite" or "just a short time." It is a unit of measurement! If it were indefinite it could have been stated as a "little time" or a "short space" but rather it is a specific unit of time.

Is it literal or symbolic time? Revelation 18 is couched in prophetic symbolism, with the main character as "Babylon," which is symbolic. Primarily, for this reason, the "one hour" should be considered symbolic. Also it is self-evident that the many events which occur under the "Fall of Babylon" as listed in *The Great Controversy* would require more than just one hour of literal time.

How then shall the "one hour" of prophetic-symbolic time be computed? There is but one tool of time conversion from prophetic-symbolic time to literal time. That is the "Year-day Computation Principle" by which the "one hour" of Revelation 17 is converted to literal time. Just as the "one hour" of Revelation 17 represents 15 literal days, so also the "one hour" of Revelation 18 represents another 15 days.

It is therefore important to understand that from the "Voice of God" deliverance of His people, it takes "one hour" or fifteen days for the fall of Babylon.

The timeline of 1290 days brings events to the end of the fall of Babylon—the destruction of the "abomination that maketh desolate:"

> And from the time that the daily...shall be taken away, and the abomination that maketh desolate set up, there shall be a thousand two hundred and ninety days [until the abomination is utterly finished]. Dan. 12:11.

Part 6. WHAT IS THE "THIRTY DAYS DIFFERENCE"?

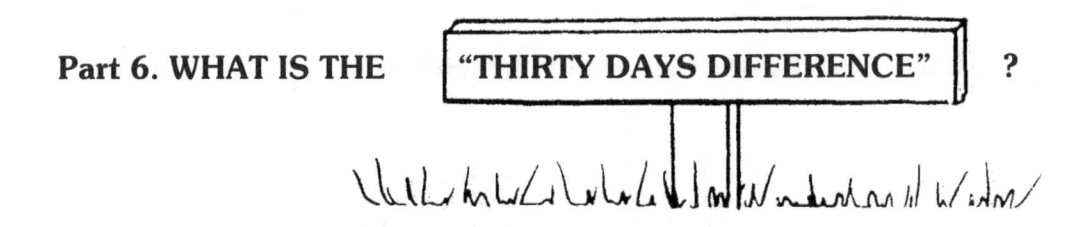

There is thirty days difference between the 1260 day timeline of Daniel 12:7 and the 1290 day timeline of Daniel 12:11. That 30 days difference is illustrated in the timelines as given below:

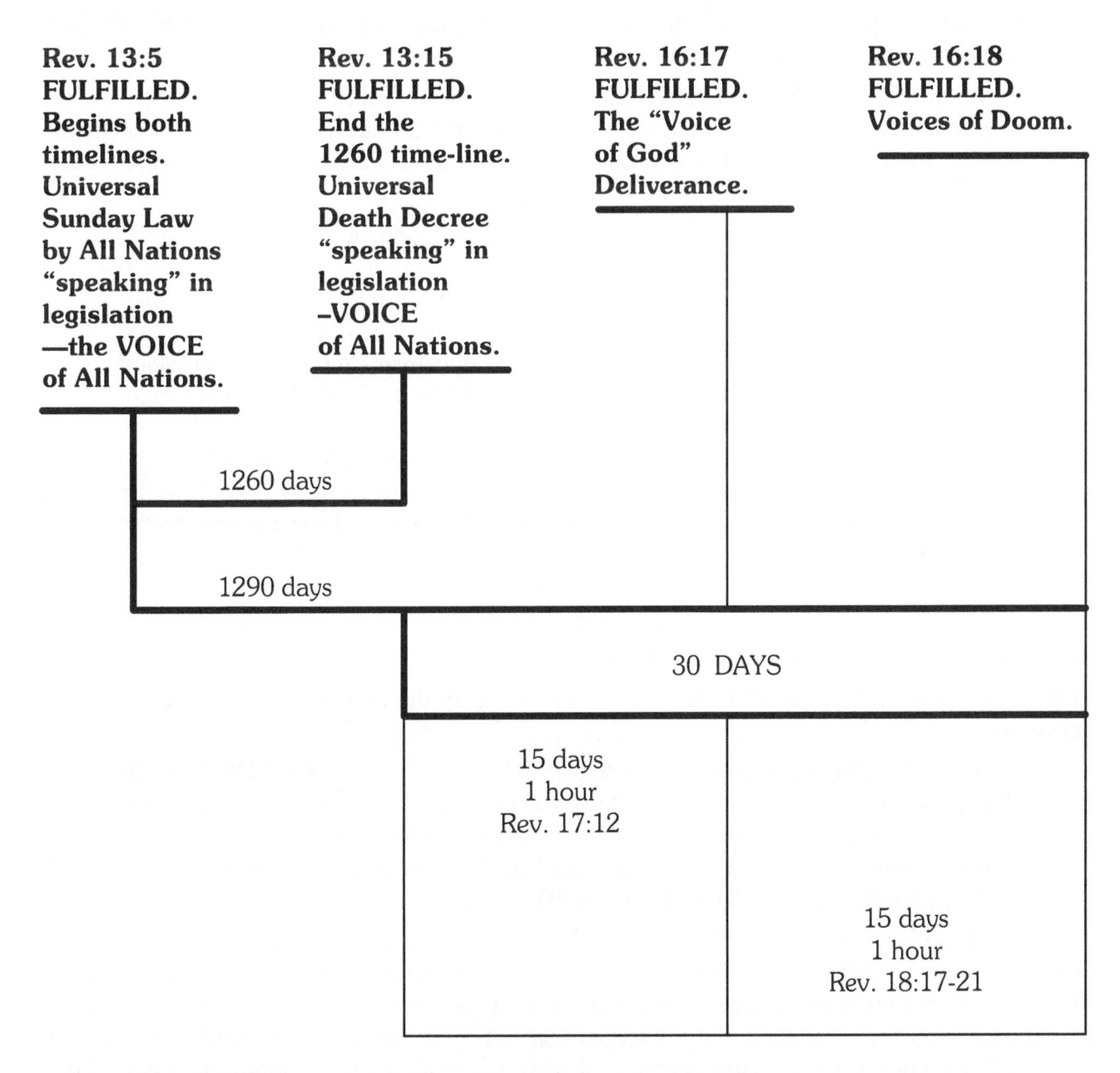

Rev. 13:5 FULFILLED. Begins both timelines. Universal Sunday Law by All Nations "speaking" in legislation —the VOICE of All Nations.

Rev. 13:15 FULFILLED. End the 1260 time-line. Universal Death Decree "speaking" in legislation –VOICE of All Nations.

Rev. 16:17 FULFILLED. The "Voice of God" Deliverance.

Rev. 16:18 FULFILLED. Voices of Doom.

1260 days

1290 days

30 DAYS

15 days
1 hour
Rev. 17:12

15 days
1 hour
Rev. 18:17-21

The thirty days difference between the 1260 day timeline and the 1290 day timeline is made up of two 15 day periods from Revelation 17 and 18. The first 15 days is a "reign" of the beast and the kings of the earth exulting in the success of their efforts to legislate a Universal Death Decree. The last 15 days is the fall of Babylon.

Part 7. WHAT IS "ABOUT THE SPACE OF HALF AN HOUR" REV 18:1?

> And when he had opened the seventh seal, there was silence in heaven **about the space of half an hour**. Rev. 8:1.

The approximate "space of half an hour" occurs within the time-setting of the seventh seal. Only after the seventh seal is opened does this "space of half an hour" occur.

The Revelation 8:1 verse does not give sufficient information about the seventh seal to identify the time or events which are connected to "the space of half an hour." Therefore it is necessary to go back to the sixth seal to get a time orientation to this "half an hour." What occurs under the sixth seal?

> And I beheld when he had opened the sixth seal, and, lo, there was a great earthquake; and the sun became black as sackcloth of hair, and the moon became as blood; And the stars of heaven fell unto the earth, even as a fig tree casteth her untimely figs, when she is shaken of a mighty wind. And the heaven departed as a scroll when it is rolled together; and every mountain and island were moved out of their places. And the kings of the earth, and the great men, and the rich men, and the chief captains, and the mighty men, and every bondman, and every free man, hid themselves in the dens and in the rocks of the mountains; And said to the mountains and rocks, Fall on us, and hide us from the face of him that sitteth on the throne, and from the wrath of the Lamb: For the great day of his wrath is come; and who shall be able to stand? Rev. 6:12-17.

In view of the fact that "the heaven" (atmosphere) has not yet "departed as a scroll" and that the other events mentioned in Revelation 6:14-17 have not yet occurred, we may conclude that these scenes are yet to be fulfilled in the **future**.

The following comment places "the heaven...rolled back" in the time-setting of the voice of God deliverance:

> The powers of heaven [sun, moon and stars] will be shaken **AT THE VOICE OF GOD**. Then the sun, moon, and stars will be moved out of their places. They will not pass away, but be shaken by the **VOICE OF GOD**. The atmosphere **parted and rolled back**; then we could look up through the open space in Orion, whence came the **VOICE OF GOD**. EW 41.

Those verses in Revelation 6:14-17 are inclusive of those events which occur from the voice of God until Jesus is seen coming in the clouds of heaven. These events which occur under the sixth seal are: the great earthquake, signs in the sun, moon and stars, the heaven (atmosphere) rolling back, and the reaction of the wicked as they view the approaching cloud as it bears up Jesus in His Second Coming. The seventh seal adds a time element of "about the space of half an hour."

Prophetic expositors of the past recognized that the "space of half an hour" referred to those events connected with the sixth and seventh seals, with reference to the voice of God and the

Second Coming of Jesus as follows:

> Silence in heaven [about the space of half an hour].—Concerning the cause of this silence, only conjecture can be offered,—a conjecture, however, which is supported by the events of the sixth seal. That seal does not bring us to the second advent, although it embraces events that transpire in close connection therewith. It introduces the fearful commotions of the elements, described as the rolling of the heavens together as a scroll, caused by the **voice of God**, the breaking up of the surface of the earth, and the confession on the part of the wicked that the great day of God's wrath is come. They are doubtless in momentary expectation of seeing the King appear in, to them, unendurable glory. But the [sixth] seal stops just short of that event. The personal appearing of Christ must therefore be allotted to the next [seventh] seal. *Daniel and the Revelation*. 1944 Edition. Uriah Smith. Southern Publishing Association, Nashville, Tennessee, p. 475, 476.

These pioneer expositors understood the "space of half an hour" and its silence in heaven, to refer to the time required for Jesus to **DESCEND** from heaven to this earth:

> When the Lord appears, He comes with ALL the holy angels with Him. (Matthew 25:31.) And when all the heavenly harpers leave the courts above to come down with their divine Lord, as He **DESCENDS** to gather the fruit of His redeeming work, will there not be silence in heaven? Ibid. 476.

Again, there is an inspired description of Christ's **descent** "which took a number of days."

> The voice of God is heard from heaven, declaring the day and hour of Jesus coming....And I saw a flaming cloud come where Jesus stood. Then Jesus... took His place on the cloud which carried Him to the East, where it first appeared to the saints on earth—a small black cloud which was the sign of the Son of man. While the cloud was passing from the Holiest to the East, **which took a number of days**, the synagogue of Satan worshiped at the saint's feet. MAR 287.

If the "silence in heaven about the space of half an hour" refers to Christ's descent from heaven to this earth, and that descent actually takes a "number of days," then it is self-evident that the "half an hour" is prophetic-symbolic time and should be decoded by the Year-day Principle.

DECODING an "half an hour"

> One twenty-four hour prophetic day represents one literal year (360 days). One twenty-fourth of a literal year is fifteen days (Simply divided 360 by 24). Therefore one prophetic hour represents fifteen literal days. And "one half hour" represents seven and a half days.

However it should be noted that the text says "**about** the space of half an hour." There is something which is not quite exact in regard to this seven days! It is seven days, slightly more or less! Is it the half day which is inexact?

There is one more reasonable observation which appears to confirm the seven days of descent of Jesus on the cloud. It is the specific statement that it will require seven days for the cloud chariot to ascend back to heaven. Approximately the same time coming as going!

> We all entered the cloud together, and were seven days ascending to the sea of glass. EW 16.

"Seven days ascending" and on the next day—the eighth day, God's people receive their crowns, the symbol of victory.

> We all entered the cloud together, and were seven days ascending to the sea of glass, when Jesus brought the crowns, and with His own right hand placed them on our heads. He gave us harps of gold and palms of victory. EW 16.

Now to total it all up: Seven days descending, seven days ascending and the 8th day receiving the crowns: 7+7+1=**15 days**.

This total of fifteen days, in which the righteous receive their crowns and palms of victory, is the parallel of the 15 days of the "Fall of Babylon" by which time the wicked are all destroyed. This neat mathematical arrangement appears to be an excellent explanation not only of the "one hour" period of the Fall of Babylon," but also of the rewards of the righteous. It all fits beautifully. However, there is a problem which must be taken into consideration!

Not by any prophetic computation can be determined the day and hour of the coming of Jesus. That will not be verified until pronounced by the voice of God. There are studies which currently bring in complications to the neat fifteen day and seven day periods as follows:

There are many today who are making a study of the ancient Hebrew economy and its implications to endtime prophetic fulfillments. As they study the feast days of Israel, they observe the statement regarding the typology pertaining to the Second Coming of Jesus as follows:

> The slaying of the Passover lamb was a shadow of the death of Christ. Says Paul: "Christ our Passover is sacrificed for us." I Corinthians 5:7.... These types were fulfilled, not only as to the event, but as to the time....In like manner, the types which relate to the second advent must be fulfilled at the time appointed out in the symbolic service. GC 399.

These students of Hebrew typology cannot locate, at the present time, any reference to a seven day descent of Jesus, but find rather a five day difference between the Day of Atonement and the Feast of Tabernacles, which for many reasons seems to point to the descent of Christ, between the voice of God and His appearance in the Eastern sky.

Then there is also the text to be considered which affects the time:

> And except those days should be shortened, there should no flesh be saved: but for the elect's sake those days shall be shortened. Matt. 24:22, Mark 13:20.

Will the approximate seven days of Christ's descent be shortened to less? Is this why it is an indefinite statement of "**about** the space of half an hour?" It is **wise** to remember well that prophecy which is yet to be fulfilled is still tentative! We also have the direct admonition that we cannot make known that day nor hour. Regarding the time of His coming there is some glorious and curious secret which will not be made plain until verified by the voice of God deliverance. It is not the purpose of this study to proclaim the day and hour of His coming and these questions serve well to remind us continually of that fact.[*]

---

[*] Note: In the statement in *Early Writings* p. 16 which says that the "cloud was passing **from the Holiest** to the East," some have assumed that "from the Holiest" refers to Christ leaving the Most Holy Place at the close of probation. This is confusion. On the typical Day of Atonement the high priest went in and out of the Most Holy place several times to perform different kinds of work. Jesus leaves the Most Holy place at the close of probation, but also leaves from the Holiest on His descent to earth.

Part 8. WHAT IS THE "DRAMA" OF THE 6th AND 7th PLAGUES?

The "drama" of the 6th and 7th plagues reaches the climax during the 30 day difference between the 1260 and the 1290 day timelines of Daniel 12:7-11. That 30 day period encompasses the greatest events of all history! It begins at the Universal Death Decree, climaxes at the "Voice of God" deliverance of the saints and closes with the complete "Fall of Babylon."

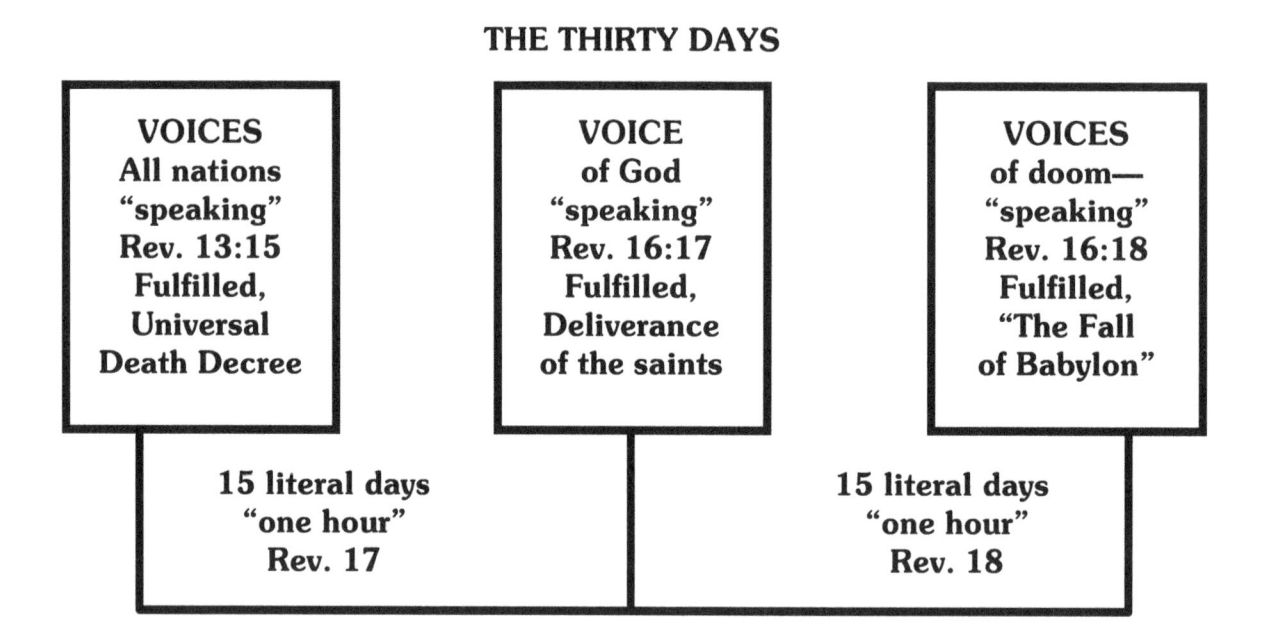

THE THIRTY DAYS

VOICES All nations "speaking" Rev. 13:15 Fulfilled, Universal Death Decree	VOICE of God "speaking" Rev. 16:17 Fulfilled, Deliverance of the saints	VOICES of doom— "speaking" Rev. 16:18 Fulfilled, "The Fall of Babylon"
15 literal days "one hour" Rev. 17		15 literal days "one hour" Rev. 18

The sixth and seventh plagues are written in the literary form of a drama. The sixth plague climaxes with the Universal Death Decree. The seventh plague begins at the "Voice of God" deliverance from that Death Decree. True to the form of drama, in the last act it not only shows the triumph of the Hero and heroine but also reveals the final judgment of the villain. In the sixth plague there are many characters on stage and they each act their part in the final crisis.

> We need to study the pouring out of the seventh vial. The powers of evil will not yield up the conflict without a struggle. But Providence has a part to act in the battle of Armageddon [sixth plague]. When the earth is lighted with the glory of the angel of Revelation eighteen, the religious elements, good and evil, will awake from slumber, and the armies of the living God will take the field. 7 BC 983.

Part 9. WHAT ARE THE "THUNDERINGS AND LIGHTNINGS"?

> And there were voices, and thunders, and lightnings; and there was a great earthquake.... Rev. 16:18.

The "voices of doom" are accompanied by "thunders, and lightnings." What is the significance of the "thunders, and lightnings"? Biblical cross-reference study reveals that the "thunders, and lightnings" accompany voices which proclaim God's **LAW**! Examples follow:

> And God spake all those words saying, [The Ten Commandments].... And all the people saw the thunderings and lightnings,.... Ex. 20:1-18.

Further study confirms the concept that the "voices, thunders, and lightnings" come from God's throne, the basis of which is the **LAW** of God.

> And out of the **throne** proceeded lightnings and thunderings and voices:.... Rev. 4:5.

> And the temple of God was opened in heaven, and there was seen in his temple the ark [which contained the **LAW**] of his testament: and there were lightnings, and voices, and thunderings, and an earthquake, and great hail. Rev. 11:19.

The "voices of doom" which bring the 1290 day timeline of Daniel 12:11 to its end in the "Fall of Babylon" under the 7th plague are accompanied by the official lightnings and thunders which emanate from God's throne, from the ark of the Ten Commandment Law. These voices from God's throne are vindicating God and His Law. They speak from the court of heaven, pronouncing verdict and sentence upon the wicked who have trampled on the Law of God. A description of this event follows:

> It is at midnight that God manifests His power for the deliverance of His people.... In the midst of the angry heavens is one clear space of indescribable glory, whence comes the voice of God like the sound of many waters, saying: "It is done." Revelation 16:17.... That voice shakes the heavens and the earth. There is a mighty earthquake.... Babylon the great has come in remembrance before God, "to give unto her the cup of the wine of the fierceness of His wrath." ...the clouds sweep back, and the starry heavens are seen, unspeakably glorious in contrast with the black and angry firmament on either side. The glory of the celestial city streams from the gates ajar. Then there appears against the sky a hand holding **two tables of stone** folded together.... **That holy law**, God's righteousness, that amid thunder and flame was proclaimed from Sinai as the guide of life, is now revealed to men as the rule of judgment. The hand opens the tables, and there are seen the precepts of the **Decalogue**, traced as with a pen of fire. The words are so plain that all can read them. Memory is aroused, the darkness of superstition and heresy are swept from every mind, and **God's ten words**, brief, comprehensive, and authoritative are presented to the view of all inhabitants of the earth.

> It is impossible to describe the horror and despair of those who have trampled upon **God's holy requirements**. The Lord gave them His **law**; they might have compared their characters with it and learned their defects while there was yet opportunity for repentance and reform; but in order to secure the favor of the world, they set aside its precepts and taught others to transgress. They have endeavored to compel God's people to profane His Sabbath. **Now they are condemned by that law** which they have despised.... Fearful will be the doom of him to whom God shall say: Depart, thou wicked servant. GC 636-640.

The "thunders and lightnings" which come from God's throne are seen and felt upon the earth! They accompany the voices of doom which condemn the wicked as sentenced for their violations of God's Law.

> Fierce **lightnings** leap from the heavens, enveloping the earth in a sheet of flame. Above the terrific roar of **thunder**, **voices**, mysterious and awful, declare the doom of the wicked. The words spoken are not comprehended by all; but they are distinctly understood by the false teachers. Those who a little before were so reckless, so boastful and defiant, so exultant in their cruelty to God's commandment-keeping people, are now overwhelmed with consternation and shuddering in fear. GC 638.

These "voices of doom," speaking from God's throne, represent His government which is founded upon His law. The "speaking" of a nation or government is its legislative or judicial action. These voices "speak" pronouncing judgment upon the wicked and initiate the "judicial action" of the Fall of Babylon which occurs in "one hour" of prophetic time or 15 literal days. Whether the voices speak only at the beginning of the "one hour" or throughout the entire time is not clear. The judicial action which they pronounce brings Babylon to its end by the close of the fifteen days of judgment.

Please note that this still does not give the day nor hour of the coming of Jesus. Men are still alive and blaspheming God "because of the hail" (Revelation 16:21) but the "wicked are slain by the brightness of His coming." Some are left to be destroyed at His coming.

> And then shall that Wicked be revealed, whom the Lord shall consume with the spirit of his mouth, and shall destroy with the brightness of His coming. 2 Thess. 2:8.

A study of the 1290 day timeline of Daniel 12:11, with its emphasis on the "Fall of Babylon" and the vindication of God and His Ten Commandment Law, expands the mind to the very heart of the great controversy between Christ and Satan.

> Lucifer went forth to diffuse the spirit of discontent among the angels....he endeavored to excite dissatisfaction concerning the laws that governed heavenly beings, intimating that they imposed an unnecessary restraint.... GC 495.

> It must be demonstrated before the inhabitants of heaven, as well as all the worlds, that God's government was just, His law perfect....

> The discord which his own course had caused in heaven, Satan charged upon the law and government of God. GC 497 498.

He denounced the divine statutes as a restriction of their liberty and declared that it was his purpose to secure the abolition of law;.... The law of God, which Satan has reproached as a yoke of bondage, will be honored as the law of liberty. GC 499, 504.

The Daniel 12:11 timeline of 1290 days spotlights the final crisis when the Decalogue will be seen in the heavens, and it will be understood that the law condemns the guilty. It is the focus of "The Fall of Babylon." It is the action spoken by the "voices" from heaven's throne and observed by all the universe! It is the vindication of God's Law and His government. The timelines of Daniel 12 do not deal with trivia. They uplift the mind to the eternal verities in the rescue of the entire universe from Satan's rebellion and power of sin!

SUMMARY OF CHAPTER VI

WHAT IS THE 1290 DAY TIMELINE OF DANIEL 12:11?

1. It does not give the day and hour of the Second Coming of Jesus.
2. It is a key to understanding closing events.
3. It is a key to understanding Revelation 16:17 through Revelation 18.
4. It cannot be understood except by cross reference with Revelation.
5. It cannot be understood without reference to *The Great Controversy*.
6. Although independent in itself, the 1290 day timeline interlocks with the 1260 and 1335 day timelines of Daniel 12:7,12.
7. It focuses on the great themes of the great controversy between Christ and Satan and the Law of God.
8. The 1290 day timeline is a fulfillment of prophetic Scripture: Revelation 18.
9. It begins and ends with "Voices" of ALL nations and the government of heaven in legislative and judicial action.
10. It begins with the "voices" of ALL nations in the Universal Sunday Law.
11. It ends with the "voices of doom" and the judicial action of judgment.
12. It ends with the "Fall of Babylon" in judicial action of judgment.
13. The "Fall of Babylon" occurs under the 7th plague.
14. The "Fall of Babylon" occurs after the "Voice of God." It occupies a span of time.
15. The "Fall of Babylon" occurs in one prophetic-symbolic "hour."
16. One prophetic-symbolic "hour" represents 15 literal days.
17. The "one hour" of Revelation 17 and "one hour" of Revelation 18 is the same as 15 days + 15 days or a total of 30 literal days.
18. There is a 30 day difference between the 1260 timeline and the 1290 timeline of Daniel 12.
19. The 30 day difference encompasses the concluding endtime climax: The Universal Death Decree, the "Voice of God", and the "Voices of Doom." These complete the "Fall of Babylon."
20. The "Voices of Doom" pronounce judgment on Babylon and vindicate God's Law before the universe with "thunderings, and lightnings."
21. The 30 day difference explains the action of the 6th and 7th plagues.

The 1290 day timeline of Daniel 12 explains the rise and fall of Papal Supremacy No. 2 as described in Revelation 13-18. It brings the prophetic expositor to the end of the judgment of Babylon but does not give light on the day and hour of the coming of Jesus. It is the torch of prophecy which lights the way!

CONCLUSION

The three timelines of Daniel 12:5-13 are the last steps in "the unrolling of the scroll." Their exposition is the last segment or application in an attempt to link this prophecy with historical events of the past to those in the immediate future. It is an accent on the last acts of the drama portrayed within the Historicist "School" of Prophetic Interpretation.

An understanding of the three timelines of Daniel 12 is "Present Truth" for the last generation. Those who study to find "Present Truth" of the endtime will be prepared for the final crisis according to God's gracious provision. "In each generation there is a new development of truth" (COL 127) and in each generation the hearts of men are tested by it regarding the deep motives of the heart.

The three timelines of Daniel provide only a bare outline of the major events of the future. They contain nothing regarding typology concerning feastdays nor the Jubilee. It is possible that some of these things can be connected or inserted into this framework, but that is not the purpose of this study. The Bible student should be aware of the fact that this outline and its specific information can be jeopardized if "decorated" with many subjective assumptions.

It is true that the astute Bible student will be aware of the fact that along these timelines there are many points of interest: The falling of the Latter Rain of the Holy Spirit; The giving of the Loud Cry Third Angel's Message, in the power of the fourth angel of Revelation 18; The Midnight Cry message, "Behold, the Bridegroom cometh, go ye out to meet him;" and the entire amplification of the three angels' messages regarding the closing of the Investigative Judgment, the Fall of Babylon and the warning against the seven last plagues. There will be the sealing of the people of God—the 144,000, and the placement of the "mark of the beast" and all that is connected with the moral and final fall of Babylon. There will be a point of the Close of Probation for the church and for the world. But none of these things are signified in the three timelines by context. The timelines provide only that basic framework by which the last generation may see the broad outlines and sequences of the conflict which lie just before us.

No one expositor possesses all truth. Each adds some facet to the "unrolling of the scroll." Your critique of this book will be valued by the author. If there is a sixty day interim between a National Sunday Law in the United States of America and a Universal Sunday Law and establishment of a worldwide Papal Supremacy, God's people may look with favor upon the rest of the study of the three timelines with faith and confidence. If not, then it will be time to consider other views and explanations which appear to be more valid.

The reader needs a chart in which all three timelines are merged into one picture. That is provided.

The Daniel 12 Timelines
(1260, 1290, 1335 Days)

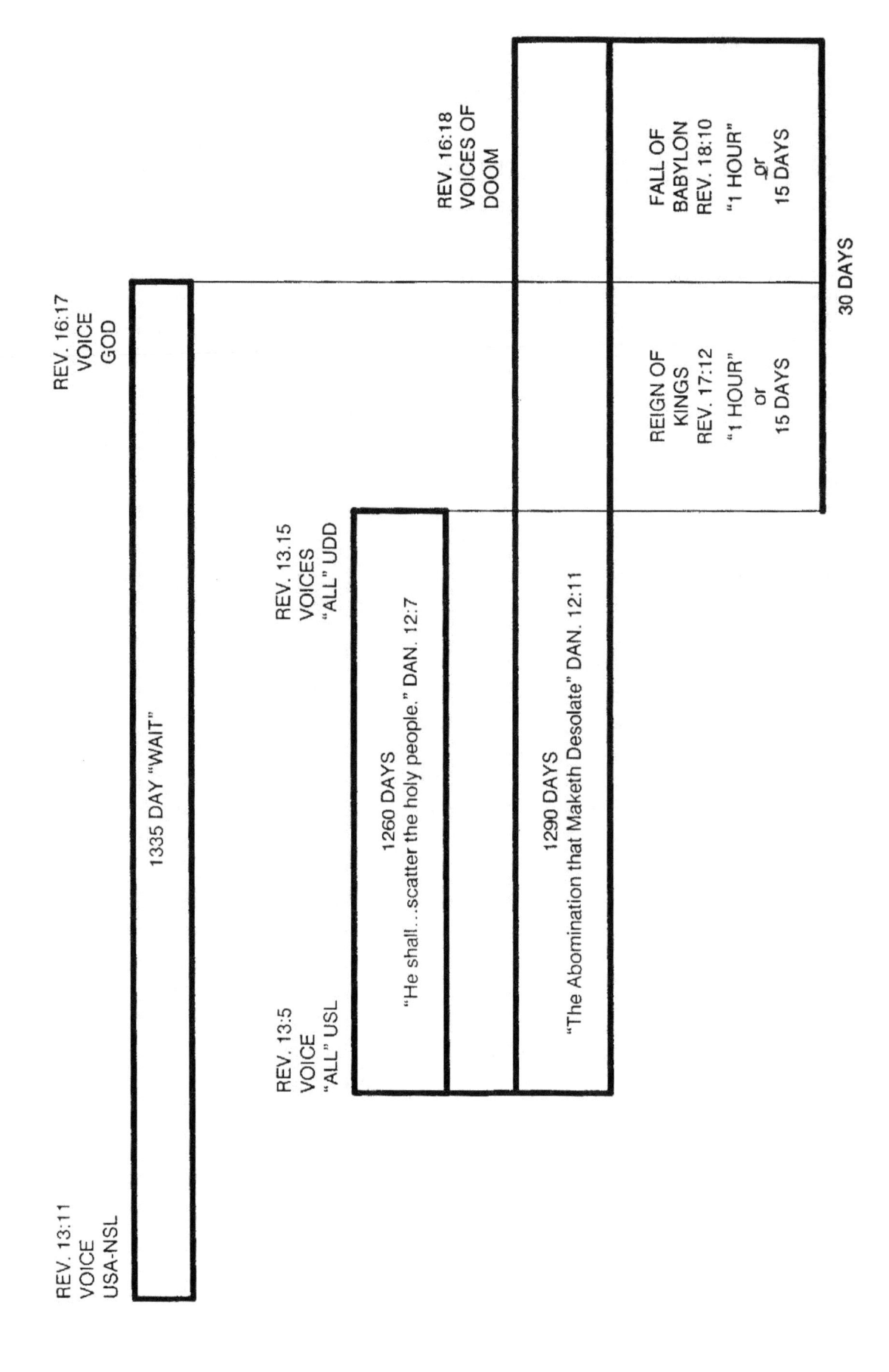

REV. 13:11
VOICE
USA-NSL

REV. 13:5
VOICE
"ALL" USL

REV. 13.15
VOICES
"ALL" UDD

REV. 16:17
VOICE
GOD

REV. 16:18
VOICES OF
DOOM

1335 DAY "WAIT"

1260 DAYS
"He shall...scatter the holy people." DAN. 12:7

1290 DAYS
"The Abomination that Maketh Desolate" DAN. 12:11

REIGN OF
KINGS
REV. 17:12
"1 HOUR"
or
15 DAYS

FALL OF
BABYLON
REV. 18:10
"1 HOUR"
or
15 DAYS

30 DAYS

THE INTERLOCKING NATURE OF THE THREE TIMELINES OF DANIEL 12

The three timelines of Daniel, when applied to future events, using the principles of hermeneutic precision, become an interlocking unit which throws light on endtime crisis. The simplicity rests in the precedent "speaking" VOICES or legislative and judicial action which begin and end the timelines. These VOICES rest in the plain statements of Scripture and are explained in Spirit of Prophecy references. Thus each unit of time is bounded at both ends by public legislation, obvious for all the world to see.

The complexity is revealed in the fact that when the three timelines are combined, they become an interlocking unit whereby each timeline is fastened into the whole in an immovable, secure position. The complexity of the interlocking devices is evidence of Divine origin. Each beginning and ending VOICE is a "key" which opens up the meaning, not only of each timeline but places each event into a correct sequence! Each key is necessary to the structure as a whole. These keys are found, most often, in the books of Daniel and Revelation. These keys which open the door of comprehension, may be listed as follows:

Key 1. **The Year-day Computation Principle**

This key unlocks the two endtime symbolic "one hour"—15 literal day periods of Revelation 17 and 18 so that they can be linked to the literal time in the three timelines of Daniel 12:7-13.

Key 2. **The "speaking" VOICES**

This is the masterkey which begins and ends each timeline with legislative or judicial action of governmental bodies.

Key 3. **The "Voice of God"**

This key provides the connecting link between: (a) The two "one hour" periods of Revelation 17 and 18, and (b) the sixth and seventh plagues in which the rising action of the sixth plague is climaxed by the Voice of God and in the seventh plague by the descending action of the drama as Babylon falls. The Voice of God brings the climax of the endtime drama into sharp focus.

Key 4. **The "one hour"—15 Literal day Periods**

This key unlocks or explains two specific intervals of time:
(a) The interim between legislation of a Universal Death Decree and its effective date.
(b) The interim between the Voice of God deliverance and the completion of the fall of Babylon under the seventh plague, all of which transpires in relation to the Second Coming of Jesus.
(c) The interim between legislation of a Universal Death Decree and its effective date is recognized as "the time of Jacob's trouble."

Key 5. **The Thirty Days**

This thirty days, the difference between the 1260 and 1290 days is provided right within the three timelines of Daniel 12:7-11. This locks right into the two fifteen day periods of Revelation 17 and 18 and the timelines are thereby locked into an immovable position.

Key 6. **The Principles of the Historicist "School" of Prophetic Interpretation**

The numerous keys provided by these principles opens the prophetic terminology in Daniel 12 and the symbolism in Revelation 12-19 to identify "the abomination that maketh desolate" which reigns for 1290 days, to be the same character as the "beast" of Revelation 13 as its healed wounded head comes back to Papal Supremacy No. 2 over ALL the world in the near future. These principles build on the foundations laid in Daniel 7, 8 and 9 and conclude the action in Daniel 12.

Key 7. **The Accuracy Test**

The sixty days interim between a National Sunday Law in the United States of America and a Universal Sunday Law over all nations becomes an accuracy TEST for those who enter the final crisis. If there is no sixty-day interlude, the Bible student will know early-on that there is error in this application. But if there is a sixty-day interlude, he may look with confidence upon it as a dependable unit. This test is a key for dependability.

CONCLUSION: All prophetic exposition which deals with the future should be held as **TENTATIVE** until fulfillment. However, prophecy is also clearly defined in Scripture as a **LIGHT** on the pathway of future events. This tension between a desire to know that which God is seeking to reveal to us regarding future events and the cautious tentative attitude is one more evidence of that delicate balance which exists between faith and works on the way to heaven. This very tension keeps the Christian humble, looking to Jesus as he makes his way day by day, step by step toward the kingdom. The three timelines of Daniel, Chapter 12 form a **paragon**, a model of perfection.

The Structure of the Book of Daniel
(The Nature and Purpose of the Book of Daniel)
Four Visions in one *Major Line* of Prophecy
from 606 B.C. to the establishment of Christ's kingdom

Directions: First, Let the Bible interpret (decode) the symbols.
Then, make an application to Historical events.

(Symbolic)	(Symbolic)	(Symbolic)	Literal Kings
Vision 1	**Vision 2**	**Vision 3**	**Vision 4**
Image	Beasts	Ram-Goat, Horns	
4 Empires	**5 empires**		**7 Empires**
Babylon	Babylon		
Medo Persia	Medo Persersia	M-Persia	Cyrus
Grecia	Grecia	Grecia	Alex.
Rome	Rome	(4 directions) Rome	Cae
	Papal Rome Little horn	Little Horn	Popes
			Stalin
		king fierce countenance	Pope
The Stone	*The Son of Man*	*The Messiah-Judge*	*The Deliverer*

(The Son of God   Palmonee--The Wonderful Numberer-Revealer of Secrets

Interlude Question	**Interlude Question**	**Interlude Question**	**Interlude Question**
How Long until all earthly empires will end? God's kingdom set up?	How Long until the 5th earthly empire will end?	How long until all men and empires face the the heavenly judgment?	"How Long until the end of time?" Until the end of the 7th empire? Until the end of all persecutions? Until the Saints will be Delivered?

Endtime Answers	**Endtime Answers**	**Endtime Answers**	**Endtime Answers**
The Stone. All empires will End! Promise that God will set up His Kingdom	1260 days timeline 5th empire ends Promise that "Saints Receive the Kingdom"	2300 days timeline Inv. Judgment begins (Legal process begins) Names retained in Lamb's Book of Life Kingdom made up	1290 Timeline ends 7th empire will end 1260 Timeline ends Persecutions end 1335 Timeline Saints delivered Kingdom set up

APPENDIX A

WHAT ARE THE SEVEN ANGEL'S MESSAGES OF REVELATION 14 & 18?

INTRODUCTION

There are three angels' messages brought to view in Revelation 14:6-12. However, Revelation 14:15-20 brings to view three more angels! It is important to be consistent in Biblical interpretation. If the first three angels, "crying with a loud voice", brought to view in verses 6-12 represent messages given by men, then also the last three angels who are "crying with a loud voice" or a "loud cry," brought to view in verses 15-20 also represent **messages** given by men.

There are six angels in Revelation 14 with messages. But in the book of Revelation the number seven represents completeness: seven churches, seven letters, seven stars, seven seals, seven trumpets, seven thunders, seven heads, seven plagues and it seems appropriate that there should be seven angels' messages also. The additional angel's message is found in Revelation 18.

The objective of this study is to examine the time setting for the proclamation of each of these seven angels' messages and to give a broad overview of the content of each as it relates to prophetic fulfillment of past, present and future. It will be discovered that the fourth and fifth **angels' messages will supply the TIME-FRAME for the proclamation of the three timelines of Daniel 12.**

1. **WHAT IS THE TIME-SETTING FOR THE FIRST, SECOND AND THIRD ANGELS' MESSAGES?**

    A. The time-setting for the first angel's message.

    ...in 1831 he [William Miller] for the first time" publicly gave the reasons for his faith. GC 331.

    In 1833 Miller received a license to preach, from the Baptist Church of which he was a member. GC 332.

    The message given by Miller and his associates announced the termination of the 2300 days of Daniel 8:14.... GC 351.

    It is this work of judgment, immediately preceding the second advent, that is announced in the FIRST ANGEL'S MESSAGE of Revelation 14:7 "Fear God, and give glory to Him; for **the hour** of His judgment **is come**." Those who proclaimed this warning gave the right message **at the right time**. GC 352.

B. The time-setting for the second angel's message.

The second angel's message of Revelation 14 was first preached **in the summer of 1844**, and it then had a more direct application to the churches of the United States, where the warning of the judgment [first angel] had been most widely proclaimed and most generally rejected." GC 389.

The Second Angel's Message, first preached in the summer of 1844 announced that "Babylon is fallen;" [apostate Christendom] had rejected the first angel's message proclaiming the coming of Jesus and judgment. After the 1844 Disappointment, God's people understood that it was investigative judgment—not executive judgment, which was to begin in 1844. This first angel's message has been given to the world ever since 1844 until the present time. The apostate condition of "Babylon" has also continued to the present day.

C. The time-setting for the third angel's message.

The passing of the time in 1844 [the Great Disappointment] was **followed** by a period of great trial to those who still held the advent faith...light directed their minds to the sanctuary above...they saw that their great High Priest had entered upon another work of administration...they were led to see also the closing work of the church. They had a clearer understanding of the first and second angel's messages, and were prepared to receive and give to the world the solemn warning of the third angel of Revelation 14. GC 431,432.

The third angel's messages presents Christ our High Priest in the sanctuary above in contrast to a false priesthood established here on earth in the Papal system—PAST, PRESENT, and FUTURE.

The most fearful threatening ever addressed to mortals is contained in the third angel's messages...the warning is **TO BE GIVEN** [future tense] to the world before the visitation of God's judgments. GC 449.

In conclusion, the first and second angels' messages began shortly before 1844 and the third angel's message began immediately after. All three messages have been proclaimed to the world ever since. The second angel's message followed the first because it was rejected. The first angel's message proclaiming a true seventh-day Sabbath in worship of the Creator is simply the positive aspect of the same message given by the third angel warning against a false sabbath.* All three of these messages are woven together in one great unit of truth. The timeframe begins around **1844**, has continued until **the present**, and will extend or be repeated into **the future**.

2. WHO IS THE FOURTH ANGEL?

In Revelation 14, the first angel and the second angel are simply described as "another angel"—not "first" or "second." Only the third angel is described numerically as the "the third."

---

* NOTE: The first and third angel's messages are simply positive and negative aspects of the same concern: The first angel says "**Worship** HIM" [God] while the third angel warns, "If any man worship [a false god]. The first angel holds the seal of God but the third angel has the mark of the beast.

Only by counting back from this third angel does one get the terms "first" and "second" angel.

In the same manner the "fourth" angel is simply introduced as "another angel" but we can know that he is fourth in line because he "unites with the third angel" and gives power to the third angel.

> Hence the movement symbolized by the angel coming down from heaven, lightening the earth with his glory and crying with a strong voice, announcing the sins of Babylon. (Revelation 18:1-4). In connection with his message the call is heard: "Come out of her, My people." These announcements, **UNITING WITH THE THIRD ANGEL'S** message, constitute the final warning to be given to the inhabitants of the earth. GC 604.

3. **WHAT IS THE TIME SETTING FOR THE FOURTH ANGEL'S MESSAGE?**

> These announcements, uniting with the third angel's message, constitute the **THE FINAL WARNING TO BE** [future tense] **given** to the inhabitants of the earth. GC 604.

> Revelation 18:1,2,4. This scripture points FORWARD TO A TIME WHEN the announcement of the fall of Babylon as made by the second angel of Revelation 14 (verse 8), IS TO BE REPEATED.... GC 603.

The above quotations give the **time-setting** for the fourth angel's message as being "forward"—into the future. It will be "the **final** warning" or the last message to the last generation as they near the close of probation.

But why do the second angel and the fourth angel both give the same message? "Babylon is fallen"? Why does the fourth angel of Revelation 18 REPEAT the second angel's message "Babylon is fallen"?

> The second angel's message of Revelation 14 was first preached in the summer of 1844, and it then had a more direct application to the churches of the United States, where the warning of the judgment had been most widely proclaimed and most generally rejected, and where the declension in the churches had been most rapid. But the message of the second angel **did not reach its complete fulfillment in 1844**. The churches then experienced a moral fall, in consequence of their refusal of the light of the advent message; **but that fall was not complete**. As they have continued to reject the special truths for this time they have fallen lower and lower. Not yet, however, can it be said that "Babylon is fallen...because she made **ALL NATIONS** drink of the wine of the wrath of her fornication." **She has not yet made all nations do this**. GC 389.

How will Babylon make "ALL" nations drink of the wrath of her fornication? She has not yet made all nations do this. How will she do it?

> Fearful is the issue to which the world is to be brought. The **POWERS OF EARTH UNITING** to war against the commandments of God, will **decree** that "**all**, both small and great, rich and poor, free and bond" (Revelation 13:16) shall conform to the customs of the church **BY OBSERVANCE OF A FALSE SABBATH**.... The Sabbath will be the great test of loyalty...the final test. GC 604,605.

"The powers of earth uniting" —ALL NATIONS, will legislate a "false sabbath"—they will pass a

UNIVERSAL SUNDAY LAW. This is the **time setting** for the fourth angel's message when the Loud Cry goes out in protest with the message that "Babylon is **completely f**allen for she has made **ALL** nations drink...."

If the Sabbath is the "Great Test" or "**Final** Test" and this is the "**final** warning" to the inhabitants of the earth, this is also the warning that ALL have come toward the close of probation. As the test is given, the decision is recorded in the judgment in heaven, and all receive either the seal of God or the mark of the beast.

Therefore, the fourth angel of Revelation gives this "final warning," adding his power to the proclamation of the third angel regarding the mark of the beast. The fourth angel of Revelation 18 points to the Universal Sunday Law and declares it to be the final or last opportunity before the close of probation. The first angel points to the true seventh-day Sabbath, while the third angel points to the false sabbath as the mark of the beast. The second angel declares apostate religion to be fallen completely and the fourth angel cries out, "Come out her my people." The fourth angel is **timed** and comes on the scene in the power of the "Latter Rain" of the Holy Spirit giving the "Loud Cry."

4. WHAT IS THE TIME SETTING FOR THE FIFTH, SIXTH, AND SEVENTH ANGELS OF REVELATION 14:14-20?

THE FIFTH, SIXTH, AND SEVENTH ANGEL'S MESSAGES

Jesus said,

The HARVEST is the end of the world;.... Matt. 13:39.

The fifth, sixth, and seventh angels' messages are given the **specific time-setting of the HARVEST**—the end of the world, or the last generation which comes to the close of probation.

> And I looked, and behold a white cloud, and upon the cloud one sat like unto the Son of man, having on his head a golden crown, and in his hand a **A SHARP SICKLE**. And another angel [fifth angel] came out of the temple, crying with a LOUD VOICE ["loud cry"] to him that sat on the cloud, Thrust in thy **SICKLE** and **REAP**, for **THE TIME IS COME** [The HOUR is come—Greek Diaglot] for thee to **REAP**; for the **HARVEST** of the earth is **RIPE**. And he that sat on the cloud thrust in his sickle on the earth; and **THE EARTH WAS REAPED**. And another angel [sixth angel] came out of the temple which is in heaven, he also having a **SHARP SICKLE**. And another angel [seventh angel] came out from the altar, which had power over fire; and cried with a loud voice ["loud cry"] to him that had the **SHARP SICKLE**, saying., Thrust in thy **SHARP SICKLE**, and gather the clusters of the vine of the earth; for her grapes are fully **RIPE**. And the angel thrust in his **SICKLE** into the earth, and cast it into the great winepress of the wrath of God. And the wine press was trodden without the city, and the

blood came out of the winepress, even unto the horse bridles, by the space of a thousand and six hundred furlongs [200 miles]. Rev. 14:14-20.

A "sharp sickle" is the instrument by which the harvest is gathered in. It is usually a curved knife by which the grain or the grapes are cut down. This "sharp sickle" is mentioned as being in the hand of Christ (verse 14) and in connection with each of the fifth, sixth, and seventh angels. The time-setting is very clear because the fifth angel announces clearly "the **TIME** is come for thee to reap" (verse 15). In verse 15 the harvest is also declared to be **RIPE**. When a harvest is "ripe" there can be no delay. Verse 16 also declares that "the earth was reaped." Therefore, the harvest is not only ready, but the action is taken and the job is completed!

The context of these three angels of Revelation 14:14-20 is that of the LAST GENERATION, and refers to the "Loud Cry" messages which bring about the close of probation for the righteous and the wicked. This time-setting is the FUTURE closing up of the Investigative Judgment. It is the last and final test and message to be given to seal the 144,000 among god's people, to call out all who will come out of Babylon, and to deliver the wicked to the "wrath of God"—the seven last plagues. This is the **REPEATING** of the three angel's messages of Revelation 14:5-12, but in the power of the Loud Cry and glory of the angel of Revelation 18:1-4.

The Content of the Fifth Angel's Message.

The Fifth Angel's Message is similar to and a repetition of the First Angel' Message, but it has a peculiar application to the closing up of the Investigative Judgment and the close of probation. Notice the similarity of the first and fifth angel's message below:

THE FIRST ANGEL	THE FIFTH ANGEL
"The HOUR	"The TIME [HOUR]
of his judgment	[of the harvest]
[Investigative Judgment]	[Investigative Judgment]
of the dead	of the living
(1844)	
IS COME"	IS COME"
Rev. 14:7	Rev. 14:15

Beginning with those who first lived upon the earth, our Advocate presents the cases of each successive generation and **CLOSES WITH THE LIVING**. GC 483.

The fourth angel which declares that "Babylon is fallen...because she made ALL NATIONS to drink of the wine...." Revelation 14:8 and 18:1-4 **sets the political scene** and provides the **time-setting** for all that follows. As soon as "**ALL** nations" have united in legislation of a Universal Sunday Law, **then** the fifth angel can proclaim his message as to what is about to happen in heaven. While the fourth angel points to that which is happening down here on **earth**, the fifth angel points to that which happens **in heaven**. This is exactly how it was with the first angel's message. As the first angel's message declared that the judgment hour (for the **dead**) had come in 1844, so the fifth angel proclaims that the judgment hour or time for the **living** "IS COME" for the last generation. As the disappointment down here on earth signaled the work going on in heaven, so the Sunday legislation down here on earth will signal that the judgment for the living has begun in heaven.

What will be the result of this fifth angel's message? The Bible says, "the earth was reaped." Revelation 14:16. (But two more reaping angels follow the fifth angel, therefore it is necessary to determine **who is reaped** by this fifth angel). The fifth angel is the first of the three to reap. Therefore he reaps the "first fruits" of the whole harvest. Who are the firstfruits? Let the Bible speak for itself:

> ...a **hundred forty and four thousand**.... These were the redeemed from among men, being the **FIRSTFRUITS** unto God and to the Lamb. Rev. 14:1,4.

In the Hebrew agricultural year there were three harvests:

1. The barley harvest—(Passover—Feast of Unleavened Bread) The BARLEY was the "FIRST FRUITS"
2. The wheat harvest —(Pentecost—Feast of Harvest)
3. The grape harvest —(Day of Atonement—Feast of Tabernacles)

See Exodus 23:14,17,15-17; Exodus 34:22; Leviticus 23:10, 33-44.

The Fifth Angel is TIME oriented

The fifth angel proclaims **"the TIME is come" (the HOUR is come)** for the judgment of the living. On what basis does he make this claim? He builds on the events spoken of by the fourth angel. But there is more. He is time oriented as he proclaims:

1. The three timelines of Daniel 12:7-12
2. The completion of the Jubilee cycles
3. The completion of the 6000 years of probation time

The fifth angel is as time-oriented as was the first angel as his message expanded toward the 1844 period. As the first angel proclaimed, "The hour of his judgment is come" the fifth angel repeats that message with a new emphasis and reinforces his message with current events in the world and Biblical time prophecies, given in the power of the Latter Rain—Loud Cry. He reaps the firstfruits—the 144,000. These come from spiritual Israel—the church.

The 144,000 are selected to do a special work—to give the "Loud Cry" to all the world. They are described as follows:

> ...they were clothed with an armor from their head to their feet. They moved in exact order, like a company of soldiers.... I heard those clothed with armor speak the truth with great power. It had effect.... I asked what had made this great change. An angel answered, "It is the latter rain, the refreshing from the presence of the Lord, the **loud cry** of the third angel." EW 271.

THE SIXTH ANGEL

> And another angel came out of the temple which is in heaven, he also having a sharp sickle. Rev. 14:17.

Just as the first angel's message is repeated by the 5th angel in the Loud Cry, so also, the second and the fourth angel's message is repeated by the 6th angel. Messages 2,4 and 6—are that which has gone on before but with new setting in the Loud Cry and amplification to bring about the final harvest out of Babylon.

> I saw that since the second angel proclaimed the fall of the churches, they have been growing more and more corrupt.... An innumerable host of evil angels are spreading over the whole land and crowding the churches. EW 273,274.

> THE LOUD CRY (Chapter heading).... "I saw another mighty angel [4th Revelation 18:1]...the earth was lightened with his glory....The work of this angel **comes in at the right time to join in the last great work** of the third angel's message **as it swells to a loud cry**. EW 277.

> I heard voices which seemed to sound everywhere, "Come out of her my people, that ye be not partakers of her sins, and that ye receive not of her plagues.... This message seemed to be **an addition** to the third message, joining it as the midnight cry joined the second angel's message in 1844. EW 277.

The midnight cry was the proclamation "Behold, the bridegroom cometh, Go ye out to meet him." This message joined that of the second angel in 1844. Again the 4th angel's message reveals **an additional voice**!

> And I saw another angel come down from heaven.... And he cried mightily with a strong voice, saying, Babylon is fallen.... And I heard **ANOTHER VOICE** from heaven, saying, Come out of her my people. Rev.18:1-4.

"Another voice" which joins that of the fourth angel is that of the sixth angel crying out "Behold, the Bridegroom cometh, Go ye out to meet him."—This is the message of the Song of Solomon—The wedding song, "Behold the Bridegroom cometh, Go ye out to meet him."

This **additional voice** which joins with that of the angels who cry out "Babylon is fallen" is described as follows as it was exhibited before 1844:

> Near the close of the second angel's message [summer of 1844] I saw a great light from heaven shining upon the people of God. The rays of this light seemed bright as the sun. And I heard the voices of angels crying, "Behold, the Bridegroom cometh, go ye out to meet him." 1 SG 140.

By these angel's messages combined with that of the third angel—all given in the LOUD CRY, the second harvest is accomplished. All the righteous in Babylon come out from her and the harvest of the righteous is completed. This is comparable to the second harvest—wheat harvest—in ancient Israel. It was celebrated at the time of Pentecost.

THE SEVENTH ANGEL

These are reaping angels. When probation closes with the 5th and 6th angels' messages, the seventh angel takes over the reaping of the wicked. It is described as follows:

> And another angel came out from the altar [See Revelation 8:3-5—the close of probation] which had power over fire; AND CRIED WITH A LOUD CRY to him that had the sharp sickle, saying, Thrust in thy sharp sickle, and gather the clusters of the vine of the earth; for her grapes are fully ripe. And the angel thrust in his sickle into the earth, and gathered the vine of the earth, and cast it into the great winepress of the wrath of God [seven last plagues]. Rev. 14:18,19.

The message of the third angel and the result of the seventh reaping angel are clearly related, as shown in the diagram below:

THE **THIRD** ANGEL	THE **SEVENTH** ANGEL
with a LOUD VOICE...	cried with a **LOUD CRY**...
tormented with fire	[he] had power over **FIRE**...
the wrath of God....	**the wrath of God**.
[the seven last plagues]	[the seven last plagues]

The three angels' messages are one unit. All three combine and swell into the Loud Cry under the outpouring of the "Latter Rain" of the Holy Spirit. It is given in the power and **timing** of the fourth angel of Revelation 18:1-4. When its work is done, the harvest of the wicked is reaped. The reaping work of the wicked is described in reference to the "sharp sickle" as it gathers the "vine" and throws it away.

> And another angel came out from the altar [See Revelation 8:3-5—the close of probation] he also having a **SHARP SICKLE**. And another angel came out from the altar, which had power over fire, and cried with a loud cry to him that had the **SHARP SICKLE**, saying THRUST IN THY SICKLE and gather the clusters of the vine of the earth; for her grapes are FULLY RIPE. And the angel thrust in his sickle into the earth, and gathered the vine of the earth, and cast it into the great winepress of the wrath of God. Rev. 14:17-19.

The third harvest of the Hebrew agricultural year was the grape harvest and it was celebrated at the time of the Day of Atonement which was a type of the **close of probation.** (All who did not surround the sanctuary and repent were "cut off" Leviticus 16). The sin offerings were burned with FIRE. "...they shall burn in the fire their skins, and their flesh, and their dung." Leviticus 16:27.

When probation closes, the wicked [grapes which are fully ripe] will be reaped and given over to the "wrath of God" which is the seven last plagues. Their second death is referred as "FIRE" and the seventh angel carries the prophecy even to the end of the millennium as follows:

> And the winepress was trodden without the city [outside the walls of the Holy City. See Revelation 20] and blood came out of the winepress, even unto the horse bridles, by the space of a thousand and six hundred furlongs [200 miles]. Rev. 14:20.

This last harvest of the wicked and the grapes in the winepress is also described in the same language in the book of Joel.

> Multitudes, multitudes in the valley of decision: for the day of the Lord is near in the valley of decision. PUT YE IN THE SICKLE AND REAP, FOR THE HARVEST IS RIPE: come get you down, for the press is full, the vats overflow for their wickedness is great. Joel 3:13,14.

The messages of the fourth and fifth angels provide the **time-setting for the proclamation of the three timelines of Daniel 12** as follows:

The fourth angel points to the Universal Sunday Law as the complete fall of Babylon. He points to that legislation which occurs **down here on earth**.

The fifth angel takes the cue from the fourth angel. That which happens down here on earth is the signal for that which occurs simultaneously **up in heaven**—the investigative judgment of the living. The fifth angel declares that "the **time [HOUR]** is come" to reap the firstfruits harvest of the 144,000.

It is the fourth and fifth angels which provide the **timesetting** for the proclamation of the Loud Cry and the detailed information contained in the three timelines of Daniel 12. The timelines merely give supplementary and complementary data.

The 6000 year limit is a time-oriented concept. The millennial Sabbath is soon to begin. The Jubilees are nearing their completion. The timelines of Daniel 12 give their testimony. The seven angels ring out their messages. All these great prophetic components merge at the end of time.

THE CONCLUSION

CONTEMPORARY RECOGNITION OF FULFILLMENT

Perhaps one of the most conspicuous lessons of all prophetic testimony through the years is the contemporary recognition, or interpretation, of each major epoch or event in the prophetic outline **at the very time of fulfillment**.

Your investigator has been brought slowly but irresistibly to the conclusion that prophecy has been progressively understood just as fast as history has fulfilled it, step by step, down through the passing centuries. L. E. Froom: *The Prophetic Faith of our Fathers*. Vol. I, pp. 890, 14.

The seven angels and their messages of Revelation have been right there "in plain sight" all this time! But they have not become "visible" and significant until the present time. Suddenly the reaping angels are brought to view! The concept of "contemporary recognition of fulfillment" places this opening insight at the very threshold of fulfillment!

This generation which recognizes the role of the reaping angels is that very generation which shall see the reaping action take place. We, dear brothers and sisters, are standing in the "endtime" of earth's history. We are just waiting for historical events to fulfill the prophetic messages of these angels—four through seven. Jesus will soon come to our names in judgment and ride down from heaven to receive His people.

THE SEVEN ANGELS' MESSAGES OF REVELATION

Content

TIME SETTING

References
Rev. 14:6,7,8,9-12

FIRST Angel's Message
1833-1844

Everlasting gospel
Fear God. Give glory to Him
THE HOUR OF HIS JUDGMENT IS COME.
(Investigative Judgment began in 1844 for the DEAD)
Worship the Creator: —
(Remember the 7th-day SABBATH)
Receive the SEAL of God.

SECOND Angel's Message
Began summer of 1844

"Babylon is fallen"
"all nations have..."
"not yet complete"
G.C. 389

THIRD Angel's Message
1845 —

If any man worship
1. The BEAST – (Papal Rome)
2. His IMAGE (Apostate Protestantism)
3. or receive His MARK (Sunday – the false sabbath)
4. He will receive the wrath of God (seven last plagues)
He will have the MARK OF THE BEAST
5. FIRE & Brimstone

FOURTH Angel's Message

"Babylon is fallen..."
"ALL NATIONS..."
"earth lightened with the Glory of God..."

"Come out of her, my people" by "another voice" [the Sixth Angel]

[Fourth Angel "unites with the Third Angel and gives power"]

Rev. 18:1-4
G.C. p. 604
Sunday Law Legislation.
THE FINAL TEST Points to the future

"LOUD CRY"

FIFTH Angel's Message
and Reaping Action from the temple

"THE TIME IS COME..."
(Investigative Judgment of the LIVING is come)

First Harvest: **Barley**
First Fruits – 144,000

SIXTH Angel's Message
and Reaping Action from the temple

"earth was reaped"

Second Harvest **Wheat**
Babylon is reaped.

"LOUD CRY"

SEVENTH Angel's Message
and Reaping Action from the altar

4. Receives the wrath of God (seven last plagues)

Third Harvest: **Grapes**
The wicked are reaped destroyed Joel 3:13-16

Rev. 14:14-20
"The SHARP SICKLE"
The Closing of the Judgment Scene.

APPENDIX B

DAILY

One of the greatest puzzles of prophetic exposition is the "daily." Five times in the book of Daniel this "daily" is mentioned: Daniel 8:11-13, 11:31 and 12:11. And in each case in the KJV the word "sacrifice" is added by the translators thus indicated by italics in some Bibles. The word "sacrifice" was not in the Hebrew text. Ellen White indicated that the word "sacrifice" should not be there! She wrote:

> Then I saw in relation to the "daily," Daniel 8:12, that the word "sacrifice" was supplied by man's wisdom, and does not belong to the text...darkness and confusion have followed. EW 74.

The word "daily" (Hebrew "tamiyd," pronounced taw-meed), as used in Numbers and Leviticus, is used to describe the "daily" sacrifices made in the sanctuary services; and is therefore an **adjective** or **adverb**. In that attributive sense it means in English "**continual**." But in the book of Daniel it is used as a **noun**, and should be a "**continuum**." When this is clear, light shines clearly on Daniel 12:11! Why has God permitted this puzzle to remain unsolved through all centuries right up to the last generation? What secret has God hidden from view until needed by those who must face the final conflict and crisis?

In past ages great prophetic expositors (who did not benefit from the counsel of Ellen White) tried to supplement the noun or subject which the "daily" describes. Their efforts are well traced by L. E. Froom in nearly 4000 pages of the four volumes of *The Prophetic Faith of our Fathers*. Let us take a look. These great men understood the "daily" to be:

1. Josephus[*]   100 A.D.   "The continual (daily) sacrifice" (of the Jews)
   Villanova   1297   "The sacrifice of Christ on the cross"
   Olivis   298   "The sacrifice of Christ on the cross"
   Wycliff   1384   "The sacrifice of Christ on the cross"
   Brute   1300   "Christ's sacrifice and priesthood"
2. Ibn Ezra[**] 1092   "Temple sacrifices"
   Obravanel   1437   "Temple sacrifices"

---

[*] *The Prophetic Faith of our Fathers,* Vol. I, pp. 202, 53, 773.

[**] The Prophetic Faith of our Fathers, Vol. II, pp. 58, 78, 79, 213, 230, 304, 306, 309, 493, 502, 535, 571, 577, 582-586, 691, 692, 721, 722, 742. 3. Ibid., Vol III, pp.64, 73, 288, 341, 363, 377, 400, 401, 410, 488, 496, 539, 553, 565, 609, 650, 732, 734-736.

	Amsdorf	1500	"The preaching of the gospel"
	Funck	1566	"The true gospel"
	Ribera	1591	"Temple sacrifices" (ref. to Antiochus)
	Viegas	1599	"The abrogation of the Mass- Eucharist"
	Downham	1634	"True Doctrine and Worship of God according to His Word"
	Tillinghast	1655	"The civil power of the Roman Empire"
	Sherwin	1687	"Civil Rome"
	Beverly	1703	"Transfer from one empire to the next" (unclear)
	Rudd	1757	"Pure worship of God"
	La Flechere	1785	"True worship of God and Jesus"
	Wood	1803	"Divine worship"
	Bell	1796	"True worship"
3.	Huit	1644	"Daily Worship of God in the church"
	Parker	1677	"True Worship"
	Cunninghame	1802	"Worship in the Church"
	Faber	1854	"Praise and Thanksgiving"
	Maitland	1865	"Spiritual Worship"
	Irving	1826	"True Worship" (of the Eastern Churches)
	Mason	1834	"Instituted Worship of God in the churches"
	Bayford	1826	"The Lamb of God in the blood sacrifice"
	Nicole	1874	"Christ's church" and sanctuary services
	Fry	1849	"Civil authority"
	Cooper	1833	"True worship"
	Keyworth	1852	"Mohammedanism"
	Hooper	1829	"Temple sacrifices" taken away 606 B.C.
	Nolan	1864	"Christ's Ministry"
	Bickersteth	1850	"The Jewish economy—nation"— Babylonian captivity. Also a future application applying to Rome
	Tyso	1838	"The Jewish nation and captivity"
	Manning	1892	The Roman Catholic Shrine and Eucharist "taken away" by schism and Protestantism
4.	Cunninghame*	1807	"Justinian (Pagan Rome)"
	Reid	1827	"True worship"

---

* The Prophetic Faith of our Fathers, Vol. IV, pp. 141, 246 255, 32, 728, 732, 748, 1073, 1115, 1118, 1119, 1120, 1121, 1134.

Campbell	1837	"Pagan Rome" (seat, power and authority)
Scott	1810	"Temple of Solomon" site taken away by Mohammedans Himes (chart) 1843 "Pagan Rome"
Miller's Broadside	1843	"Pagan Rome—abomination"
Dowling	1843	"Jewish temple sacrifical system" Rhodes-
Nichols	1850	"Pagan Rome" (civil power) 508 A.D. - 538 A.D.
Arnold	1848	"Jewish sacrifical system"
Crosier	1846	"Ministry of Christ"
U. Smith	1853	"Pagan Rome—Paganism"
Bell	1869	"Paganism"

5. (Contemporary—20th century)

Haskell	1906	"Paganism"
Jones	1905	"Christ's service in heaven"
Bunch	1930	"Christ's ministry in heaven"
SDA (Smith)	1944	"Paganism"—Revised Editions
Ford	1978	"Temple sacrifices (types)

5. 20th century expositors.

Maxwell	1981	"Christ's ministry"
Wheeling	1986	"Perpetual Sabbath"—Covenant
This book	1990	"Scepter of Power"*

---

* Note: The religious background and time in history affected the expositor's conclusions: Jewish expositors saw the "daily" referring to the daily temple sacrifices "taken away" by enemies or Rome. Early Christians saw the "daily" "taken away" as Christ's sacrifice on the cross in 31 A.D. Reformers saw the "daily" to be true worship "taken away" by apostasy. Jesuits saw the "daily" "taken away" as the mass or eucharist removed by the Reformation. By the 17th century some began to see it as civil power taken away from Pagan Rome and absorbed or usurped by Papal Rome.

FROOM CHART ON DAILY #1

Careful analysis of this tabular chart, made by following the lines through, both vertically and horizontally, results in certain inevitable conclusions: (1) There was greater unity of belief among the leaders of the North American Advent Movement than in the Old World Advent Awakening that slightly preceded it. (Cf. tabular charts, Vol. III, pp. 744, 745.) (2) There was startling similarity between the positions of Miller and his associates, and those of many contemporary expositors in both the New World and the Old, including many of the most learned and illustrious interpreters of post-Reformation and Reformation times. There was even striking similarity to certain early church teachings.

The general conclusion seems inescapable that the Millerites did not introduce new and strange interpretations. Every position they held was previously taught by other recognized scholars. They simply revived and unitedly stressed the standard, orthodox positions of past and contemporary writers.

Specifically, they held the standard, established Historical School interpretation of the outline prophecies of Daniel 2, 7, 8, and 11. Their list of the divisions of the Roman fourth empire was what scores, if not hundreds, of others had used. They applied the composite prophetic symbols of Antichrist to the Papacy—Antichrist, Man of sin, Son of Perdition, Mystery of Iniquity, Little Horn, Beast, Babylon, and Harlot. They were supported by hundreds of predecessors in applying the year-day principle to all the prophetic time periods of Daniel—the 1260, 1290, 1335, and 2300 year-days.

They had been anticipated by scores in the Old World and in the New in recognizing the 70 weeks of years as the first part of the 2300 years, cut off for the Jews and beginning synchronously with the longer period in 457 B.C. The chief variance was the nature of the event expected to occur at the end of the 2300 years. Many liberals fondly expected their terminal point to mark the ushering in of a thousand years of spiritual triumph, world conversion, and universal peace, before the second advent.

But scores upon scores of expositors across the years had held that the 2300 years would lead to the second advent, just as the Millerites universally believed. Like most interpreters before them, the Millerites first placed the cross in A.D. 33, at the end of the seventieth week. But others had likewise anticipated their later revised position in the "midst" of the prophetic "week," in A.D. 31.

There was an unparalleled uniformity in the Millerite dating of the 1260, 1290, and 1335 years. But here again there were numerous antecedents for each position. And the "Seven Times" of the Gentiles had been widely taught in the Old World Advent Awakening, as from 677 B.C. to 1843/4.

It is therefore to be logically concluded that the basic positions on prophecy held by the Millerites were not in any sense original with them. Nor were they revolutionary or fanciful innovations, but they stood in the line of that honored and respected company of predecessors of high standing and orthodoxy in the various historic communions.

her years, who, with her parents, had been disfellowshiped from the Methodist Church because of espousing the second advent views of the Millerites, had begun to display a singular spiritual activity. Her influence, establishing confidence in God's past leadership, and in His future guidance in the Advent Movement, began to be felt by a sizable group around Portland, Maine. In time these three groups and teachings united.

FROOM CHART ON DAILY #2

More study was given by the Sabbatarian Adventists to the book of Revelation than had been the case with the Millerites. Painstaking consideration was given to all its component prophecies—the seven churches, seals, trumpets, witnesses, and the earthquake, the symbolic women, beasts, angelic messengers, and vials, Babylon and its fall, the millennium and the new earth. But this was more for the perfecting and revision of detail, as the rugged outlines had been built up through the centuries.

The area of special study and development was Revelation 13 to 17, and more particularly the specifications embraced in the third angel's message. These involved the identity of the second as well as the first beast, the image, mark, number, and name, the time of the plagues, and the duration of the torment. In the matter of the millennium the location of the saints during the thousand years had special consideration, and aspects of the new heaven and new earth. Theirs was basically a reaffirmation of the clearly established positions of the centuries, and now the related end events of the several prophecies all climaxing in the last days. They strove for a consistent and harmonious understanding of the whole.

Unlike the composite positions of any previous period or group of expositors, there was virtually no variance of belief on the fundamental points of all major aspects of Daniel, as is evident from a scrutiny of this tabular listing of the positions of the Sabbatarian Adventists. Upon careful review, the interpretation of Daniel was taken over almost intact from the final positions of the scholarly Millerite writers in the seventh-month phase of the movement. That involved the culmination of Daniel's grand time of time in the autumn of 1844, instead of within the Jewish sacred year "1843." And all related or consequent changes were made accordingly.

A few explanations will clarify: The general abbreviations are essentially the same, but "H-V-O" under the "3 Horns" of Daniel 7, stands for "Heruli, Vandals, Ostrogoths." No page on the text is cited, as these positions are often gathered from various pages, and details on the chart are frequently from supplemental writings—books, pamphlets, periodicals, and occasionally a manuscript. Differences were minor—whether the "daily" be paganism, or the high priestly ministry of Christ; and whether the king of the north of Daniel 11:45, be the Papacy or Turkey. On essentials there was unity.

NELLIE HICKEY LETTER FROM WHITE ESTATE

Ellen G. White Estate, Inc.
Proprietor of
ELLEN G. WHITE PUBLICATIONS

EGW

General Conference
of Seventh-day Adventists
6840 Eastern Avenue, NW
Washington, D.C. 20012

January 8, 1987

Ms. Nellie Hickey
Route 1, Box 122
Hardinsburg, IN 47125

Dear Sister Hickey:

Thank you for your recent letter to our office. The passage in Early Writings to which you refer is found on pages 74 and 75. Ellen White makes the statement there that "the Lord gave the correct view of it [the daily] to those who gave the judgment hour cry." I do not believe she ever singled out O. R. L. Crosier concerning his views on the daily, but rather, the consensus of opinions held by those giving the first angel's message in 1843-1844.

I have enclosed a photocopy from L. F. Froom's Prophetic Faith of Our Fathers, Vol. 4, that gives the interpretations of the principal Millerite leaders, and you will readily see that the consensus was that it represented Roman paganism.

In view of the fact that Ellen White later stated that she had no light on the correct interpretation of the "daily" (see The Later Elmshaven Years, chapter 19), many understand this Early Writings statement to refer to the danger of time-setting, that this is the thrust of her vision, rather than a specific view or interpretation of the daily. At least her statement in 1910, now in Selected Messages, book 1, p. 164, suggests that she did not feel the question should be decided by any reference to her writings.

If we can be of any further help to you on this matter, please let us know.

Sincerely yours,

Tim Poirier
Assistant to the Secretary

TP:ldl
Enclosure

THE "DAILY" AND "THE MINISTRY OF CHRIST"

General Objectives: To establish the concept that the "Daily" of Daniel 8-12 cannot refer to the ministry of Christ.

Specific Objectives:

1. To define "the ministry of Christ"
   a. The "wider ministry of Christ"
   b. The mediatorial ministry of Christ
2. To link the mediatorial ministry of Christ with sacrificial atonement
3. To recognize the objection to sacrificial ministry as linked with the "Daily"
4. To recognize the problems encountered when the ministry of Christ is linked to the "Daily" of Daniel.

POSITION No. 1. **Christ has a "Wider Ministry which is NOT "taken away" at the close of probation.**

Christ does have a "wider ministry"—wider than His mediatorial role—as defined by Ellen G. White and referenced by the Word of God as follows:

> So in the heavenly courts, in His ministry for all created beings: through the beloved Son, the Father's life flows out to all; through the Son it returns, in praise and joyous service, a tide of love, to the great Source of all. And thus through Christ the circuit of beneficence is complete, representing the character of the great Giver, the law of life. DA 21.

Christ's "wider ministry" for all created beings is everlasting. This "wider ministry" is described in Scripture in His many offices and roles as follows: Creator (Col. 1:16), Sustainer (Col.1:17), Lifegiver (Jn. 5:21-26, 11:25), The Word (Jn. 1:1-4), Covenant-Maker (Gen. 3:15), Communicator (DA 21), Son of God (Heb. 1), Son of man (Matt. 1), Servant-Minister (Phil. 2:5-8) and Sacrificial Lamb (Rev. 1).

From the foundation of the world, He has been the Sin-bearer, stepping into this ministry at the fall of man. Not until the great controversy is ended and when the entire universe is clean, will His role in meeting the challenge of sin be removed.

THEREFORE: The "wider ministry" of Christ will not cease at the close of probation. This "wider ministry" of Christ, as defined above, is not the "Daily" of the book of Daniel which will be "taken away" at the close of probation.

POSITION No. 2. **Christ has the role of ministry as MEDIATOR—HIGH PRIEST which He now fills in the Most Holy Place, during the Antitypical Day of Atonement, which will cease at the Close of Probation.**

The following quotations reveal those roles of ministry which will cease when Christ leaves the Most Holy Place and completes the work of the Investigative Judgment:

> And He saw that there was no man, and wondered that there was no **INTERCESSOR**. Isa. 59:16.

> When He leaves the sanctuary, darkness covers the inhabitants of the earth. In that fearful time the righteous must live in the sight of a holy God without an **INTERCESSOR**. GC 614.
>
> I also saw that many do not realize what they must be in order to live in the sight of the Lord without a **HIGH PRIEST** in the sanctuary in the time of trouble. EW 71.
>
> But there will be no...**MEDIATOR** to plead their cause before the Father. EW 280.
>
> ...now there was **NO ATONING BLOOD** to cleanse the guilty, no compassionate Saviour to plead for them. EW 281.

The above statements reveal that the specific roles of Christ which will cease at the close of probation are: Intercessor, High Priest, and Mediator AND that these roles, when finished, will be such that there will be "no atoning blood" applied for God's people.

These roles of "intercessor"—"high priest" and mediator" are a part of the applied blood sacrifice for sin. When one ceases the other also ceases.

THEREFORE: It is not a "wider ministry" of Christ which will cease at the close of probation but these specific roles as enumerated above, which are involved in an application of the atoning blood sacrifice.

POSITION No. 3. The role of Intercessor-Mediator and High Priest is validated only by the Atoning Blood Sacrifice.

The book of Hebrews defines the validity of the role of Christ as our High Priest and Mediator, only as specifically based upon His atoning blood sacrifice:

> For every high priest taken from among men is ordained for men in things pertaining to God, that he may offer both gifts and **sacrifices** for sins. Heb. 5:1.
>
> "A **MINISTER** of the sanctuary, and of the true tabernacle.... For every high priest is ordained to offer gifts and **SACRIFICES wherefore it is of necessity that this man have somewhat to offer.** Heb. 8:2,3.[*]
>
> ...into the second [Most Holy place] went the high priest alone once every year, NOT WITHOUT BLOOD.... Heb. 9:7.
>
> How much more shall the blood of Christ who through the eternal spirit OFFERED HIMSELF without spot to God.... **And for this cause he is THE MEDIATOR.** Heb. 9:14,15.

The ministry of Christ as High Priest, Intercessor and Mediator in the antitypical "Day of Atonement"—"Cleansing of the Sanctuary" is connected inseparably with His blood **sacrifice** on Calvary. During the entire Investigative Judgment, Christ's ministry as Mediator is that of

---

[*] NOTE: The Daniel 8:14 2300 day-year prophecy marks the beginning of the "**cleansing**" of the sanctuary." This "cleaning" is accomplished by an application of Christ's Calvary "atoning blood" sacrifice. This blood sacrifice enables Christ to make atonement for sin in a legal procedure which, name by name, gathers each individual into His kingdom. This second phase of atonement is called the antitypical "Day of Atonement." Atonement is performed only by spilling or application of blood sacrifice. Christ's ministry in application of the atoning blood sacrifice will cease at the close of probation.

making an application of His atoning blood offered on Calvary. At the close of probation there will no longer be "atoning blood" applied. (See EW 281,282).

POSITION No. 4. **The ministry of Christ as High Priest- Mediator is validated by His atoning blood SACRIFICE. The Lord, through His prophet, declares that the word [concept] of "sacrifice" may not be linked to the "Daily" which is "taken away" of Daniel.**

The Lord, through His messenger, has informed us that the word or concept of "sacrifice" (and all that has to do with or connected with "sacrifice") has nothing to do with the "daily" which is "taken away" in the book of Daniel. She also declares that such teachings bring in "darkness and confusion." See the following warning:

> Then **I saw** in relation to the "daily" [Daniel 8:12] that **the word "sacrifice,"** was supplied by man's wisdom, and **does not belong to the text**, and that the Lord gave the correct view of it to those who gave the judgment hour cry. When union existed before 1844, nearly all were united on the correct view of the "daily"; but in the confusion since, 1844, other views have been embraced, and darkness and confusion have followed. EW 74, 75.

The "Atonement" is accomplished in two phases: First, Christ spilled His blood on Calvary; then in 1844 He began the antitypical "Day of Atonement" to apply that blood sacrifice in His **MINISTRY** as High Priest-Mediator- Intercessor. Ellen G. White "**was shown**" two things:

1. When the antitypical "Day of Atonement" comes to its end in the heavenly sanctuary and when Christ's work there is ended, there will be no more "atoning blood" sacrifice applied. (EW 281).
2. The word (words stand for concepts)—entire concept of "sacrifice"—does not belong to the texts which have to do with the "daily" of Daniel which are "taken away." She also saw that to violate this principle is to bring in darkness and confusion.

THEREFORE: Whatever ministry of Christ that is connected to, or bears significance to the concept of sacrifice—atoning blood sacrifice—must not be connected to the "daily" of Daniel.

The "daily" of Daniel which is "taken away" has nothing to do with:

1. The wider ministry of Christ
2. The specific Mediatorial ministry of Christ, 1844 onward
3. The Investigative Judgment—Day of Atonement
4. The Close of Probation

POSITION No. 5. **To assume that the "daily" "taken away" in Daniel refers to the ministry of Christ, initiates confusion.**

A. **The Imperative of Consistent Interpretation**

The "daily" "taken away" is mentioned in five verses of Daniel: Daniel 8:11, 8:12, 8:13, 11:31 and 12:11.

If the "daily" of Daniel 12:11 refers to the ministry of Christ literally "taken away" **in heaven**, then to be consistent the "daily" "taken away" in all the previous verses should refer to the same thing.

However, historicist prophetic expositors understand Daniel 8:9-13 and 11:31 to refer to the historical rise of the Papacy and its 1260 years of Papal Supremacy over Europe. It is a DESCRIPTION of the rise of the "little horn" power (Daniel 8:9-13). This passage is a description of the political scene as a religio-political power takes control.

While it is true that the Papacy substituted a counterfeit human ministry down here on earth (as many other false religions had done previously) this action did **not bring Christ's ministry to a close in heaven**. The literal FACT is that the "daily" "taken away" in Daniel 8 did not bring to an end Christ's ministry in heaven back then, nor would it do so in the future.

B. **The Imperative of OBVIOUS fulfillment of prophetic timelines**

The "daily" "taken away" of Daniel 12:11 is connected to a timeline. Timelines, to be of any value, must have **OBVIOUS** points of beginning and endings. A timeline which would begin with some event which could not be observed on earth, would be of "no earthly value"!

God's people have been warned by the Lord, through His messenger, Ellen G. White, that we cannot know the time for the close of probation. We cannot know the time for the close of Christ's ministry in the Most Holy Place. If we cannot know it, it would be impossible for it to be a marker for God's people in regard to the timeline in which it is couched.

> And from the time that the daily sacrifice shall be taken away, and the abomination that maketh desolate set up, shall be a thousand two hundred and ninety days. Dan. 12:11.

The 1290 days timeline cannot begin nor end with an invisible action which occurs in heaven of which God's people can have no knowledge! Prophetic timelines are given as a light to guide the feet of God's people through times of crisis. The 1290 days timeline must begin with an obvious action down here on earth, which can be observed by the people of God. Prophecy is not given for God's benefit—but for the instruction of the saints!

The "daily" "taken away" of Daniel 12:11 must pertain to an event which occurs down here on earth and one which will be visible to all—to the whole world. It would be well to look at the precedent "VOICES" or legislative actions of timelines which have occurred in the past, and of this timeline prophecy. (Daniel 12:11).

C. **The Imperative of Sequential Action**

The timeline prophecy of Daniel 12:11 links two actions:

1. "The daily taken away," and
2. The abomination that maketh desolate set up (established)

It appears that the first occurs so that the second can be accomplished:

> The clause may be translated literally, "and from the time of the taking away of the continual (daily), **even in order to set up** the abomination." This would indicate that the "taking away" was done with the direct intent of setting up the abomination. 4BC 880.

If the "daily" "taken away" were to refer to the ministry of Christ, then it would be said that the ministry of Christ would be taken away or the close of probation would occur **before** the abomination is set up. Yet it is the oppression of the abomination power which brings about the final test by which men will be judged. This puts the "cart before the horse." It brings about "darkness and confusion."

POSITION No. 6. MODERN PROPHETIC EXPOSITORS NEED TO ALIGN THEIR VIEW OF THE "DAILY" WITH THAT OF THE PIONEERS THAT THE UNITY WHICH THEY HAD MAY EXTEND TO THE PRESENT.

> ...the Lord gave the correct view of it to those who gave the judgment hour cry. When union existed before 1844, nearly all were united on the correct view of the "daily";.... EW 74, 75.

For nearly two thousand years various theologians had assumed that the "daily" referred to the ministry of Christ. They perceived it as His ministry here on earth, or his ministry in the intercessory priesthood, or the doctrine of his ministry. However, those who gave the judgment hour cry before 1844 were given the "**correct view**" and "nearly all" were united on it. They abandoned the assumptions of nearly two millennia, and perceived that this "daily" referred, not to Christ's ministry, but to a transfer of the scepter of power, seat, and authority from pagan to Papal Rome.

By this "correct view" they traced in Daniel 8 the rise of the Papacy (538-1798) and interpreted the 1260 years—"time, times and a half" of persecution and Papal supremacy. In 1798, "those who gave the judgment hour cry" saw the Pope taken from his throne! They focused their prophetic vision upon events occurring in their own day! By this "current event" they made application to the "daily" "taken away" in Daniel 8 to the transfer of power in 538 and ending in 1798.

It is this comprehension of the meaning of Daniel 8 and the rise and reign of the "little horn" Papacy which is the basis of the third angel's warning of Revelation 14. It is the platform of the warning of future events found in Revelation 13! This view of the "daily" ties the past to the future!

The pioneers did not prepare and leave for us a theological rationale on the "daily." Unfortunately they abbreviated their concept of a transfer of power, seat and authority from pagan to Papal Rome to one word: "Paganism" taken away. However, there are many sources by which we may understand their position:

1. Early articles by James White
2. Ministers's Manuals by Loughborough
3. *Daniel and the Revelation* by Uriah Smith
4. Statements in *Early Writings*
5. *Great Controversy* statements on past and future Papal Reign

The Daniel 8 reference to the "daily" "taken away" referred to Papal Reign in the past. Daniel 12 "daily" "taken away" refers to Papal Reign in the future. It is part of the third angel's warning message of past and future import. Just as the "daily" "taken away" established the first Papal Supremacy in 538 (as described in Daniel 8) the "daily" "taken away" in Daniel 12:11 will establish the next Papal Supremacy in the future (See Revelation 13). On this we need to be united as were the pioneers in their day.

The encyclicals of John Paul II urging the world to unite in observance of the false Sabbath, the revelation of the goals of the Papacy in "The Keys of This Blood" by Malachi Martin for John Paul II to become the head of the New World Order, the plans to initiate the new millenium with celebrations in Jerusalem in the year 2000, and the increasing apparitions of Mary around the world, reveal the nearness of prophetic fulfillment of Revelation 13 and Daniel 12.

SUMMARY

1. The "wider ministry" of Christ for all created beings is everlasting. It does not cease at the close of probation.
2. The "wider ministry" of Christ is not the "daily" "taken away" in Daniel 8 and 12.
3. Christ's mediatorial-high-priest-intercessory ministry is validated by the blood sacrifice in 31 A.D.
4. At the close of probation "atoning blood" will no longer be applied.
5. The concept of "atoning blood sacrifice" and ministry connected with it is not the "daily" "taken away" of Daniel 8 and 12. (The prophet warned against this line of reasoning).
6. The "daily" "taken away" was perceived in "correct view" as given by the Lord to the pre-1844 pioneers of the Great Advent Movement.
7. Pioneers of Adventism viewed the "daily" "taken away" as a transfer of the scepter of power from pagan to Papal Rome.
8. Pioneers of Adventism abandoned the view that the "daily" "taken away" referred to Christ's ministry.
9. Pioneers of Adventism were in unity and established their views in numerous publications that the "daily" taken away" referred to the establishment of the Papacy in 538 A.D.
10. The "daily" "taken away" in Daniel 8 describes the establishment of Papal Supremacy in the past (538- 1798).
11. The "daily" "taken away" in Daniel 12 describes the establishment of Papal Rome Supremacy in the future.
12. The "daily" "taken away" in Daniel 8 is the basis and beginning of the third angel's warning and the fulfillment of Revelation 13. Daniel 12 simply extends the concept to a future similar fulfillment.
13. The "daily" "taken away" in Daniel 8 and 12 must receive consistent, logical application.
14. The "daily" "taken away" in Daniel 12 does not apply to the close of probation—an event which cannot be observed, but applies to a transfer of power, seat and authority to establish or set up a future Papal Reign. This observable event begins the 1290 days timeline of Daniel 12:11.

Ellen G. White Publications Office Document, Q. and A. 4-D-4

Subject: *EARLY WRITINGS* REFERENCE TO 1844, "CORRECT VIEW" OF "THE DAILY"

Prepared by: Arthur L. White

In your inquiry you refer to the statement found in Early Writings, pages 74 and 75, which speaks of the "daily," and you ask if there are any articles now extant that would enlighten us on just what that "correct" view was. I wish the question of the identity of the "daily" could be settled by merely digging up some old articles, but it cannot be disposed of so easily. All through our experience there have been divergent views in regard to just what was referred to in the "daily." This was true also in the Miller movement preceding the Seventh-day Adventist movement. We find that what is sometimes referred to as *the "new view" is, if anything, the older of the two*. See Crozier's article on the sanctuary in *Facsmilies of the Two Earliest S.D.A. Periodicals*, "Advent Review," No. 3, p. 43.

There have been times when there has been some agitation over this question. I am happy that there is not much general agitation at the present time. From time to time there have been those who have endeavored to buttress their views by this statement from *Early Writings*.

In 1910 Mrs. White wrote two communications to our brethren who were agitating this question, and she forbade their using her writings to sustain their arguments, for she said: "I have no instruction on the point under discussion and I see no need for the controversy." You may be interested in reading these two statements found in *Selected Messages*, Book I, pages 164-168.

When this controversy was raging one leading worker reproduced the old 1843 chart, and at the bottom printed this statement from *Early Writings*. Mrs. White forbade his using the statement in that connection, and so he pasted a piece of paper over the statement. We have one of these charts in our possession.

The question naturally arises then, To what did Mrs. White refer in her statement on pages 74-75 of *Early Writings* when she speaks of the "daily." I think this is partially answered when one reads the statement in its setting. You will observe that she is writing about the 2300-day period and its termination in 1844. She speaks of the chart and then she says that the word "sacrifice" has been supplied. After referring to the unity which existed before 1844 on the question, she speaks of the confusion since that time and specifically states that time has not been a test since 1844 and will never again be a test. This places the reference to the question of the "daily" in a time-setting element. The statement doesn't carry as much significance to us today as it did to those who read this from Ellen White's pen when it was first written, for at that time, among the Adventists who failed to accept the third angel's message, there were many who were setting time from year to year. They disclaimed confidence in the integrity of the 1844 termination of the 2300 days and felt around for new periods which would terminate just a little later. In this endeavor new times were fixed, based upon the "daily sacrifice" of the Jews, one of which placed its commencement at 446 B.C. and thus carried the time span to 1854. I have before me as I write, one such chart. (See chart on page 257). Thus the setting of the new time was very definitely based upon the word "sacrifice" as used in Dan. 8:11-13. See the rough reproduction of the chart attached.

When Mrs. White was shown that the word "sacrifice" was a supplied word and not a part of the original, it knocked the pins entirely out from under the arguments of the First-day Adventist in their setting of the new time.

Along about 1910 Elder Daniells, accompanied by Elder W. C. White and C. C. Crisler, went to Mrs. White with this statement from *Early Writings* and endeavored to seek from her some information as to just what she had in mind—something which would settle this question of the "daily," and I quote here from Elder Daniells' account of this interview, as written in a letter to Elder W. C. White.

> When we were having some controversy regarding what we called the "daily" of Dan. 8:9-14, those who argued for the old view claimed that it was supported by the following statement on page 74 of *Early Writings* (statement quoted).
>
> I first read to Sister White the statement given above in *Early Writings*. Then I placed before her our prophetic chart used by our ministers in expounding the prophecies of Daniel and the Revelation. I called her attention to the picture of the Sanctuary and also to the 2300-year period as they appeared on the chart.
>
> I then asked if she could recall what was shown her regarding this subject.
>
> As I recall her answer she began by telling how some of the leaders who had been in the 1844 movement endeavored to find new dates for the termination of the 2300-year period. This endeavor was to fix new dates for the coming of the Lord. This was causing confusion among those who had been in the Advent Movement.
>
> In this confusion the Lord revealed to her, she said, that the view that had been held and presented regarding the dates was correct, and that there must never be another time set, nor another time message.
>
> I then asked her to tell what had been revealed to her about the rest of the "daily," the Prince, the host, the taking away of the "daily" and the casting down of the sanctuary.
>
> She replied that these features were not placed before her in vision as the time part was. She would not be led out to make an explanation of those points of the prophecy.
>
> The interview made a deep impression on my mind. Without hesitation she talked freely, clearly, and at length about the 2300-year period, but regarding the other part of the prophecy she was silent.
>
> The only conclusion I could draw from her free explanation of the time and her silence as to the taking away of the "daily" and the casting down of the sanctuary was that the vision given her was regarding the time, and that she received no explanation as to the other parts of the prophecy.—A.G. Daniells' Letter to W. C. White, Sept. 25, 1931.

From this as well as the other evidence I have presented it seems that Mrs. White was not given light on the question of the identity of the "daily," and it is therefore a question which must be settled entirely on the basis of earnest Bible study but we should guard against its becoming a point of issue by sincere Bible students.

I would direct your attention to rather secondary evidence which appears in *Great Controversy*, page 65 of the trade edition. You will notice that in lines four and five she speaks of *truth* being *cast down* to the ground by *the papal power*, and refers to the prophecy which, of course, is Dan. 8:12. We could not take this as settling the question, but it is of interest in connection with the study of this point.

Washington 12, D.C. December 15, 1959

PROPHECY'S PLACE IN THE MASTER PLAN OF GOD—PAST, AND FUTURE

Prophecy is a beacon light through the ages calling men and women from apostasy. Prophecy sustained the early Christian martyrs as they recognized God's controlling hand over the nations. It nerved the Waldenses to withstand Rome and lit the flaming torch of Wyclif in Britain and the Hussites in Bohemia. It was invoked by Luther when he defied Rome, as he declared the identity of Antichrist in contrast to the Christ of Scripture. Adventist pioneers believed it would enlighten the multitude of God's children still entangled in the subtleties of modern apostasy. They believed that the most marked guidance of prophecy would yet be experienced just before the world's final crisis. They held that prophecy shows where mankind has come from, just where he is now in the stream of time, and where under God he is going. It is the luminous torch in the hands of faithful heralds of the everlasting gospel that will enlighten man in his final march toward the kingdom of God.

Man's honest attempts at prophetic interpretation have been but the record of his quest for a sound understanding of prophetic truth and principle. Its fulfillment has been recognized as progressive over the centuries. It has unfolded slowly to the minds of men, in proportion as history has fulfilled each succeeding epoch or major event of prophecy. Standing on this firm platform, men are in position to recognize those remaining portions that are rapidly taking shape before their eyes.

As fast and as far as history has fulfilled the succeeding segments in the master outline of prophecy, men have been able to recognize with certainty the actul fulfillments as they have taken place; thus they grasp the vast prophetic panorama of the ages. And it is simply the extension of this same perception and confidence that they are to hold today toward the final phases of prophecy now about to take place before the eyes of the world.

Prophecy therefore adds meaning and depth to all doctrine and life. It brings the baffling events of history into sharp perspective. It draws aside the curtain, so man can see the hand of God and the outworking of the great controversy behind many otherwise baffling events, enabling him to glimpse the larger meaning of it all. It draws a master portrait of God's redemptive love for a lost race.

Prophecy gives light in the darkness of time's last hour. The darksome path of history, through prophecy and fulfillments discloses the principle of God's dealing with nations as well as with individuals. It is a rainbow of promise, painted by the finger of God. It gives assurance of coming deliverance from the final cataclysm of the ages now bearing down upon the world. Rightly understood, it results in ever-radiant optisism. It assures mankind that the Paradise of Eden is soon to be restored, and that sin will not rise up a second time. Nothing short of this can prepare God's people for their final deliverance. That is the recognized challenge of prophecy for time's last hour. That was the faith of Sabbatarian Adventists.

HOW DOES SATAN ATTEMPT TO SEIZE THE "DAILY" (SCEPTER OF POWER, SEAT, AND AUTHORITY)?

INTRODUCTION

The description of Satan in the prophetic symbolism of Revelation 12 pictures him as, "a great red dragon," and "having seven heads and...seven crowns upon his heads." Revelation 12:3. These "crowns" reveal Satan's determination to rule—to be a king over a kingdom, and to wear the crown and hold in his hand the "daily"—scepter of power, seat and authority.

> Satan's agents are constantly working under his direction to establish his authority and build up his kingdom.... GC 507.

The seven heads of the great red dragon and their seven crowns represent a sequence of seven attempts of Satan to establish his kingdom: past, present and future. (The number seven is symbolic representing completeness—or a complete sequence in time from his rebellion in heaven until he will be destroyed in the lake of fire at the end of the millennium.)

The seven "heads" are also symbolic. The Bible provides its own key to interpret the "heads." The **two** keys, which interpret the symbol of "heads" are found in Revelation 17:9,10; and Daniel 2:35,44.

In Revelation 17:9,10, the first "key" states that: "The seven heads are seven mountains." But a "mountain" is also a prophetic symbol and we therefore need a second "key" to unlock this combination lock! The second "key" is found in Daniel 2:35 in which Nebuchadnezzar (and Daniel) saw a symbolic mountain. Daniel explained in Daniel 2:35,44 that this symbolic mountain represents a kingdom—God's kingdom.

> ...the stone that smote the image became a great **mountain**,.... Dan. 2:35. And in the days of these kings shall the God of heaven set up a **kingdom**. Dan. 2:44.

Therefore we understand that **a symbolic "head" is the same as a symbolic "mountain"**—both of which represent literal kingdoms. The entire focus of the great controversy between Christ and Satan is over the possession of the kingdom! Who shall hold the "daily"—scepter of power!

In Revelation 17:9,10, the concept that "heads" and "mountains" both represent kingdoms is reinforced by the following verse where it reiterates or reinforces the concept by repetition saying that:

> The seven **heads** are seven **mountains**.... And there are seven **kings**:.... Rev. 17:9,10.

It is characteristic of prophetic symbolism to repeat at least twice—the interpretive concept—to give assurance of correct interpretation. (Seven kings would of course represent kingdoms). While it is true that the Revelation 17:9,10 verses provide a key verse to interpret the seven heads of the beast of Revelation 13 that same key verse will also unlock the symbolic "heads" of the great red dragon.

This study is a study of the seven heads of the great red dragon and those seven crowns or attempts to grasp the "daily"—scepter of power in the past, as well as its endtime efforts as the time comes for Jesus to return, and at last in the future as Satan seeks to wrest the Holy City at the end of the millennium.

Not until these seven heads are fully understood, can the Daniel 12:11 timeline of the 1290 days be understood clearly. Therefore this study is an explanation of Satan's seven attempts to take the kingdom—a study of the seven heads of the great red dragon.

This study gives answer to the following questions regarding the seven heads of the great red dragon of Revelation 12:

1. What is represented by the first head?
2. What is represented by the second head?

3. What is represented by the third head?
4. What is represented by the fourth head?
5. What is represented by the fifth head?
6. What is represented by the sixth head?
7. What is represented by the seventh head?
8. What relationship exists between the seven heads and the Daniel 12 timelines?
9. Summary

Part 1. **WHAT IS HEAD NO. 1 OF THE GREAT RED DRAGON?**

Satan's first attempt to seize the "daily"—scepter of power, seat and authority, was in heaven, when he established a rebellion and gained control over certain of the angels. This is one of the first concepts established in Revelation 12 concerning his long career.

> And his tail drew a third part of the stars of heaven, and did cast them to the earth.... And the great dragon was cast out...into the earth, and his angels with him. Rev. 12:4-9.

> Satan...is a mighty general who controls the minds of evil angels.... GC 507.

Part 2. **WHAT IS HEAD NO. 2?**

Satan's second attempt to seize the "daily"—scepter occurred in the Garden of Eden. By virtue of creation the earth belonged to God. He gave this dominion of the earth over to Adam. (Genesis 1:26). When Adam, through sin, placed himself under Satan's control, he submitted the dominion of the earth into Satan's possession. "Legally"—the usurper gained dominion or the scepter of power and authority of this earth and he appeared at heavenly councils as its representative. (See Job 1). There he declared himself to be the "god of this world," or the "prince of this world." He protested the plan of salvation to the universe, claiming every human being to be his lawful captive. He complained bitterly when any soul was rescued from his grasp. The contest was over every human soul—whether it should be in Satan's dominion or in the kingdom of Christ.

Satan's dominion prospered so that in the days of Noah, only eight persons retained integrity to God and entered the ark. It was Satan's intention to blot out the people of God from the entire earth—to establish a universal dominion, and thereby secure the earth as his planet for eternity. But God saved the human race just in the nick of time—by sending the flood which destroyed Satan's kingdom entirely as it existed prior to the flood.

Part 3. **WHAT IS HEAD NO. 3?**

Satan's third attempt to seize the "daily"—scepter began shortly after the flood in the plains of Shinar and the tower of Babel.

> For a time, the descendants of Noah continued to dwell among the mountains where the ark rested. As their numbers increased apostasy soon led to division. Those who desired to forget their Creator and to cast off the restraints of His law...journeyed to the plain of Shinar.... Here they decided to build a city, and a tower...to found a **monarchy [dominion]** that should eventually embrace the whole earth. Thus their city would become the metropolis of a **universal empire**.... PP 118,119.

But God did not intend that Babel should so quickly bring the whole earth under Satan's rulership. God separated the nations by confusion of tongues and in this way Satan's purpose was thwarted. (See Genesis 11).

The land of Shinar with its tower of Babel emerged at last as the great Babylonian empire, which gained universal dominion in the then known civilized world surrounding the people of God. But this earthly empire rose and fell. It reached its climax under Satan's strategy when it took captive God's people, the Jews, in 606 B.C., with the intent and purpose that they should be obliterated, swallowed up and lost in Babylon. But God delivered them and took them back to their homeland where they rebuilt the temple and the city in Jerusalem. Therefore the third head of the dragon was also thwarted by God and failed of its intended purpose.

Part 4. WHAT IS THE FOURTH HEAD?

Satan's fourth attempt to seize the "daily"—scepter of power, seat and authority was to take the King Himself. If the King could be captured the kingdom was assured. The life of Jesus here on earth was a long struggle for the "daily" scepter of power. Satan attempted to get the kingdom during the forty days temptation in the wilderness.

> Again, the devil taketh him up into an exceeding high mountain, and sheweth him all the kingdoms of the world, and the glory of them; And saith unto him, All these things will I give thee if thou wilt fall down and worship me. Matt. 4:8,9.

And the crucifixion was the last great effort on Satan's part. This battle for the "daily" scepter was described as follows:

> Now the tempter had come for the last fearful struggle. For this he had been preparing during the three years of Christ's ministry. Everything was at stake with him. If he failed here, his hope of mastery was lost; the kingdoms of the world would finally become Christ's; he himself would be overthrown and cast out.

> But if Christ could be overcome, the earth would be Satan's kingdom, and the human race would forever be in his power. With this issue of the conflict before Him, Christ's soul was filled with dread of separation from God. Satan told him that if He became the surety for the sinful world, the separation would be eternal, He would be identified with Satan's kingdom, and would nevermore be one with God. DA 687.

But this fourth head attempt to seize the scepter also ended with failure. At the resurrection, Jesus arose triumphant with His kingdom assured.

Part 5. WHAT WAS THE FIFTH HEAD OF THE DRAGON?

After the resurrection, the Christian church was established. God's people inhabited Europe for the next 1900 years. Satan determined to size the "daily"- scepter of power of the governments of Europe and set up a counterfeit system by which God's true saints could be put to death. This system was known in prophecy as "the little horn" (Daniel 7:20-25) and the beast (Revelation 13-20) and it referred to the European Papal Supremacy which reigned over Europe for 1260 years, with the intent and purpose to destroy utterly all the saints of God. But again, this fifth attempt to establish a universal system under Satan's control failed. It failed because there were always those who kept touch with the Word of God. Through the efforts of the European reformation, and the French power which took the Pope captive in 1798, that scheme to take the scepter also failed in its universal objective.

Part 6. **WHAT IS THE SIXTH HEAD?**

We now live under the sixth head of the great red dragon. The deadly wound inflicted in 1798 is now being healed. "The Pope is coming"—back to power. This is the subject of the Daniel 12 timelines! (Papal Supremacy No. 2).

Dan. 12:7 **1260 literal days** of persecution to induce all to come under one banner, by keeping the mark of the beast, so that Satan can align all humanity under his scepter of power.

Dan. 12:11 **1290 literal days** of Papal Reign No, 2 (Revelation 13) in which the kings of the earth hand over the "daily" scepter of power to one man who is Satan's agent to destroy God's people.

Dan 12:12 **1335 literal days** from a National Sunday Law in the USA, until God's people are delivered from a final Universal Death Decree.

The sixth head of the great red dragon is the present attempt—already in process to destroy God's people and to establish a universal kingdom under Satan by common consent of the wicked. We have not seen the last of it yet. We have hardly seen the beginning. But we will see this sixth head attempt, and will know that it is in full swing when the National Sunday Law in the USA has been passed!

Under this sixth head—many final crisis events transpire: The Sunday Laws, the time of trouble (persecution) and at last under the sixth plague: the "gathering of the kings of all the earth" to legislate a universal death decree against God's people. These timelines of Daniel 12 bring Revelation 16 (the seven last plagues—especially the sixth and seventh) into clear focus. We cannot understand the Daniel 12 timelines without a clear view of Revelation 16,17 and 18.

But we may understand that the sixth head attempt to seize the scepter, even when Satan personates Christ and proclaims himself "King of kings," will also end in failure as the Voice of God delivers the saints and brings that kingdom to its end.

SATAN'S PERSONATION OF CHRIST

The beast that thou sawest was, and is not; and shall descend out of the bottomless pit, and go into perdition: and they that dwell on the earth shall wonder, whose names were not written in the book of life from the foundation of the world, when they **behold** the beast that was, and is not, and yet is. Rev. 17:8.

> As the crowning act in the great drama of deception, Satan himself will personate Christ.... Now the great deceiver will make it appear that Christ has come. In different parts of the earth, Satan will manifest himself among men as a majestic being of dazzling brightness, resembling the description of the Son of God given by John in the Revelation. Revelation 1:13-15. The glory that surrounds him is unsurpassed by anything that mortal eyes have yet beheld. The shout of triumph rings out upon the air: "Christ has come!".... The people prostrate themselves in adoration before him, while he lifts up his hands and pronounces a blessing upon them.... His voice is soft and subdued, yet full of melody. In gentle compassionate tones he presents some of the gracious, heavenly truths which the Saviour uttered; he heals the diseases of the people, and then in his assumed character of Christ, he claims to have changed the Sabbath to Sunday and commands all to hallow the day which he has blessed. He declares that those who persist in keeping the seventh day are blaspheming his name by refusing to listen to his angels sent to them with light and truth. This is the strong, almost overmastering delusion. GC 624.

God's people, the 144000, are a Mordecai in the gate who will not bow down, and therefore are confronted with a Universal Death Decree as in the days of Queen Esther. They are a Daniel who continue to serve the God of heaven and was thrown to the lions. If [Satan] "could blot them from the earth, his triumph would be complete." GC 618.

Part 7. WHAT IS THE SEVENTH HEAD OF THE DRAGON?

Satan's last and final attempt to seize the "daily"—scepter of power, seat and authority will be at the end of the millennium.

> And when the thousand years are expired, Satan shall go forth to deceive the nations which are in the four quarters of the earth; Gog and Magog, to gather them together to battle: the number of whom is as the sands of the sea. And they went up on the breadth of the earth, and compassed the camp of the saints about, and the beloved city: and fire came down from God out of heaven, and devoured them. Rev. 20:7-9.

The last attempt to seize the "daily" scepter is no more successful than those which preceded it. Nevertheless, each attempt signified as a "head" provides a graphic prophetic picture of Satan's mighty efforts and rebellion against God and His people.

CONCLUSION

Satan's seven attempts to grasp the "daily" scepter are listed below:

1. War in heaven—dominion over fallen angels
2. Fall of man in Eden—to the flood
3. The tower of Babel and the confusion of languages
4. Temptation and Crucifixion of Christ and His resurrection
5. Papal Supremacy No. 1 (538-1798)
6. Papal Supremacy No. 2 which is future. This climaxes with the battle of Armageddon and the Voice of God deliverance
7. Battle of Gog and Magog which ends with the lake of fire

Daniel 12:11 timeline describes Satan's sixth attempt to grasp the "daily"—scepter as he first takes it away from the kings of the earth, and places it with his representative on earth—the "abomination of desolation" and then personates Christ visibly in the role of "King of kings" wearing the crown and holding the scepter—as though he had won the kingdom at last!

Part 8. WHAT RELATIONSHIP EXISTS BETWEEN REVELATION 12 AND DANIEL 12?

The seven heads of the great red dragon of Revelation 12 explain in detail the nature and purpose of Satan as he wages the great controversy. His nature is to persecute and destroy (God's people particularly) and to establish his universal empire on this planet. It is his purpose to get a unanimous consent by earth's inhabitants so that he can "legally" claim this planet as his own before the universe. To do this he must destroy God's people. This persecution of God's people at the end of time is the subject of the timelines of Daniel 12!

The nature and purpose of Satan is registered in the following Scriptures:

...to devour her child as soon as it was born.... Rev. 12:4.

...he persecuted the woman.... Rev. 12:13.

The dragon was wroth with the woman, and went to make war with the remnant of her seed, which keep the commandments of God.... Rev. 12:17. ...and have the faith of Jesus. Rev. 14:12.

The dragon gave him [the beast of Revelation 13] his ["daily"—scepter of power, seat and authority]..... Rev. 13:3,4.

And it was given him to make war with the saints, and to overcome them.... Rev. 13:7.

And that no man might buy nor sell.... Rev. 13:17.

...as many as would not worship the image of the beast should be killed. Rev. 13:15.

>...he shall have accomplished to scatter [persecute and destroy] the power [hand] of the holy people.... Dan. 12:7.
>
>...the abomination that maketh desolate [persecutes] set up [establish].... Dan. 12:11.
>
>Blessed is he that waiteth [it out].... Dan 12:12.

Although it is Satan's purpose—according to his seven heads—to get a universal empire over which he shall reign as "King of kings" in his personation of Christ, yet there will be 144,000, whom he cannot touch and who will be delivered by the Voice of God! His present and near future attempt, as described in the three timelines of Daniel 12, will not be any more successful than have those of the past!

APPENDIX C

ADDITIONAL NOTES ON DANIEL 12

Ellen G. White indicated that Daniel 11:30-36 has future significance. While it describes the rise of the Papacy in the past (538-1798), "much of this prophecy will be repeated" in the future when the Papacy rises again in Papal Supremacy No. 2 as described in Revelation 13:1-10.

> Soon the scenes of trouble spoken of in the prophecies will take place. The prophecy in the 11th. of Daniel has nearly reached its complete fulfillment. Much of the history that has taken place in fulfillment of this prophecy will be repeated. In the 30th. verse a power is spoken of that "Shall be grieved, and returned, and have indignation against the holy covenant: so shall he do; he shall even return, and have intelligence with them that forsake the holy covenant. And arms shall stand on this part, and they shall pollute the sanctuary of strength, and shall take away the daily sacrifice, and they shall place the abomination that maketh desolate." [Quote continues from Dan. 11:30 to 11:36]. Scenes similar to those described in these words will take place. Letter 103, 1904 (Published in RH July 8,1976).

The following matching phrases and words and diagram reveal the similarity of context, wording and structure between Daniel 11:30-35, Daniel 12:4 and Daniel 12:6-13. These two passages are undeniably related. If Daniel 11:30-35 has reference to future events, then Daniel 12:6-13 also pertains to future fulfillment.

The **matching phrases and words** from Daniel 11 and 12 are listed together for ease of comparison:

> **Dan.11:31** "shall take away the daily sacrifice" (5493, 8548)
> **Dan.12:11** "the daily sacrifice shall be taken away" (5493, 8548)
>
> **Dan.11:31** "and they place the abomination that maketh desolate" (8251, 4150)
> **Dan.12:11** "the abomination that maketh desolate set up" 8251, 4150)
>
> **Dan.11:35** "and some of them of understanding" (7919)
> **Dan.12:10** "but the wise" (7919)
>
> **Dan.11:35** "for a time appointed" (4150)
> **Dan.12:7** "times" (4150)
>
> **Dan.11:35** "to the time of the end" (6256, 7093)
> **Dan.12:9** "till the end of time" (6256, 7093)
>
> **Dan.11:35** "to try them, and to purge, and to make them white" (6884, 1305, 3835)

Dan.12:10 "shall be purified, and made white and true" (1305, 3835, 6884)

Dan.12:4 "Daniel shut up the words, and seal" (1840, 5640, 1697, 2856) [Dan. 12:1-4 is part of Dan. 11]

Dan.12:9 "Daniel: for the words are closed up and sealed" (1840, 5640, 2856, 1697)

The following words: Dan. 11;35 "the end" (7093) and Dan. 12:4 "the end" (7093) appear in Dan. 12:6 "the end" (7093), Dan.12:9 "of the end" (7093), Dan. 12:13 "till the end" (7093), Dan. 12:13 "at the end" (7093). These additional words are not connected by lines in the following chart.

As can be seen in the listing above and the diagram on the next page some nineteen Hebrew words which appear in Daniel 11:30-35 and Daniel 12:4 are also found in Daniel 12:5-13.[*]

---

[*] Note: Daniel 11:30-40 describes Papal Supremacy No. 1. Daniel 12:7-11 describes Papal Supremacy No. 2.

CHART OF DANIEL 11 AND DANIEL 12 COMPARED

CHAPTER 11

30 ¶ For the ships of Chittim shall come against him: therefore he shall be grieved, and return, and have indignation against the holy covenant: so shall he do; he shall even return, and have intelligence with them that forsake the holy covenant.

31 And arms shall stand on his part, and they shall pollute the sanctuary of strength, and shall take away the daily *sacrifice*, and they shall place the abomination that maketh desolate.

32 And such as do wickedly against the covenant shall he corrupt by flatteries: but the people that do know their God shall be strong, and do *exploits*.

33 And they that understand among the people shall instruct many: yet they shall fall by the sword, and by flame, by captivity, and by spoil, many days.

34 Now when they shall fall, they shall be holpen with a little help: but many shall cleave to them with flatteries.

35 And *some* of them of understanding shall fall, to try them, and to purge, and to make *them* white, *even* to the time of the end: because *it is* yet for a time appointed.

CHAPTER 12

4 But thou, O Daniel, shut up the words, and seal the book, *even* to the time of the end: many shall run to and fro, and knowledge shall be increased.

CHAPTER 12

5 ¶ Then I Daniel looked, and, behold, there stood other two, the one on this side of the bank of the river, and the other on that side of

6 And *one* said to the man clothed in linen, which *was* upon the waters of the river, How long *shall it be to the end* of these wonders?

7 And I heard the man clothed in linen, which *was* upon the waters of the river, when he held up his right hand and his left hand unto heaven, and sware by him that liveth for ever that *it shall be* for a time, times, and an half; and when he shall have accomplished to scatter the power of the holy people, all these *things* shall be finished.

8 And I heard, but I understood not: then said I, O my Lord, what *shall be* the end of these *things*?

9 And he said, Go thy way, Daniel: for the words *are* closed up and sealed till the time of the end.

10 Many shall be purified, and made white, and tried; but the wicked shall do wickedly: and none of the wicked shall understand; but the wise shall understand.

11 And from the time *that* the daily *sacrifice* shall be taken away, and the abomination that maketh desolate set up, *there shall be* a thousand two hundred and ninety days.

12 Blessed *is* he that waiteth, and cometh to the thousand three hundred and five and thirty days.

13 But go thou thy way till the end *be*: for thou shalt rest, and stand in thy lot at the end of the days.

MAN ON THE WATER IN DANIEL 8:16

The Man on the water in Daniel 12:7 has been previously identified as Christ during the period of the Investigative Judgment (after 1844). In Daniel 8:16 is found another case of a man on the water.

> And I heard a man's voice between the banks of the Ulai, which called, and said, Gabriel, make this man understand the vision. Dan. 8:16.

The following argument will reveal the identity of the man between the banks of the river (on the water):

1. The man between the banks of the river is definitely not Gabriel.
2. The man on the water was Gabriel's superior for he gave him orders.
3. Since Gabriel is a covering cherub, his superior could only be one of the Godhead—Christ.
4. Therefore the man on the river must be Christ.
5. The fact that the man was on the water (between the banks of the river) implies again that it was Christ.

We invite you to view the complete
selection of titles we publish at:

www.TEACHServices.com

Scan with your mobile
device to go directly
to our website.

Please write or email us your praises, reactions, or
thoughts about this or any other book we publish at:

TEACH Services, Inc.
PUBLISHING
www.TEACHServices.com • (800) 367-1844

P.O. Box 954
Ringgold, GA 30736

info@TEACHServices.com

TEACH Services, Inc., titles may be purchased in bulk for
educational, business, fund-raising, or sales promotional use.
For information, please e-mail:

BulkSales@TEACHServices.com

Finally, if you are interested in seeing
your own book in print, please contact us at

publishing@TEACHServices.com

We would be happy to review your manuscript for free.

CPSIA information can be obtained
at www.ICGtesting.com
Printed in the USA
BVHW06233505052
636133BV00005B/362